PANCHAYATI RAJ IN ACTION

PANCHAYATI RAJ IN ACTION

A Study in the Context of Andhra Pradesh

E.A. NARAYANA

PUBLICATIONS
KALPAZ PUBLICATIONS
DELHI-110052

Panchayati Raj in Action : A Study in the Context of Andhra Pradesh

Rs. 750

ISBN: 81-7835-678-3

Published in 2008 in India by
Kalpaz Publications
C-30, Satyawati Nagar,
Delhi-110052
E-mail: kalpaz@hotmail.com
Phone : 9212729499

Lasser Type Setting by: Rudra Computer Graphics, Delhi
Printed at : Singhal Print Media, Delhi

Dedicated

to

My Parents

Contents

Foreword

The 73rd and 74th amendments to the Indian Constitution are the magna carta for local bodies. The 73rd Amendment Act has opened a new chapter in providing constitutional guarantees for rural local bodies and in initiating the process of establishing a structure for a strong decentralised administrtion in the country-side. Greater responsibility was entrusted to the state governments to enable the functioning of the Panchayati Raj Institutions more effectively through comprehensive devolution of powers to them. It was expected that the state governments would take appropriate steps in line with the constitutional mandate by (a) constituting the bodies; (b) conducting elections; (c) taking appropriate measures in entrusting powers and functions; and (d) providing necessary resources to enable them to perform their assigned functions. While the first two phases of the post – 73rd Constitution Amendment Act were completed smoothly, most state governments are dragging their feet in fulfilling the third and fourth phases. The successful implementation of these two phases determines the overall direction of the PRIs. Some delegation of power did take place although resource crunch continued to haunt the PRIs, as in the past. Their hopes on financial devolution were also belied as reports of State Finance Commissions were either delayed or not implemented. Thus arose a paradox – newly generated enthusiasm not matched by substantial devolution of authority.

Lack of resources is part of the problem of democratic decentralisation in India; developing political capacity for demanding accountability for the utilisation of resources is equally important. Acts of political engagement, therefore, require new commitments and political skills, especially on the part of marginalised groups, to evolve relationships of accountability. Until and unless this requirement is fulfilled there will be a divide between the normative assertions of Panchayati Raj and Panchayati Raj in practice.

There are several other issues and problems the functioning of the PRIs has thrown up. They need to be highlighted and discussed in depth. It is in this context that the study of the Panchayati Raj System by Prof. Narayana gains importance. In this book, the author makes a sincere attempt to discuss the various issues and problems and offers valuable suggestions to activate the PRIs.

The functioning of PRIs and their achievements were studied by several scholars. However, there are very few studies on the functioning or achievements of PRIs after the implementation of 73rd Constitution Amendment Act. The study of Prof. Narayana, which is based on extensive field research, attempts to fill this gap in a modest way. The study covers a broad spectrum of PRIs..... organisational structure, powers, functions, personnel, finances and overall performance.

Prof. Narayana's study should interest all those concerned with democratic decentralisation. However, it will be of special interest to students, research scholars and teachers of Political Science and Public Administration and to policy makers, bureaucrats, journalsists and social activists. I congratulate Prof. Narayana for publishing the study in a book form for wider circulation and use.

102, Jaya Residency
A.C. Guards,
Hyderabad – 500 004.

Prof. C.V. Raghavulu
Ex-Vice-Chancellor
Acharya Nagarjuna Universit

Acknowledgements

I had received valuable help and co-operation from various organisaitons and individuals in completion of this study. I shall be failing in my duty if I do not record my appreciation for them.

First and foremost thanks and appreciation are due to the University Grants Commission, New Delhi, for supporting the study.

I sincerely acknowledge the administrative support provided by the Andhra University. I am thankful to all my collegues in the Department of Politics and Public Administration for their constant help and support in completing the study.

The officials and people's representatives of Panchayati Raj Institutions in the selected districts i.e., West Godavari, Cuddapah and Warangal are the natural claimants of my thanks. I really very much appreciate their help and co-operation. They had not only provided necessary information but also given valuable suggestions on the problem. My thanks are also due to the people respondents from all the three districts.

Dr. B.V. Chalapathi, Head, Department of Public Administration, S.V.U. P.G. Centre, Cuddapah, Dr. P. Hussain Khan, Head, Department of Political Science, Kakatiya University, Warangal, and Dr. K. Ramachandra Murty and Dr. B.V.V. Balakrishna, P.G. Department of Politics, Sir C.R.R.

College, Eluru, were kind enough to help me in data collection in their respective areas. I am thankful to them for the help I received from them.

I acknowledge the services of my research students - Mr. S.R. Subhani, Mr. M.Satyanarayana, Mr. A. Bun, Mr. V. Janardhanarao Naidu, and Mr. P. Ratnasekhara Rao - who assisted me in the data collection.

I am grateful to the staff of various libraries which I referred to during the course of study for their co-operation and cheerful assistance whenever required; particular mention may be made of the Libraries of the Indian Institute of Public Administration, New Delhi, and the National Institute of Rural Development, Hyderabad.

I would like to record my appreciation of the assistance from Sri M. Appa Rao, Sri M. Suri Babu and Sri D.V. Jagannadham who typed the hard pages of my manuscript with all sincerity and dedication.

I would like to place on record my heartfelt thanks to my wife Smt. Vasantha Lakshmi, son Aravind and daughter Haritha for their loving understanding, encouragement and co-operation in the completion of the study.

I am very much thankful to Prof. C.V. Raghavulu, Professor in Political Science and Public Administration and former Vice-Chancellor of Nagarjuna University who has indepth knowledge in Panchayati Raj for agreeing to contribute 'Foreword' to this volume.

E.A.Narayana

List of Tables

1

Panchayati Raj in India : A Historical Prespective

Independent India inherited local self-government as a small wing of the national governmental system. The rural local bodies were the Village Panchaya Councils and the District Boards with some organizational linkage between them. The third rural body (local board) which was at the intermediate level between these two local bodies were established in most of the places, but were abolished subsequently during the second quarter of twentieth century. The independent India thus inherited a modern type of rural local self-government in place of traditional village panchayats.

The Constitution of India promulgated in January 1950 for setting up a democratic and semi-federal system also includes a provision relating to the panchayats. The Article 40 in the chapter on "Directive Principles of State Policy" states that "the states should take steps to organize village panchayats and endow them with such powers and authority as may be necessary to enable them to function as units of self-government. Article 40 of the Constitution is an important authoritative affirmation and impetus for the laws in states under general guidance of union government.[1]

Measures were taken by states to bring their laws in conformity with Article 40 of the Constitution. In the states, where no law was existing to provide for panchayats, new laws were passed. By 1951-52 there were over 70,000 village panchayats functioning in the country.[2] Since 1950, the major landmarks in the evolution of panchayati raj system in India have been launching of Community Development Programme and National Extension Service, appointment of Balwantray Mehta Committee, introduction of three-tier system of Panchayati Raj, appointment of Asoka Mehta Committee, reform efforts by union and state governments and the constitutional amendments.

Community Development Programme and National Extension Service

In tune with the twin goals of democracy and development, the Government of free India launched the Community Development Programme on 2nd October, 1952 to synchronize the birth anniversary of Mahatma Gandhi. President Rajendra Prasad hailed this programme as "the small seed which will grow into a huge and mighty tree. Jawaharlal Nehru described this programme as "real, solid, constructive work which would bring about a great revolution in a peaceful manner and not by breaking heads and yelling".

The basic premise on which the CDP rests is to motivate the rural people to undertake self-reliant community based approach to improvement of economic and social condition of their life and environment. The government is to provide necessary guidance and technical and financial assistance to the rural people for undertaking the activities needed by the people. The CDP is programme for all sided development as distinguished from the development of a particular aspect of rural life like agriculture, education, health, animal husbandry, sanitation and cottage industries. The target aimed at by the CDP is giving the villager a fuller and richer life.

The Community Development Programme was started on pilot basis in selected areas called community projects. Fifty-five community projects started functioning in the country in 1952 in the areas endowed with irrigation facilities or assured rainfall. A year later a development programme with limited scope and funding named as National Extension Service (NES) was launched as a prelude to the launching of CDP in the remaining rural areas of the country. The NES started in 1953 had, in a decade, covered the entire country.

A new basic administrative unit named development block was created in most parts of the country to serve as the locale of the CDP and NES. About 300 villages were covered under a block. The development block was headed by the block development officer and comprised of several specialist extension officers. As the last link in the administrative set up for the community development, the village level worker was conceived as a multi-purpose worker looking after 5 to 10 villages.

The state development committee consisting of the Chief Minister and the ministers in charge of development departments was set up in most states for enunciating general principles of policy. The development commissioner at the state level was the secretary of this Committee. At the Central level there was an Administrator of Community Projects. He was responsible for planning, directing and coordinating the community projects throughout India. He worked under the general supervision of central committee constituted to lay down the broad policies for the implementation of Community Development Programme and National Extension Service. The CPA was assisted by an executive staff to advise him on administration, finance, personnel and other matters related to CDP and NES. The central committee consisted of the members of the planning commission.

For providing people's participation in local planning and implementation of these two programmes advisory bodies with citizen membership were set up at block and district levels. The block level advisory committee consisted of the representatives of village committees and cooperative societies, the members of central and state legislatures and progressive farmers. The district level advisory committee consisted of citizens and heads of various technical departments.

The CDP and NES failed to achieve their objectives mainly because of lack of public participation which is considered as one of the critical variables in the achievement of development goals. Their organization and administration reposed little trust in the citizens. In other words, the CDP and NES instead of people's programmes with government assistance, became government's programmes with varying degrees of people's participation.[3] Furthermore, the existing institutions of local government, both rural and urban, were completely kept out of the administration of these programmes thereby impoverishing both. The Advisory Committees, created to enlist popular support and participation in the Community Development Programme, lacked capacity, vitally and power to represent people's point of view.[4] Indeed, only lip service was paid to local initiative and cooperation. It was under these circumstances that the National Development Council constituted a Committee on Plan Projects which appointed a Study Team under the Chairmanship of a senior legislator, Balwantray Gopaljee Mehta in 1957 to diagnose the maladies and imbalances of CDP and NES.

Balwantray Mehta Committee Report

The Balwantray Mehta Committee was appointed to review CDP and NES and arrangements for execution of these schemes and improving efficiency in their implementation. The Committee was asked to examine the extent to which the CDP Movement had succeeded in utilizing local initiative and in creating institutions to ensure continuity in the process of improving economic and social conditions in the rural areas. The Committee was also asked to assess the requirements of personnel for CDP and NES. The Mehta Team had kept its terms of reference in view while formulating recommendations about reorganizations of institutional arrangements for the CDP and NES.

The Balwantray Mehta Report published in 1957 is an essay on the science and art of democratic decentralization, dealing both with its theory and practice, with its basic postulates and institutional premises. The report had suggested the scheme of democratic decentralization as a measure remedial to the failure of the Community Development Movement to evoke people's intiative and mobilise their voluntary and spontaneous participation. As a preface to the scheme of democratic decentralization, the authors of the report observed:

"Admittedly, one of the least successful aspects of the Community Development Programme and National Extension Service work is its attempt to evoke popular initiative".[5]

The Mehta Team recommended the creation of institutions which were to be statutory, elective, comprehensive in duties and functions, equipped with necessary executive machinery with adequate resources and with enough freedom and autonomy. To secure this the Committee envisaged the three-tier system of rural local government, namely village panchayat at the village level, the panchayat samithi at the block level and the zilla parishad at the district level. Of these three, however, the most effective body was visualized at the block level. All developmental programmes at these levels should be channelled through these institutions. The Committee also recommended that the system of rural local government evolved should be such as will facilitate further devolution and dispersal of power and responsibilities in future.

The Panchayat Samithi would be located at the block level to provide for institutionalized participation of people in planning and implementation of development programmes. Above the Panchayat Samithi, there would be an institution at the district level named Zilla Parishad to replace district board. The Zilla

Parishad would be primarily concerned with guiding the panchayat samithi. The existing village panchayats would continue to function at the village level and work under the overall supervision of the panchayat samithi. All these three units of rural local government should be organically linked up and should be in operation simultaneously. The Mehta Report mentioned that the composition of panchayati raj institutions should be suitably representative of all sections of people. The report underlined the need of comprehensive, appropriate and effective training of the people's representatives in the panchayati raj units.

The National Development Council, while endorsing, in January 1959, the introduction of panchayati raj at district and block levels suggested that each state should so evolve its panchayati raj structure as would be suited to the peculiar conditions prevalent in the state. Acceptance of panchayati raj with necessary variations to suit conditions in states was also favoured by the Central Council of Local Self-Government. This does not, however, suggest or imply deviations from fundamental principles and pattern envisaged by the Committee.

The Union Government held meetings of state ministes and administrators to persuade the state governments to establish the three-tier system of panchayati raj. The Union Government agreed to guide and support the system. As a result a network of PRIs began to be built by the state governments. The lead in the establishment of panchayati raj system was taken by the states of Rajasthan and Andhra Pradesh. The scheme of democratic decentralization was launched in Rajasthan on October 2, 1959. In Andhra Pradesh the scheme was introduced on 1st November 1959.

The necessary legislation had also been passed and implemented in Assam, Bihar, Gujarat, Karnataka, Madhaya Pradesh, Maharastra, Orissa and Punjab. In West Bengal the West Bengal Panchayat Act, 1956 was in force and legislation for setting up of bodies at the block and district level was undertaken. In Kerala a new and comprehensive panchayat act was passed in 1960 and was implemented. Legislation for the upper tier was also undertaken.[6] The original Acts of many states have been amended and brought several changes in the panchayati raj system in their respective states based on the recommendations of the large number of committees appointed by the Central and State Governments to evolve and evaluate the functioning of the Community Development Programme and the structure that would be appropriate for its effective functioning. Some states had repealed old Acts and enacted new legislations. The panchayati raj was, thus, implemented in all states except in the hill states of Nagaland, Meghalaya and Mizoram and Union Territory of Lakshadweep in which the traditional councils of village elders are still in existence.[7]

Ashok Mehta Committee Recommendations

The creation of panchayati raj in 1959 with the object of entrusting the authority and responsibility for rural development to rural people is considered not only an innovation, but also a revolution.[8] A.H. Hanson and Janet Douglas considered panchayati raj as India's distinctive contribution to the theory of local government.[9] Norman D. Palmer described it as the most exiting experiment in democratic decentralization in any developing country.[10] It is assumed, by the national political leadership, that once the pattern of institutional structures and legitimacy are established the panchayati raj institutions would take over functions of government and serve as vital institutions of policy planning and administration at the grassroot level. But what eventually happened to the structural and functional aspects of the PRIs is quite disheartening. A number of developments have undermined the system and made it ineffective. As these institutions took a shape, the MLAs, MLCs and other politicians came to realize the strategic importance of PRIs and started looking at the representatives of these bodies as the political rivals. Therefore, they seemingly started a non-co-operation movement against these institutions. The declining support coupled with indifferent attitude of local level bureaucracy led further diminution of the development and administrative role of the PRIs making the political role more prominent. So much so that during the seventies it created an impression of 'a God that failed'. Thus the earlier enthusiasm and promising performance began to decline rapidly.[11] The need for evaluation of the system was felt by both the Union and State Governments. A number of committees had been appointed by the Government of India to examine and report on one or the other aspects of panchayati raj. In a number of states also committees had been set-up to deal with the various issues relating to panchayati raj.[12] However, the appointment of the Asoka Mehta Committee is to be regarded as an event of far-reaching significance in the annals of panchayati raj for the reason that the committee's endeavor has been to take a systematic and total view of panchayati raj in the country.

The Janata Government, which came to power at the Centre in 1977 accorded highest priority to rural development. The Government considered that the maximum degree of decentralization, both in planning and implementation of rural development programmes was necessary. Accordingly, the Government set up a committee to enquire into the working of the PRIs and to suggest measures to strengthen them so as to enable a decentralized system of planning and development to be effective. Ashok Mehta was the chairman of the Committee. The Committee elicited views through questionnaire, through meetings at the state level and through studies and discussions with several knowledgeable persons. A total view of all the aspects of PRIs was taken by the Committee. The Committee submitted its report on 21st August, 1978 to the Prime Minister.

Diagnosing the ills afflicting the PRIs, the Asoka Mehta Committee pointed out that haphazard programmes, non-performance, rise of vested interests, lack of political will on the part of the Central and State Governments, lack of adequate financial resources, etc., have positively contributed to its decline. It also felt that the concept of panchayati raj itself got lost in the haze of conflicting interpretation. However, the Committee hastened to add that this failing was not peculiar to panchayati raj only. It was only symptomatic of the decline afflicting the entire body politic of the nation. Without going into the details of the report of the Committee let us look at the major recommendations and the model suggested by it.

1. The district should be the first point of decentralization, under popular supervision below the state level.
2. Below the district level the Mandal Panchayats should be constituted by grouping a number of villages.
3. At the village level, the people would be involved in Mandal Panchayats through Village Committees which would look after the municipal functions and related welfare activities.
4. The Village Committee should organize two Gram Sabha meetings every year to explain the people what programmes the Mandal Panchayat is executing in their area and to channelise the people's feedback to the Mandal Panchayat.
5. Whatever be the structural arrangements, the directly elected element must preponderate over the others at all levels.
6. The chairman of Zilla Parishad will be elected directly. The President of Mandal Panchayat may, however, be elected directly or indirectly as the states may decide.
7. The term of all elected bodies should be 4 years.
8. In the elections, the Scheduled Castes and Scheduled Tribes should get representation on the basis of their population.
9. The Panchayati Raj elections should be conducted by the Chief Election Officer of the State in consultation with Chief Election Commissioner.

10. The State Government should not supersede the panchayati raj institutions on partisan grounds and if supersession becomes necessary these should be replaced by an elected body within six months.
11. The State Government should not postpone elections of PRIs.
12. The political parties should be permitted to take part in the election to PRIs and participate in their working.
13. The states and union territories should have evolve their own list of functions to be devolved on PRIs. Periodical adjustments should be made in the functions devolved upon PRIs to suit the changing requirements.
14. All the development functions relating to the district should be placed under the Zilla Parishad.
15. With the decentralization of the functions of the State Government, all the concerned district level officials should be placed under the Zilla Parishads and lower tiers.
16. Apart from the budgetary devolution from the State Government the PRIs also should mobilize enough resources of their own.

Being conscious of the operational realities of PRIs the Asoka Mehta Committee adopted a flexible approach to the problem and recommended a "two-tier" model of panchayati raj.[13] Keeping in view the development necessities the first point of decentralization below the state should be the district. Apart from being the basic unit of devolution, the district level should be treated as the unit of planning. The Committee recommended that all development functions relating to a district which are now being performed by the State Government should be entrusted to Zilla Parishad. The Committee also felt that the funds should be transferred to Zilla Parishad automatically. An important related recommendation is that all the staff with decentralized functions should be under the Zilla Parishad. Administrative expenditure on the salaries and allowances of such transferred staff should be borne by the government.

For the second tier, the Committee thought in order to be viable the unit has to be bigger than the existing panchayat. It, therefore, suggested the creation of mandal panchayats each consisting of a cluster of villages covering a population of 15,000 to 20,000. The Committee further felt that a mandal panchayat would alone be able to ensure a balance between technological requirements and possibilities of popular participation in decision-making. The Committee recommended direct election for both the tiers with reservation of seats for Scheduled Castes and Scheduled Tribes in proportion of their population and also two seats for women. The Committee categorically favoured the participation of political parties in panchayati raj.

A Conference of Chief Minister was called in Delhi in August 1979 to discuss the recommendations of the Asoka Mehta Committee. In the light of the discussions, to bring uniformity in panchayati raj pattern for the whole of the country, a model bill was prepared with a hope that every state government will pass it and will follow an uniform pattern. But unfortunately, in the course of events, the model bill did not attract the attention of state governments and the bill could not be passed. However, some states have tried to implement a few recommendations, but not all, of the Asoka Mehta Committee to revitalize the PRIs in their respective states. Andhra Pradesh, Karnataka and West Bengal have tried to follow the model envisaged by the Committee.[14]

The Janata Government which came to power in 1983 in Karnataka enacted new legislation, namely the Karnataka Zilla Parishads, Taluka Panchayat Samithis, Mandal Panchayats and Nyaya Panchayats Act, 1985, based on the recommendations of the Asoka Mehta Committee. It established a new pattern of rural local bodies, which comprised Mandal Panchayat, Taluk Panchayat Samithi and Zilla Parishad. Under the new dispensation of Karnataka, the Gram Sabha is the basic tier of the system and is a college comprising all eligible voters in the village. The Gram Sabha is required by law to meet at least twice an year. It discusses and reviews all development programmes of the village, selects beneficiaries for all beneficiary-oriented programmes transferred to the panchayati raj system and plans for local improvement. The Mandal Panchayat, covering a group of villages is the first elected tier of the system. It is entrusted with all civic functions and powers and responsibility for development and welfare programmes with an intra-mandal orientation. The number of seats in a Mandal Panchayat is one for every 400 persons. Twenty-five per cent of the membership is earmarked for women and 18 per cent for Scheduled Castes and Scheduled Tribes. The President and Vice-President are elected by the members of the Mandal Panchayat. The Taluk Panchayat Samithi is a purely nominated body comprising ex-officio members, all the presidents of mandals in the taluk, all MLAs / MLCs representing any part of the taluk, members of the Zilla Parishad representing any part of the taluk; presidents of taluk level cooperative societies and cooperative banks, plus five co-opted members belonging to SCs, STs, backward classes and women. The MLA representing the major part of the taluk is the Chairman of the Taluk Panchayat Samithi. This body is entrusted with advisory, supervisory, review and inter-mandal coordination functions in relation to the mandals of the taluk. The Zilla Parishad is the second directly elected tier of the panchayati raj system in Karnataka. One member for every 28,000 population is elected to the Zilla Parishad. MPs and MLAs whose constituencies cover the district or a part thereof are members of the Zilla Parishad,but do not have the right to hold office in the Zilla Parishad. Reservations for women, SCs and STs, as in the case of mandals, are provided at the Zilla Parishad level also. The Adhyaksha and Upadhyaksha are elected by members of the Zilla Parishad.

At the apex of the panchayati raj system is the State Development Council, which is chaired by the Chief Minister and comprises the Adhyakshas of all Zilla parishads in the state, six ministers of state and the Development Commissioner as its member-secretary. It is intended to provide a forum for continuous review and direction of the functioning of panchyati raj in the state. There is also a statutory provision for setting up a Finance Commission every five years to determine the principles on which the resources are to be shared between the state government and PRIs and the basis on which allocations would be among the zilla parishads / mandal panchayats.

The Left Front Government in West Bengal introduced some changes in the organization of panchayari raj system. In the first place, the Department of Community Development was taken out from the Department of Agriculture and merged with the Department of Panchayats to speed up the process of rural development in a concerted manner. Secondly, the District Magistrate had been made the Executive Officer of the Zilla Parishad with a view to integrating panchayat administration with development administration at the district level. The Zilla Parishad had been given the services of all the officers and employees of the State Government at the district level. Similarly, all the block level officers had been statutorily associated with the Panchayat Samithi. The government had also placed the services of the gram sevak, a village level extension worker of the erstwhile Community Development Department, at the disposal of the gram panchayats. In order to ensure financial discipline and to assist the panchayati raj bodies in the maintenance of accounts, a new audit and accounts organization was created under the government. A provision was made in the State Panchayati Raj Act for village assembly of voters to review performance of the village panchayats. The political parties were allowed to participate in panchayati raj elections.

In several other states amendments were made to their statutes for providing changes in panchayati raj. The representation for scheduled castes, scheduled tribes and women was enlarged. The number of tiers of panchayati raj system was increased from the existing one to two or from two to three. There was some increase in devolution of powers, functions and resources. Efforts were made to hold elections which had remained postponed on one plea or the other.

Other Union Government Initiatives

The Planning Commission has stressed in its five year plans the role of panchayati raj in promotion and management of rural development. According to the Commission effective people's participation through panchayati raj in rural development would contribute to better responsiveness to people's needs and aspirations and to coordinated and accelerated progress of this development. The Prime Minister wrote to the Chief Ministers of State Governments in 1984 to take appropriate action without further delay for holding of overdue elections to PRIs as well as revitalizing their functioning. Another important step taken by the Union Government was to appoint two committees successively in 1985 and 1986 respectively to suggest ways and means for strengthening panchayati raj as vibrant local institutional set-up for playing an active and purposeful role in management of local services and appropriate development programmes.

The Committee on Administrative Arrangements for Rural Development (CAARD) set-up under the chairmanship of G.V.K. Rao, a senior administrator, in 1985 recommended the following measures:[15]

(a) The PRIs should be given greater powers in relation to planning, implementation and monitoring of rural development programmes;

(b) The elections to PRIs should be held regularly;

(c) A post of District Development Commissioner who should act as incharge of all development departments at the district level and be the Chief Executive Officer of the Zilla Parishad should be created; and

(d) The post of Block Development Officer should be revamped.

The L.M. Singhvi Committee of the Union Department of Rural Development set-up in 1986 advocated that the panchayati raj should primarily be viewed as the local self-government system.[16] It should be strengthened so as to serve better as one of the foundation stones of the country's democratic political system. In order to strengthen the status of panchayati raj its main features should be mentioned in the Constitution itself.

A sub-committee of the Parliamentary Consultative Committee attached to the Union Ministry of Personnel, Public Grievances and Pensions set up in 1988 under the Chairmanship of P.K. Thungon pleaded for the constitutional recognition of panchayati raj. The Thungon Committee recommended that the Zilla Parishad should be the most effective level in the panchayati raj system. The Committee recommended for a detailed list of subjects for panchayati raj to be incorporated in the Constitution and setting up of the State Finance Commission to laydown the principles for devolution of financial resources to PRIs.

The Sarkaria Commission which was mainly concerned with the Centre-State relations also considered the devolution of powers to local bodies. The Commission observed that the objectives of decentralized planning could not be achieved unless the panchayati raj and other local bodies were allowed full scope to play their role. They were of the view that for this purpose, it was necessary that the elections were held regularly and adequate finances were devolved on these institutions. The Commission recommended that the regular elections to and sessions of Zilla Parishads and Municipal Corporations should be ensured by legal provisions analogous to those Articles 172 and 174 of the Constitution and these institutions should not remain superseded for long period.

Constitutional Status to the Panchayati Raj Institutions

The Constitution of India has not foreseen integrated administrative development and percolation of genuine democracy to the grassroots. Left to the whims of the states local self-government was not developed into a live and viable infrastructure of Indian democracy. A constitutionally provided network of local self-government ensures grassroots participation in government and development. It is very often stressed that the Constitution of India must be suitably amended to enable the panchayati raj to be enshrined in the supreme document of land itself. Late Jayaprakash Narayan had vociferously pleaded for the constitutional sanctity to the PRIs. While striking a note of caution on centralization of power, he had stated; I feel the idea of a three-tiered decentralized government cannot be successfully put into effect unless and until the PRIs are assigned due place in the Constitution and they are empowered to function as governments at their respective levels. Though the Asoka Mehta Committee was not categorical on this issue, but it felt it was desirable to request the Central Government to give careful consideration to the document prepared by 21 eminent citizens. The document contains specific suggestions for giving PRIs constitutional mandate.

The High Power Committee on Panchayati Raj under the chairmanship of C. Narasimham, constituted by the Government of Andhra Pradesh in 1981, also pleaded for according constitutional sanctity to the PRIs.[17] It warned that the social cost of governing a vast country like ours by remote control, from the level of Union Government, or the State Government, for that matter, is very high. The Narasimham Committee had pointed out in its report that giving constitutional status to panchayati raj bodies, ensuring their continuance by regular elections to be conducted by an autonomous authority, embodying the welfare of the weaker sections to be brought about by these bodies in all appropriate and uniform legislative measure and giving them enough financial teeth, the local bodies would become real and effective institutions at the grassroots level and prove to be the harbingers of democracy in the country, attended by growth with justice – social, economic and political in the constitutional parlance. An independent status to panchayati raj would promote democratization at the grassroots levels, provide them with adequate responsibilities and matching resources, facilitate judicial review of arbitrary action towards panchayati raj, and make PRIs fully accountable to their electorate.[18] The demand for constitutional status to the local bodies was more widespread during 1980s. At many conventions and conferences including All India Mayors Conference and academic gatherings appeals had been made to the Union Government to accord constitutional status to the local self-governing institutions. None other than Ramakrishna Hegde, former Chief Minister of Karnataka and pioneer in the genuine decentralization in his state, called for constitutional amendment to establish a four-tier federal system consisting of mandal panchayats, zilla parishads, state and union governments.

Sixty-Fourth Constitution Amendment Bill

In view of these demands and also because of political compulsions the Congress (I) Government at the Centre had come up, in May 1989, with a bill in favour of a constitutional amendment for the resurrection of panchayati raj backed by the slogan 'power to the people'. In the words of Rajiv Gandhi "unless PRIs were strengthened power goes not to the people but to the power brokers". He wanted what he called "syndrome of dependence" of PRIs ended so that they become grassroots institutions with maximum devolution of powers and maximum democracy. He declared that the Centre had to step in where the states had failed and discharge its joint responsibility towards development under Article 40 of the Constitution.

The Sixty-Fourth Constitution Amendment Bill makes it obligatory for all states to establish a three-tier system of panchayats at the village, intermediate and district levels with a fixed tenure of five years and due reservation for Scheduled Castes, Scheduled Tribes and women. It enables state legislatures to endow, by law, the panchayats with adequate powers and authority so as to involve them in the preparation of plans for economic development and social justice and in the implementation of schemes on a wide range of subjects. The Bill provides for a State Finance Commission to go once in five years into the nature and quantum of taxes and other levies that may be assigned or appropriated by the panchayats and distribution of net proceeds between the state and panchayats and among panchayats themselves besides determining the grants-in-aid payable to the panchayats from State funds. The Bill vests in the Election Commission the superintendence, direction and control of elections to the panchayats at three levels. The Bill empowers the Comptroller and Auditor-General to audit the panchayat accounts, through his state level functionary, and cause his report to be laid before the state legislature concerned. The Bill also seeks to add a new schedule after the tenth schedule to the Constitution to supplement the provisions that already exist in the laws regarding panchayats in most states.

The non-Congress (I) State Governments particularly in the south opposed the Bill. They saw a threat to the autonomy and powers of the state governments. They questioned the intentions of the Union Government for empowering the people with a measure seeking to transfer some of the powers and functions of the State Governments to the PRIs without implementing the measures proposed by the Sarkaria Commission. In spite of the opposition from the non-Congress

(I) state governments and opposition parties, the Congress (I) Government got the Sixty-Fourth Amendment Bill passed in Lok Sabha. The Bill was, however, defeated in Rajya Sabha in which the Congress (I) Party could not command a two-thirds majority to push through the legislation. The National Front and other opposition parties opposed the manner in which the Bill was presented hurriedly and they termed it as election eve stunt. Thus, first attempt to accord constitutional status to PRIs had failed.

Seventy-Fourth Constitution Amendment Bill

The National Front which came to power in November, 1989 also promised to strengthen the panchayati raj set up in the country. A constitutional amendment bill (74th Constitution Amendment Bill) seeking periodical elections to the PRIs and reservations for Scheduled Castes and Scheduled Tribes on the basis of their population was introduced in September, 1990. The Government had fallen before it could fulfil it's promise.

Seventy-Third Constitution Amendment Act

The Constitution (72nd Amendment) Bill seeking to amend the Constitution for strengthening PRIs was introduced by the then State Minister of Rural Development, G. Venkataswamy in the Parliament in September, 1991. This Bill is a modified form of 64th Constitution Amendment Bill and more akin to the 74th Constitution Amendment Bill introduced by the V.P. Singh Government. The Parliament did not take up the Bill immediately due to serious differences between the Government and the opposition on various issues of the bill. The Congress (I) Government under the leadership of P.V. Narasimha Rao also did not push it because it had no majority in either House of the Parliament. It tried to convince the opposition for the need to pass the Bill. A Joint Parliamentary Committee under the chairmanship of Nathuram Mirdha was appointed to examine the Bill and report to the Parliament. The Parliament took up the Bill and JPC Report on December 1, 1992. The Bill became the Seventy-Third Constitution Amendment Act finally on April 23, 1993 with the assent of the President to the Bill.

The Act enshrines in the new part IX of the Indian Constitution certain basic features of the panchayat system "to impart certainty, continuity and strength of them". A list of specified subject matters for which the panchayats may be empowered forms of new Eleventh Schedule of the Constitution. The main provisions of the Act are given below:

1. The Gram Sabha shall exercise such powers and perform such functions as the state legislature legally provides.
2. A three tier panchayat system shall be constituted in every state. It shall comprise panchayats at the village intermediate and district levels. However, a state with population not exceeding 20 lakhs may not have the intermediate level panchayat.
3. Membership seats in the panchayats at all levels shall be filled by direct election from territorial constituencies.
4. In all panchayats directly elected membership seats shall be reserved for.

i) Scheduled Castes (SCs) and Scheduled Tribes (STs) in proportion to their respective population in total population in panchayat area. One-third of these reserved membership seats shall be reserved for Scheduled Castes and Scheduled Tribes women.

ii) Not less than one-third of seats, including the seats reserved for Scheduled Castes and Scheduled Tribes women shall be reserved for women.

5. Office of chairperson of panchayats at all levels shall be reserved for Scheduled Tribes and Scheduled Tribes in proportion to their respective population in a state; and

not less than one-third of the chairperson office shall be reserved for women.

6. The state legislature may provide for reservation of membership seats and chairperson offices in the panchayats for backward class citizens.
7. The normal term of every panchayat shall be five years; if dissolved earlier, fresh elections shall be completed within six months of the expiry of date of dissolution.
8. The Governor of the State shall appoint a finance commission within one year of the commencement of the Seventy-third Constitution Amendment Act and there after every five years to review financial position of the panchayats and make recommendation for principles which should govern distribution of resources between the state and the panchayats.
9. The state legislature may legally endow the panchayats with such powers and authority as may be necessary to enable them to function as institutions of self-government.
10. The state legislature may authorise a panchayat to levy and collect taxes, duties, tools and fees as well as may assign to panchayat taxes, duties, taxes and fees levied by the state government and also provide for grant-in-aid from the state government to the panchayats.
11. A State Election Commission shall be appointed by the State Governor and shall be vested with authority for supervising, directing and controlling preparation of electoral rolls and conduct of all elections.
12. The Eleventh Schedule of the Act contains a list of twenty-nine subject matters as reference for the state legislature while deciding about devolution of powers. These relate to: Agriculture and allied sectors, rural industries, basic infrastructure and services, social services and social welfare and family welfare, poverty alleviation

programmes, public distribution system, maintenance of community assets and a few miscellaneous subjects.

Both the Union Government and State Governments had taken steps towards implementation of the Amendment Act. The Union Government asked the states to enact legislation within one year from the Amendment Act comes into force. The State Governments and Union Territory administration passed fresh laws or made amendments to the existing ones in conformity with the 73rd Constitution Amendment Act. The elections to panchayats were held in States under the direction of newly appointed State Election Commissions. After elections panchayats had been reconstituted as constitutionally mandated institutions. The State Finance Commissions had been set up to report on panchayat finance. Administrative action is being taken on these reports recommending improvement of the financial of position of PRIs. The devolution of powers and transfer of functions along with appropriate finance and personnel have been promised by the state governments.

References

1. B.S. Khanna, *Rural Local Government in India and South Asia,* Deep & Deep Publications, New Delhi,1999, p. 14.
2. V. Venkatesan, *Institutionalizing Panchayati Raj in India,* Concept Publishing Co., Delhi, 2002, p. 10.
3. Rajeswar Dayal, *Panchayat Raj in India*, Metroplitan Publications, Delhi, 1970, p. 6.
4. B. Maheswar, *Studies in Panchayati Raj*, Metropolitan Publications, Delhi, 1963, p. 8.
5. Government of India, *Report of the Team for the Study of Community Projects and National Extension Service,* Vol.I, Committee on Plan Projects, New Delhi, 1957, p. 5.
6. For details on statewise panchayati raj, see G. Ram Reddy (ed.), *Patterns of Panchayati Raj,* Macmillan, Delhi, 1977.

7. Vasant Desai, *Panchayati Raj: Power to the People,* Himalaya, Bombay, 1990, p. 85.
8. Henry Maddick, *Panchayati Raj: A Study of Rural Local Government in India*, Longman, London, 1970, p. 3.
9. A.H. Hanson, and Janet Douglas, *India's Democracy,* Vikas, Delhi, 1972, p. 184.
10. Norman D. Palmer, *The Indian Political System*, Boston, Houghton, Miffin, p. 104.
11. G. Ram Reddy and K. Seshadri, *The Voter and Panchayati Raj*, National Institute of Community Development, Hyderabad, 1972.
12. To name a few, the following committees are appointed to look into several aspects of Panchayati Raj: (1) Santhanam Committee on Panchayati Raj Finance (1963); (2) Maharastra Evaluation Committee on Panchayati Raj (1970); (3) Rajasthan High Power Committee on Panchayati Raj (1971); and C. Narasimham Committee of Andhra Pradesh (1972).
13. Government of India, *Report of the Committee on Panchayati Raj Institutions*, Department of Rural Development, Ministry of Agriculture, New Delhi, August, 1978.
14. C.V. Raghavulu and E.A. Narayana, "Reforms in Panchayati Raj: A Comparative Analysis of Andhra Pradesh, Karnataka and West Bengal", *The Indian Journal of Public Administration*, Vol.XXXVII, No.1, January-March, 1991, pp.34-46.
15. Government of India, *Report of the Committee on Administrative Arrangements for Rural Development and Poverty Alleviation Programmes* (Chairman: G.V.K. Rao), Ministry of Agriculture, Department of Rural Development, New Delhi, 1985.
16. Government of India, *Report of the Committee on Panchayati Raj* (Chairman: L.M. Sighvi), Ministry of Agriculture, Department of Rural Development, New Delhi, 1986.
17. Government of Andhra Pradesh, *High Power Committee on Panchayati Raj*, Panchayati Raj Department, Hyderabad, 1981.

18. For clarification on the issues and implications of constitutional status to local government, see Abhijit Datta, "Constitutional Status of Local Government of India", *The Indian Journal of Public Administration*, Vol. XXXIII, No. 2, April-June, 1987, pp.309-317.

2

Panchayati Raj at Work : The National Perspective

The PRIs come under the direct responsibility of the state governments as the local government falls in the state list of subjects enumerated in the Constitution. However, the central government was never neglected the rural local government. The responsibility of the central government becomes direct and undivided with regard to panchayati raj in the union territories. The central government is also called upon to perform several functions with regard to panchayati raj in the states. The Centre has a responsibility for ensuring that the system of panchayati raj is implemented by the states according to the Constitution and its directives. The Central Government can point out to the state governments the latter's errors and lapses in dealing with panchayati raj. The Central Government make available to the states funds for support of PRIs. As a grant giver, the Central Government owes it to the tax – payer and parliament. So it keeps a general watch over the functioning of PRIs. As a matter of fact, the very concept of panchayati raj had been originally conceived by a committee set up at the central level – the Team for the Study of Community Projects and

National Extension Service, popularly known as the Balvantray Mehta Committee. The Central Government persuaded the states to accept the scheme of democratic decentralization recommended by the Committee. It also set up a number of committees to examine the various aspects of panchayati raj. All these serve to focus the interest of the central government in the progress of panchayati raj.[1]

The Union Ministry of Rural Areas and Employment has been playing the role of motivator, guide and supporter for implementation of the 73rd Constitution Amendment Act in states and union territories.[2] The union ministry has also been convening conferences of elected representatives of PRIs to know their view points about the working of their institutions. The ministry is also helping the state governments financially to improve and expand requisite training programmes for these representatives as well as for panchayati raj personnel. It has been convening conferences of the state panchayati raj ministers and secretaries from time to time to review periodically progress of implementation of the Act in letter and spirit. The Conference of Ministers has set up a national committee for regular monitoring and guiding the panchayati raj reorganization process. The committee has been guiding the states to take appropriate measures for ensuring effective democratic functioning of the panchayati raj system.

The conference of panchayati raj ministers held on July 11, 2001 had resolved that a task force should be set up to suggest steps for administrative decentralization of funds, functions and functionaries to the PRIs with regard to 29 subjects mentioned in the 11th schedule of the Constitution. Accordingly, a task force was appointed under the chairmanship of Additional Secretary and Financial Advisor of the Ministry of Rural Areas and Employment. The task force submitted its report within its time frame. All state governments and union territories have been requested to complete the process of devolution of powers to the PRIs by March 2002. The Task Force has suggested a broad framework for the devolution of powers to the PRIs. The state governments can make amendments to this framework as per their requirements.

Panchayati Raj in Indian States

The panchayati raj system has existed formally in most of the major states of India since the early 1950s. However, the system was not an effective body of governance until the early 1990s. Elections were not held and the PRIs did not assume any active role. The 73rd amendment to the Constitution of India has provided for the framework of a three-tiered panchayati raj system with regular elections through out India. The state governments and union territories passed fresh panchayati raj laws or amended their existing ones in conformity with the 73rd Constitution Amendment Act. This process was completed within one year of the commencement of the Amendment Act i.e., by April 1994. Elections were held to the PRIs in accordance with the conformity legislation in the states. These elections were held under the direct supervision of newly appointed State Election Commission. The states had set up their respective finance commissions to report on the sharing of financial resources between the state government and local government bodies. The reorganized panchayati raj system has been at work in states and union territories since a decade. A brief description of the panchayati raj system in major states is being given in the following pages.

Rajasthan

The state of Rajasthan had enacted legislations strictly in accordance with the provisions of the Constitution by introducing the Rajasthan Panchayati Raj Act, 1994. A three-tier structure adopted in this State from the very beginning continued and was incorporated under the new Act also. After constitution of new panchayati raj structure there are now 32 zilla parishads, 237 panchayat samithis and 9185 panchayats in the State. An independent Election Commission had also been appointed by the State Government. The 1st election of all reconstituted PRIs, at all levels, was held in January, 1995. After completion of a term of 5 years 2nd elections of PRIs were also conducted well in time in January 2000. Apart from reservations for SCs and STs and women as per provision o the Constitution, 15 per cent reservation had been provided by the State Government for OBCs.

A provisions has been made under section 50, 51 and 52 read with schedule 1, 2, 3 appended to the State Act in respect of powers and functions to the panchayats, panchayat samithis and zilla parishads respectively. These provisions seem to be mandatory in nature because word 'shall' has been used. As per Schedule 1 under section 50 of the Act, 33 subjects have been enlisted for village panchayats. Schedule 2 under section 51 prescribes 30 subjects for panchayat samithis and schedule 3 under section 52 enlists 19 subjects for zilla parishads. Out of 29 subjects enlisted in 11th Schedule of the Constitution 16 subjects have already been transferred to the PRIs. Apart from this, 4 subjects viz., poverty alleviation programmes, rural housing, markets and fares and maintenance of community assets were reported to be already there with PRIs. Out of the remaining 9 subjects, 4 subjects including fuel woods and fodder, cultural activities, local roads, bridges, culverts, ferries, waterways and other means of communication and social forestry and farm forestry are indirectly being looked after by the PRIs. In view of this, there remains only 4 subjects for which it has been mentioned that necessary action for transferring of these activities is to be taken under the second phase of transferring of functions to PRIs.

No efforts have been made to provide necessary administrative support to the PRIs in order to easily carry out their statutory functions. The zilla parishads continue to function with a skeleton staff which includes one Additional Chief Executive Officer deputed by the Government, one Assistant Engineer, two Senior Deputy Inspectors of Schools, one Assistant Secretary and some accounts staff. All district level officers concerning rural development programmes are functioning independently under their HODs and District Collector in his capacity of district development officer. Similar is the case of panchayati samithis where block staff and sectoral officers posted at the block level continue to maintain their separate identity. The panchayat samithis despite having sufficient workload and multifarious activities of development programmes are simply having a Block Development Officer, selected from various development services, a few Extension Officers like Panchayats, Education, Cooperatives, Agriculture, Animal Husbandry, a Junior Engineer, and a very few ministerial and accounts officials. As regards panchayats, there is not even a full time Secretary in all the panchayats. A VLW-cum-Group Sachiv designate looks after 3 to 4 gram panchayats at a time in many cases and all other village level functionaries of various departments function independently outside the purview of gram panchayats.

The CEO of Zilla Parishad and BDO of Panchayat Samiti have been authorised only to incure administrative expenditure on salaries. The financial powers have been delegated for various purposes to different authorities which includes Vikas Adhikari, Collector, Divisional Commissioner and Director RD and PR and Administrative Department in the Government. Even in the case of own income, major powers have been retained with the official hierarchy mainly with the District Collector, Divisional Commissioner and the State Government and only a small expenditure on various items has been empowered to be incurred with the approval of Standing Committees of the PRIs.

The State Government had been providing funds to PRIs for staff and other expenses under the non plan and for various schemes of the Rural Development and Panchayati Raj Department being implemented by PRIs under the plan. The total amount provided both under the non-plan and plan increased year after year. An amount of Rs.5,458.44 lakhs under plan and Rs.25,739.99 lakhs under non-plan was devolved to PRIs in 1995-06. These amounts were increased to Rs.20,790.42 lakhs under plan and Rs.64,078.88 lakhs under non-plan in 1999-2000.

The First Finance Commission was constituted by the State Government immediately after enactment of the new Act and the Commission had submitted its report on 30.12.1995. The allocation of resources under per capita grants to PRIs from 1999-2000 have been increased. It has been further provided that the general grant of panchayats would be increased every subsequent year. The pancayat samithis would also be provided 50 per cent of the total land revenue collected in their respective areas.

District Planning Committees have been constituted by the State Government as provided under section 121 of the Act, 1994. There are 25 members of which, 5 members are nominated by the Government and 20 members are elected out of the members of Zilla Parishad and Municipal Committees and municipal corporations in the district in proportion to the urban and rural population of the District. The Pramukh, Zilla Parishad, has been appointed as Chairman of District Planning Committee. The District Planning Committee is empowered to prepare a consolidated plan for the entire district and has been entrusted to take decisions regarding distribution of physical and natural resources like water, etc., integrated development of the infrastructure and conservation of environment and other matters related to the common interest of urban local government institutions and PRIs in the district.

Maharashtra

Maharashtra, instead of adopting a new Panchayati Raj Act, amended its Bombay Village Panchayat Act, 1958 and Maharashtra Zilla Parishads and Panchayat Samithis Act 1961 in order to make them conform to the provisions of the 73rd Consitutional Amendment. The amended Act No.XXI came into force in the state on 24th April, 1994. There is a three-tier structure from the beginning. The same organizational structure has been continued under the amended Act. The amended Act provides for two statutory meetings of gram sabha in every financial year. It is the duty of the Sarpanch and in his absence the upasarpanch to call these statutory meetings.

Constitutional reservations for SCs and STs was a part of the composition of PRIs in Maharashtra since inception. One-third elected seats of PRIs in the State are reserved for women since 1992 elections. The provisions for 27 per cent reservation for other backward classes and 33 per cent reservation for women in all categories for membership and office were provided by the amended Act of 1994 in the State. The elections to PRIs in the State were held under the amended Act in 1997.

The PRIs are expected to be responsible for execution and maintenance of development works and schemes in rural areas. All the three tiers of panchayati raj system in Maharashtra have been involved in this process and given the opportunity to carry out this responsibility with adequate powers. The activities which can be undertaken by the panchayat samithis and zilla parishads are enumerated in the Zilla Parishads and Panchayat Samithis Act, 1961 and the subjects which can be entruted to the gram panchayats are given in the Bombay Village Panchayat Act. 1958.

A village list incorporated in schedule 1st assigning 79 subjects and activities in respect of 12 sectors to village panchayat has been appended under section 45 of the Village Panchayat Act. Each gram panchayat has been provided a full-time

Secretary by integrating the functions of Gram Sevaks and Agriculture Assistant and distributed them amongst all the village panchayats.

As regards Panchayat Samithi, a provision of assigning 75 subjects and activities including development activities in respect of 14 sectors have been assigned. Each Panchayat Samiti has been provided with the Extension and office staff for day-to- day working and with BDO as the executive head.

As per 1st schedule under section 100 of 1961 Act as many as 129 activities including development activities of 113 subjects namely agriculture, forest, medical (ayurved), buildings, communications (roads), public health engineering, publicity, community development, social welfare, education, rural housing and various other development programmes were assigned to Zilla Parishad. An officer of I.A.S. cadre has been made Chief Executive Officer of Zilla Parishad under the control of president of Zilla Parishad. The C.E.O. of Zilla Parishad is assisted by two Deputy C.E.Os. and 7 class I heads of departments namely General Administration, Finance, Agriculture, Works, Education, Development, Women and Child Welfare departments. Each department has supporting Class II officers and other required supporting staff.

In Maharashtra, the Zilla Parishad is an apex body having tremendous importance as all the important powers are concentrated around it which is distinct from other states of India. The district was accepted as a unit for devolution of powers and panchayat samithis as executive arms of Zilla Parishad. There is a very strong and powerful system of committees at Zilla Parishad level. There are as many as 10 committees including the standing committee which is presided over by the president and consists of the chairman of subject committees and 8 elected councillors and 2 coopted persons having knowledge and experience of the related subjects. The other 9 subject committees are Finance, Works, Agriculture,

Health, Education, Social Welfare, Animal Husbandry and Dairy, Women and Child Welfare, Water Conservation and Drinking Water Supply. Each of these committees consists of 8-10 elected councillors and 2 members having special knowledge of the subjet. This shows that effective participation of all the directly elected members in day to day working of Zilla Parishad has been ensured by electing them as members of one of the committees through a system of proportional representation by means of single transferable vote and by ensuring that a member should not be a member in more than one committee. The meetings of subject committees are conducted once in a month where concerned Heads of the Department and district level officers are the ex-officio secretaries of the subject committees.

The PRIs in Maharashtra are having wide range of administrative and financial powers directly given to them under the Act. These institutions raise their finance through levying cess, taxes, tolls, fees, rates, etc. and commission for agency charges received from the government for carrying out works on the agency basis. This is apart from grants, assigned from the Government. They also receive government grants in respect of the government schemes transferred to them for execution.

Gujarat

The Government of Gujarat amended their Panchayat Laws and a new legislation known as Gujarat Panchayats Act, 1993 was enacted in order to comply with all the provisions of the 73rd Constitutional Amendment. Apart from all other mandatory provisions relating to the Panchayats at all levels, reservations have been provided for women (33 per cent), Scheduled Castes and Scheduled Tribes (in proportion of population) and for OBCs (10 per cent). Direct elections were held per sarpanch and members of Taluk Panchayats and District Panchayats. An independent Election Commission was appointed to conduct elections to PRIs.

There are 13216 Gram Panchayats in the State. Gram Panchayat may constitute various committees for the effective working but formation of a Social Justice Committee at the Panchayat level has been made mandatory. The Act provides that a District Panchayat may, with the previous sanction of the State Government, make bylaws for a village panchayat. The services of Talati have been made available to the village panchayats. He functions as a secretary, even prior to the introduction of new panchayati raj in the state. There are 12352 talaties-cum-village panchayat secretaries in the state. The State Government bears the full expenditure on account of salaries and training cost of these officials but recovers 35 per cent of land revenue collection of the state as part of contribution from the panchayats. The Panchayats are also empowered to appoint other officers and servants as per their requirement.

There are 182 Taluka Panchayats in the state. It is mandatory for a Taluka Panchayat to constitute an Executive Committee to discharge various functions of the Taluka Panchayat and a Social Justice Committee for performing such functions as are considered essential for securing social justice to the weaker sections of the society. The term of executive committees is only 2 years while that of the social justice committee is co-extensive with that of the Taluka Panchayat. In Tribal Block areas an officer of higher status of Deputy District Development Officer is posted as Taluka Development Officer. Taluka Development Officer is appointed by the State Government to function as Secretary and Chief Executive of the Taluka Panchayat. Other functionaries like Extension Officer, Gram Sevaks, Stockman, Primary School Teachers, Talati-cum-Village Panchayat Secretaries are functioning under the Taluka panchayat.

The Taluka Panchayat in Gujarat is entrusted with the functions of planning and execution of agricultural programmes and works, timely and equitable distribution of inputs and full use of water available under irrigation schemes; besides facility of pure drinking water, construction and maintenance of village approach roads, establishing information and community recreation centres, training of Gram Sevaks, welfare activities of women and child, planning for increased employment and production, pr^motion of cooperative societies and village and small scale industries, provision for hostels for backward classes, scheduled castes and scheduled tribes, rural housing schemes and establishing village defence corps, etc.

The Taluka Panchayats are empowered to impose education cess and have concurrent powers to levy taxes and fees leviable by Gram Panchayats. It also receives 15 per cent of the land revenue and can raise the rate of stamp duty upto 15 per cent on transfer of immovable property. A large amount of funds are also received by Taluk Panchayat for execution of schemes from District Panchayats apart from a grant from the District Equalization fund.

There are 25 district panchayats in the state. District panchayats are functioning with the help of statutory committees. An officer of the status of the Collector has been posted as the Chief Executive of the District Panchatyat who has also been designated as District Development Officer. The Sate Government have also posted Class I & II Officers of the State Services under the District Panchayat on deputation in respect of the District Level Officers of Agriculture, Family Planning, Education, Social Welfare, Animal Husbandry, Cooperation, Block Development, Panchayats, Revenue Administration, Accounts and Public Works Department. In addition Government have transferred all other Class III and Class IV of the State Service officials in respect of the respective Government functions transferred to the Panchayats. The Chief Executive Officer of the District Panchyat is also the Chairperson of the DRDA.

The Gujarat Panchayats Act provides for devolution of functions as listed in Schedule I, II and III in favour of the Village, Taluka and District Panchayats respectively. This has been done in conformity with the 29 subjects listed in Schedule 11th of the Constitution. In addition a special provision has been made under the new Act that previous delegation of powers and transfer of functions made under the earlier Act shall be kept intact and further devolution of powers and responsibilities can be made under the new provisions of this Act. Out of the 29 activities listed in 11th Schedule of the Constitution 15 activities are completely within the purview of the Panchayats at all levels.

A large number of statutory functions have also been transferred to PRIs in respect of Acts and Rules on land revenue, agricultural and non-agricultural loans and cooperatives. As a result of this they have been empowered for collection of land revenue, cesses and other dues. The maintenance of accounts for this purpose, permission for non-agricultural use of land and imposing penalties, maintenance of boundary marks, disposal of certain village sites, tank-bed land, minor produce like murham, sand, etc. and flowing water for irrigation use in the condition of scarcity and flood damage are also provided through panchayats.

A large amount of resources have been transferred by the government to PRIs in Gujarat to make them financially viable and strong. An amount of Rs. 2210.45 crores was spent through the three tier panchayats during 1997-98 transferred to the PRIs in the form of grant by the Government. For the financial year 1999-2000 a provision of Rs. 2791.87 crores have been kept constituting 75.46 per cent of the State Government Budget under the plan and non-plan schemes allotted and transferred to panchayats. This also constitutes around 15.42 per cent of the total budget of the State Government. The State Government have also provided untied funds constituting nearly 20 per cent of the total state plan in order to enable PRIs to formulate their District Plans in true sense.

There are statutory funds at the district and taluk levels which have been created out of the income from taxes or fees, sale proceeds of all dust, dirt etc., sums contributed by the State Government, funds received by way of loans and Government contribution, income from the property vested in these bodies, net proceeds of cess and stamp duty along with all sums realized by way of rent, penalty, etc. Hundred per cent of the land revenue collected in the district is also assigned to the PRIs of which 35 per cent is transferred to the Government towards contribution for salaries of Talaties and 5 per cent for state equalization fund. Rest of the 60 per cent of total land revenue grant is distributed among PRIs in the district. The PRIs are also authorized to recover upto 30 paise per rupee of land revenue as cess on land revenue, and 20 paise on every rupee of water rate is also leviable as cess on water rate. The PRIs are also authorized to impose taxes and fees on professions, trade, minor minerals like sand and quarry fees, which is distributable at the rate of 75 per cent and 25 per cent respectively between district panchayats and taluk panchayats.

Madhya Pradesh

Madhya Pradesh took the lead in implementing the panchayati raj system as envisaged in the 73rd Constitution Amendment Act and was the first state to conduct elections to PRIs in 1994. The Madhya Pradesh Panchayati Raj Act, 1993 was enacted to create and amend existing laws for the establishment of PRIs. The conformity Act contains all mandated provisions of the Constitution. The structure of the panchayati raj continues to tbe three-tiered one. Gram sabha has been included in the new Act. The gram sabha consists of all people in the voter list of every village. The gram sabha should meet at least four times in a year. The sarpanch or upa-sarpanch presides over the meeting and the secretary of the Gram Panchayat convenes the meeting.

Each village or cluster of villages is required to have a Gram Panchayat with a tenure of 5 years. The Gram Panchayat consists of elected panches from the wards, an elected sarpanch and upa-sarpanch. Each Gram Panchayat is required to have three standing committees. These committees exercise powers asassigned by the Gram Panchayat. Under section 49 of the State Act gram panchayats are expected to perform several civic, administrative, regulatory, development and maintenance functions. Properly tax on land or building, lighting tax, professional tax, market fee and fee on registration of cattle sold in markets are the important sources of revenue of the Gram Panchayats. The Panchayat Secretary or Village Karmi is to function as the secretary to the Gram Panchayat.

The Janpad Panchayat, the second tier of the panchayati raj system is constituted at the block level and consists of members elected from the constituencies, members coopted from the marketing societies or cooperatives and all members of the state legislative assembly representing constituencies of the block. Every Janpad Panchayat makes five standing committees from its members. These committees are General Administration Committee, Agriculture Committee Education Committee, Communication and Works Committee and the Cooperation and Industries Committee. The Janpad Panchayat is entrusted with development, maintenance and regulatory functions. According to Section 51 of the Act, it is obligatory on the part of the Janpad Panchayat to act as an agent of government in respect of such functions entrusted by the State Government on matters relating to development activities. The Janpad Panchayat can impose tax on theater and other public entertainment places. It can also collect fees for any licence or permission for use and occupation of lands or other properties vested in or maintained by the Janpad Panchayat. A Chief

Executive Officer appointed by the government is responsible for keeping and maintaining the records of the Janpad Panchayat.

Every district has a Zilla Panchayat consisting of members from the constituencies, chairperson of District Cooperatives and Development Bank, members of the Lok Sabha representing the district and members of Rajya Sabha returned from the state whose names appear in the voter list of a Gram Panchayat within the district. The president and the vice-president of the zilla panchayat are elected for 5 years. The Zilla Panchayat controls and supervises the administration of the District Rural Development Agency. All functions and schemes assigned to DRDA by the State Government are being implemented by the Zilla Panchayat. The Zilla Panchayat also exercises such powers which the state government entrust it from time to time. The Zilla Panchayat is not vested with any taxation power. An amendment to the 1993 Act in 1997 empowers the Zilla Panchayat to increase the rate of cess on land revenue to the extent of Rs.10. A government appointee called the Chief Executive Officer acts as the Secretary of the Zilla Panchayat and is responsible for keeping and maintaining records.

The State Government have been continuously devolving powers and authority to the PRIs and initiating innovative measures to empower, strengthen and institutionalize the PRIs. The Government of Madhya Pradesh have formulated some guiding principles for devolution of powers and functions to PRIs. According to these guidelines all the state subjects have been bifurcated into two categories i.e., State Sector and Panchayat Sector. The State Government have transferred various schemes pertaining to 20 departments to PRIs and have issued comprehensives orders for execution of such schemes. Necessary funds and staff which were available for such schemes with the state government have also been transferred to PRIs. The State Government have also changed and issued office orders and amended the Panchayati Raj Act itsef to address the problems of PRIs. Thus willingness and flexibility of the state government to tackle bottele-necks has given strength to the panchayati raj system in Madhya Pradesh.

West Bengal

The West Bengal Panchayat Act, 1973 was amended in 1992 itself to make provisions for reservation of one-third of the seats for women as well as the SCs and STs. The State Act was further amended in 1994 and 1995 so as to conform to the provisions of the 73rd Constitution Amendment Act. The amended state legislation has provided for a three tier panchayati raj system. The three-tiers are Gram Panchayat, Panchayat Samithi and Zilla Parishad. It has also provided for the creation of Gram Sabha, a body consisting of persons registered in the electoral rolls relating to a village. The Act has gone further and created a new and unique body called Gram Sansad to guide and advise gram panchayat in regard to schemes for economic development and social justice. The first elections, on the basis of these amended provisions, to the PRIs were held in 1993.

There are, at present, in West Bengal 3325 Panchayats, 340 Panchayat Samithis and 17 Zilla Parishads. Each Panchayat Samithi and Zilla Parishad has 10 Sthayee Samithis (standing committees) which cover the matters related to public importance. Besides, a Samanvaya Samithi headed by the chairperson of the Panchayat Samithi or the Zilla Parishad, as the case may be, coordinates the functions between a standing committee and the panchayati raj institution and also amongst different standing committees. In order to ensure inter-tier institutional co-ordination, a very strong system has been created in the State, where, firstly, panchayat samithis have been given powers to oversee activities of the gram panchayat and Zilla Parishad to those of panchayat samithis. Directly elected members of Panchayat Samithis are ex-officio members of the concerned gram panchayat and pradhans of gram panchayats are in turn ex-officio members of the concerned Panchayat Samithis. Similar inter-linkages have been established in case of Zilla Parishad and Panchayat Samithis by making directly elected Zilla Parishad members as ex-officio members of the concerned Panchayat Samithis and Sabhapatis of Panchayat Samithis as ex-officio members of Zilla Parishad.

The required paraphernalia of staff has been provided to the PRIs at all levels. At the gram panchayat level a Job Assistant, 3 Panchayat Karmis, 3 Tax Collectors and a full time secretary have been provided as core staff who are being paid directly by the State Government through BDO. At the Panchyat Samithi level there is an Executive Officer who exercises control over all officers and employees of the Pancayat Samiti and is also empowered to award punishments. Apart from an Executive Officer, there is a Secretary and Extension Officers and other ministerial staff.

The District Magistrate has been made as ex-officio Executive Officer of Zilla Parishad. He is assisted by an Officer in the rank of ADM as full time Additional Chief Executive Officer who is further assisted by a Secretary appointed by the Government from State Civil Services. The District Engineer, Executive Engineer, Assistant Engineer and other staff of the rural development department are placed on deputation of Zilla Parishad. There is an Accountant supported by two Assistant Accountants and one cashier who are responsible for management of finances and maintenance of accounts.

A wide range of powers, duties and functions have been assigned to PRIs in West Bengal. Apart from vast administrative and financial powers, Gram Panchayats perform multifarious local activities, which have been categorized as obligatory functions and assigned functions. Under the obligatory functions, there are 14 items ranging from sanitation, drainage, prevention of public nuisance, curative and preventive measures in respect of malaria and small pox, etc., supply of drinking water, arrangement and care of public tanks, public common grounds, burning ghats and public grave yards; to organizing voluntary labour for community working and works for the upliftment of its area and supply of any information which the Zilla Parishad or Panchayat Samithi may require.

There are as many as 21 items under the assigned functions which include primary, social, technical and vocational education, rural dispensaries and health centers, irrigation, care of infirm destitutes, rehabilitation of displaced persons, breed improvement and prevention of cattle diseases, land reform measures and poverty alleviation programmes. Other discretionary functions include maintenance of lighting public streets, planting and maintenance of trees on the sites of public streets, sinking of wells and excavation of ponds and tanks, construction and regulation of market, promotion and encouragement of cottage industries; and establishment and maintenance of libraries and reading rooms, etc.

The Panchayat Samithis have also been assigned to perform various functions and programmes related to 18 sectors like agriculture, fisheries, livestock, khadi, cottage and small scale industries, etc. The zilla parishads have been given an active role in all the sectors assigned to Panchayat Samithis. The zilla parishads have also been delegated with the following administrative and financial powers:

(1) A Zilla Parishad can undertake or execute any scheme if it extends to more than one block.

(2) A Zilla Parishad has the power to advise the State Government on all matters relating to the development work among gram panchayat and panchayat samithis.

(3) A Zilla Parishad is empowered to take over the maintenance and control of any road, bridge, tank, ghat, well, channel or drain belonging to a private owner or any other authority on such terms as may be agreed upon.

(4) A Zilla Parishad has authority to exercise general powers of supervision over Panchayat Samithis and Gram Panchayats in the district and it would be the duty of these authorities to give effect to any direction of the Zilla Parishad.

(5) A Zilla Parishad is empowered with the approval of the State Government, to raise loans for the purpose of the Act and create sinking fund for repayment of such loans.

(6) Every Zilla Parishad is required to prepare in each year a budget of its estimated receipts and disbursements for the following year and submit it to the State Government.

In addition to the above functions, the State Government have transferred all 29 items under Eleventh Schedule grouped in 17 items to the panchyats under section 207 B of the West Bengal State Panchayat Amendment Act, 1994. Apart from this some departments have also assigned as many as 24 departmental schemes for implementation to different levels of PRIs.

The sources of income of PRIs are taxation and income generating activities, assigning revenue and schematic grants from the State Government. A system of statutory audit by independent audit wing has been created. Apart from this, a unique system of constituting district councils has been introduced for examining and scrutinizing the accounts of Panchayats and satisfying itself that financial norms and procedures are applied with the Pancayats in the district. The district councils consist of an Adhyaksh who is the leader of the largest recognized political party in opposition in the district, one Upadhyaksh and 5 more members elected by the members of Zilla Parishad and 3 government officers nominated by the Government as members. The Additional Executive Officer, Zilla Parishad functions as its Member Secretary.

Kerala

In March 1994, the State Government introduced the Kerala Panchayati Raj Bill in the State Legislature. The provisions in this bill were very restrictive and led to a great deal of criticism both from intellectuals and public men. As a result of strong public opinion, substantial changes were made in the bill by the Select Committee. A very much improved Kerala Panchayati Raj Act was introduced and the District Administration Act, 1979 repealed. The new Act conformed to the mandatory provisions of the Constitution. The State Act provides for the constitution of Gram Sabha, Gram Panchayat, Block Panchayat and Zilla Panchayat in the state. A brief description of their composition, powers and functions is given in this part.

Gram Sabhas are to be formed ward-wise in Kerala in view of the large size of the panchayats. They are to have a number of supervisory and monitoring powers relating to development activity and are also to assist in the identification of beneficiaries as well as in mobilization of community efforts. The village panchayat is bound to place a report before each gram sabha on the development schemes and the development activities of each year and those proposed for the next year, and the reasons for non-implementation of the recommendations of the gram sabhas would have o be explained by the president of the panchayat.

According to Section 7 of the Kerala Panchayati Raj Act, 1994, there should be Gram Panchayat for a village or a group of villages. The total number of the members of Gram Panchayat will be decided on the basis of population. It will varies from Panchayat to Panchayat. Total number of the members in the Gram Panchayat shall be between 8 and 15. All members are elected directly by the people. A fixed number of seats should be reserved for SCs and STs depending on their population. The reserved constituencies should be changed on rotation basis. One-third of the total seats of the Gram Panchayat should be reserved for women. The members of the Gram Panchayat will elect its president and vice-president from among themselves. Sections 166, 167, 168, 169, 170 and 171 of the State Act enumerate the following powers, duties and functions of the village panchayats.

1. It shall be the duty of the Village Panchayat to meet the requirements of its area in respect of the matters enumerated in the Third Schedule of the Act.
2. The Village Panchayat shall have exclusive power to administer the matters enumerated in the Third Schedule of the Act
3. Village Panchayat shall also have powers to enhance employment facilities, undertake developmental activities and start manpower banks.
4. All grants-in-aid sanctioned by the Government in respect of the matters enumerated in the Third Schedule shall be distributed through the village panchayat concerned.
5. The district panchayat or the block planchayat may transfer to the village panchayat, the management and maintenance of any institution or the execution or maintenance of any work or the exercise of any power or the discharge of any duty work within the village panchayat area whether provided in this Act or not.
6. The Government may authorise a village panchayat to exercise any power or discharge any function such as collection of land revenue, maintenance of survey and village records, collection of village statistics, supervision and control over government primary schools, execution of community development work, etc.

Section 8 of the Kerala Panchayati Raj Act states that there should be a block panchayat at the block level. Total number of members in block panchay shall be in between 8 and 15. Each block panchayat consists of :

1. Members who are directly elected by the people;
2. Presidents of the Gram Panchayats within the territorial limits of the block; and
3. Local Member of Legislative Assembly and Member of Parliament.

A fixed number of seats of the block panchayat should be reserved for SCs and STs, depending on their population in the block panchayat area. One-third of the total seats of the block panchayat should be reserved for women. The members of the block panchayat will elect its president and vice-president from among themselves. The powers and duties of Block Panchayats as mentioned in Section 172 of the State Act are:

1. Subject to the rules made under this Act, it shall be the duty of the block panchayat to meet the requirements of its area in respect of the matters enumerated in the Fourth Schedule of the Act.
2. Subject to the other provisions of this Act and the directions of the Government, the block panchyat shall have exclusive power to administer the matters enumerated in the Fourth Schedule of the Act.
3. The Government and the district panchayat shall, subject to availability of resources, provide necessary financial, technical and other assistance to the block panchayats to enable them to discharge their functions.
4. All grants-in-aid sanctioned by the Government in respect of the matters enumerated in the Fourth Schedule shall be distributed through the block panchayat concerned.
5. The Government shall, as soon as may be, after the commencement of this Act, transfer to the block panchayats all the institutions, projects, buildings, and other properties and assets and liabilities connected with the matters referred to in the Fourth Schedule.

Section 9 of the Kerala Panchayati Raj Act states that there should be a Zilla Panchayat at the district level. Total number of members in the Zilla Panchayat shall be in between 15 and 25. Each Zilla Panchayat consists of :

1. Members who are directly elected by the people;
2. The Presidents of Block Panchayat;
3. The MLAs and Members of Lok Sabha, within the territorial limits of the Zilla Parishad; and
4. The Rajya Sabha members who are included in the voter list of the district.

A fixed number of seats of Zilla Panchayat should be reserved for SCs and STs depending on their population in the district. One-third of the total seats of the Zilla Panchayat should be reserved for women. The members of the Zilla Parishad will elect its president and vice-president from among themselves. The powers and functions of Zilla Panchayat according to Section 173 of the State Act are:

1. Subject to the rules made under the Act, it shall be the duty of the district panchayat to meet the requirements of its area in respect of the matters enumerated in the Fifth Schedule of the Act
2. Subject to the other provisions of this Act and the directions of the Government, the District Panchayat shall have exclusive power to administer the matters enumerated in the Fifth schedule of the Act.
3. The Government shall, subject to availability of resources, provide necessary financial, technical and other assistance to the district panchayats to enable them to discharge their functions.
4. All grants-in-aid sanctioned by the Government in respect of the matters enumerated in the Fifth Schedule shall be distributed through the district panchayat concerned.
5. The Government shall, as soon as may be, after the commencement of this Act, transfer to the district panchayats all the institutions, projects and buildings and other properties and assets and liabilities connected with the matters referred to in the Fifth Schedule of the Act.

The Government of Kerala had appointed a Finance Commission on 22nd April, 1994 for the Panchayati Raj Institutions as mandated by the 73rd Constitution Amendment Act. The three member Commission was headed by P. Abraham, former Union Transport Secretary. The other two members were K. Ummer, former State Finance Secretary and K. Mohan Das, State Local Administration Secretary. The Commission had submitted its report before the Governor of Kerala in the first week of July, 1996. The State Finance Commission had recommended major changes in the structure of building and property taxes and entertainment tax; revision of rates for services offered by the local bodies and the fees for various licenses, constitution of rural and urban pools for the devolution of the statutory and non-statutory non-plan grants to the PRIs and Municipalities. The SFC has also suggested the regrouping the existing panchayats into four on the basis of their annual income – Rs. 20 lakh and above for the first group, in between Rs. 15 lakh and Rs. 20 lakh for the second group, in between Rs. 15 lakh and Rs. 10 lakh for the third group and Rs. 5 lakh and below for the last group. The Government accepted 64 recommendations of the Commission and gave the force of law.

There should be a standing committee for each Gram Panchayat, Block Panchayat and Zilla Panchayat for fixing taxes, checking accounts, and for all kinds of planning operations. The presidents and vice-presidents are ex-officio members of the standing committee. The chairman of the standing committee will be elected from among its member.

There is a District Planning Committee which is clothed with powers to examine and propose changes in the draft for development projects prepared by the panchayats and municipalities. The Government is to consider the proposals and priorities in the draft prepared by the District Panchayat Committee when the State Plan is prepared. The District Planning Committee has power to monitor and evaluate the implementation of the Plan.

The people's planning was launched in 1996 in Kerala to ensure maximum participation of the people in conformity with the 73rd Constitution Amendment Act and its subsequent legislation of the state in 1994. The local self-government bodies as part of people's planning movement, formulated their schemes and implemented them with people's cooperation. The movement had brought out the qualitative changes in the power decentralization sector in general and development sector in particular. People's planning has more or less acquired by now the ability to cut and clear its own path and forge ahead. The people's planning has become the urgent obligation of the local self-government bodies of the state. The main aims of peoples' planning are

1. To solve the crisis existing in the production sector (including agriculture and industry) and ensure development;
2. To end the fall in the standard of the quality in service sectors including in the health and education and improve the tribal/fish worker sectors, which have not yet reached the mainstream of development;
3. To raise the socio-economic life standards of people of the above sectors step by step and bring them to the mainstream of life;
4. To ensure balanced development in the environmental sector of the state; and
5. To deliver the womenfolk who constitute more than half of the society from the different kinds of exploitation they face today and take them to the mainstream of development.

As part of people's planning large-scale financial aid was transferred to the local self-government bodies in the state. It was only a very meager amount that the local self-government bodies in the state used to get before the beginning of this movement. In 1997-98 a sum of Rs.749 crores was provided in the budget and given as grant out of which an amount of Rs. 39 crores was earmarked for Tribal Sub Plan and an amount Rs.194 crores was provided for Special Component Plan. In 1998-99 and 1999-2000 years the plan allocation for the local self-government bodies rose to Rs. 950 crores and Rs.1020 crores respectively. An amount of Rs. 1042 crores was earmarked for the year 2000-2001.

All the aims and objectives were not achieved. There is, however, a sense of optimism developed among the people, that if worked on the basis of people's participation with will power and determination, a lot of things could be implemented. Objectives and transparent style of taking decisions based on distinct priorities and norms have come to stay in the majority of the local self-government bodies. The most important achievement of the village assemblies is that they could prove that they have a very crucial role in the planning.

The people's plan programme envisaged a structural change in the formulation and implementation of development plans. Every stage of planning was shaped by people's participation. The previous practice of planning from above, i.e., from Kerala State Planning Board at the capital city, gave way to the new practice of planning from below. The grassroot level plan formulation and implementation necessitated a lot of structural changes in the formulation and finalization of plan projects.

The people's planning programme gave a new vigour to panchayats in all the key issues related to economic development of their area.[3] Panchayats became centres of a hub of activities. The traditional concept of panchayat gave way to a new notion. The panchayat presidents and other elected representatives began to assume more responsibilities and increased powers. Along with the traditional functions they began to perform the duty of local planning of development activities also. Project formulation through gram sabhas and ward sabhas was one of the most important features of the decentralization process.[4] Through the people campaign power had not only been transferred to the local bodies, but also to the hundreds of people who had attended the Gram Sabhas and Ward Sabhas. Their aspirations were later translated into development projects.

The Government of Kerala has appointed high power committee under the Chairmanship of S.B. Sen, Chairman of West Bengal Finance Commission, to consider and recommend modifications for decentralization of powers under the Kerala Panchayati Raj Act, 1994 and other related Acts and Rules. The ten member Committee was appointed on 4th July, 1996. The Committee had detailed interaction with the State Planning Board, District Panchayat Presidents, Mayors, representatives of Municipal Chairpersons, Block and Grama Panchayat Presidents, District Collectors, Directors of Panchayats, Municipal Administration and Local Funds Audit Departments. After fourteen sittings the Committee had submitted its interim report on 14 August 1996, with the following major recommendations.

1. The Block and District Panchayats should be accorded the importance that the Block and District level administrative machinery now has.
2. The Block Development Officers shall continue as Secretaries of Block Panchayats.
3. The District Rural Development Agencies and District Development Committees shall be dissolved.
4. The concept of social audit to check corruption at the Panchayat level shall be introduced.
5. A Women's Vigilance Committee to monitor the implementation of specific schemes shall be set up in each panchayat.
6. The present practices relating to grant of various sanctions should be revised. Both the administrative sanction and technical sanction for schemes formulated by the panchayats shall be sanctioned at that level itself, so that

panchayat authorities should not be required to wait at the doors of bureaucrats for obtaining sanction for schemes prepared by their own technical personnel.

7. The Functional Committees shall be set up in all Grama Pancayats to deal with specific functions. These Committees would be in charge of implementation of specific schemes drawn up by each Grama Panchayat.
8. The PRIs should have total control over the officials placed under them.
9. The State Government shall appoint District Collectors as ex-officio secretaries of the District Panchayats and junior IAS officials to assist the Collectors.

The Kerala Legislative Assembly made amendments to Panchayati Raj Act in February 1999 on the basis of the principles propounded and recommendations made by the Sen Committee. The amendments to the Panchayat Raj Act were intended to strengthen the power decentralization process and to expand the powers and responsibilities given to the three-tier system as per the 73rd amendment to the Constitution. As a result of amendment to the State Act, the PRIs have been meaningfully empowered through massive transfer of resources as well as administrative powers. In order to make participation meaningful, the amended Act has clarified the role of Gram Sabha in an elaborate manner and given substantial power and responsibility to the institution. The State Election Commission is armed with ample powers. Besides conducting election to the local self government bodies, the powers like division of wards, reservation of wards, disqualification of people's representatives, implementation of Prohibition of Defection Act, etc. are vested with the Election Commission. Prior to this, these powers were vested in the Government.

Tamil Nadu

The Government of Tamil Nadu passed the Tamil Nadu Panchayats Act, 1994 to give effect to the 73rd Constitution

Amendment Act. The Act has provided for a three-tier system with a Village Panchayat at the grassroot level, Panchayat Union at the intermediate level and District Panchayat at the district level. The Act has also provided for Gram Sabha. A specific number of positions at all levels of the PRIs are reserved for women (one-third) and SCs and STs (in proportion to their population). An Election Commission headed by the State Election Commissioner was appointed by the Governor of Tamil Nadu. The Election Commissioner enjoys powers and privileges and status of a judge of a High Court. The State Finance Commission consisting of a chairman and four other members was also constituted by the Tamil Nadu Government. The elections to PRIs in the state were held in October, 1996 under the new legislation. There are at present 12,618 Village Panchayats, 385 Panchayat Unions and 28 District Panchayats in Tamil Nadu.

Under the 1994 Act for the first time in Tamil Nadu's history of local self-governance, provisions have been made for convening Gram Sabha meetings in each Village Panchayat.[5] The Gram Sabha under the new panchayati raj system in the State is intended to be an important instrument of participatory decision making. The Gram Sabha shall meet thrice in a year and the president of the Village Panchayat shall convene its meetings. The Gram Sabha will meet

(1) to approve the village plan, the annual village budget, village audit report on the village panchayat's accounts of previous years, list of beneficiaries selected and location of community facilities identified by the village panchayat;

(2) to review the progress of the implementation of the schemes entrusted to the village panchayats;

(3) to mobilize voluntary labour, cash and other contributions for community welfare and development programmes; and

(4) to promote harmony among the various groups residing in the village.

A village panchayat is constituted for a minimum population of 500. The number of wards of Village Panchayat varies from 5 to 15. The ward members and the President are to re-elected directly by the voters. The Vice-President of the Village Panchayat is elected indirectly among the ward members of the Village Panchayats. The President of the Village Panchayat has been designated as executive head and has been entrusted with powers and responsibilities.

For each development block, a Panchayat Union is formed. Each Panchayat Union has a chairperson and a vice-chairperson elected indirectly by the members of the Panchayat Union. The Union Panchayat members are elected directly by the people. For every 5,000 population, one Union Council member will be elected by the people. The MPs and MLAs elected from the area are ex-officio members of the Panchayat Union Council. There are two administrative divisions in the Panchayat Union. One is headed by the Block Development Officer and the other by the Assistant Block Development Officer. The two sections work independently with their supporting staff.

The District Panchayat is constituted with the directly elected members. The chairperson and vice-chairperson have to be elected among the council members. The MLAs and MPs of the district are the ex-officio members of the District Panchayats. There are three offices to enable the District Panchayat office to perform the earmarked functions. The Divisional Development Office, which is nearer to the district headquarters will supervise the District Panchayat activities. Another office, which is away from the headquarters will look after the auditing of the District Panchayat Accounts. The third office will be attached to the District Panchayat.

Originally, the 29 subjects have been incorporated in the State Act without specific responsibilities delineation among the three tiers. Subsequently some measures have been initiated by the State Government to clearly assign functional responsibilities among the three tiers. A Commission under the Chairmanship L.C. Jain was appointed in 1997 to provide the guidelines for entrustment of powers and responsibilities to the PRIs. The Jain Commission had classified the functions to be entrusted to PRIs under four heads namely planning, implementation, supervision and coordination. The Commission has also proposed inter-tier allocation of the 29 subjects. The State Government issued orders, which delineate functional responsibilities among the three tiers.

The Tamil Nadu Act assigned five taxes for Village Panchayats and one local surcharge for Panchayat Union. In addition there are 11 items of fees and duties and 14 other non-tax revenue sources. The statutory, non-statutory and development grants are also available to the village panchayats and Panchayat Unions. The State Government had accepted the recommendations of the First State Finance Commission. Under Pool-A, assigned revenue, local cess, local cess surcharge, surcharge on stamp duty, and seigniorage fees on minor minerals are fully assigned to the village panchayats. Local cess surcharge is fully assigned to the Panchayat Union. Under Pool-B, divisible pool, as recommended by the SFC, the State Government follow the policy of sharing with the PRIs by grouping all the state tax revenue except entertainment tax. This makes the level of devolution more predictable since the total revenue does not fluctuate as much as proceeds from each tax.[6]

The Government of Tamil Nadu have, thus, initiated measures in tune with the Constitutional Amendment. The efforts of the State Government deserve to be commended. There are, however, some areas which need improvement. The bureaucracy has armed with itself with certain arbitrary powers such as dissolution of the PRIs and preparation of the budgets of the Village Panchayat and Panchayat Union. The District Collector has the controlling authority on PRIs. The government officers shall not be given major role in PRIs and the functional autonomy shall be given to the elected representatives. The resource requirement to meet the functions assigned for the PRIs should be quantified and the revenue should be allocated accordingly.

Karnataka

The Karnataka Panchayati Raj Act, 1983 was substituted by a new law in 1993, i.e. the Karnataka Panchayati Raj Act, 1993 to accommodate the mandatory provisions brought in by the 73rd Constitutional Amendment. The 1993 Act replaced the existing two-tier structure and provided for a three-tier structure of pancnayat raj system. The three tiers are – Gram Panchayat, Taluk Panchayat and Zilla Panchayat. The Act also provides for a Gram Sabha.

Of the three tiers of PRIs, Gram Panchayat is the most important tier as it is directly involved in local governance. The Gram Panchayat is constituted for a population of not less than 5,000 and not more than 7,000. The area of a village or a group of villages will be considered as a panchayat area and there will be one member for every 400. At the Gram Pancnayat level there are three different committees for production, social justice and amenities to execute the developmental programmes.

A model staffing pattern has been prescribed by the government for village panchayats which includes a Secretary who is a government servant paid from the Zilla Panchayat funds and other employees like Bill Collectors, Jawans, Waterman, etc. Any increase in the strength and appointment of employees is to be made with the approval of the Chief Executive Officer of Zilla Panchayat.

The financial resource of Village Panchayats consists mainly of tax on building, entertainment, markets and levey on water, etc., share of cesses on land revenue, statutory grants of Rs.1 lakh by the Government every year, grants from the

Government of India under Finance Commission awards and other funds transferred for various schemes by the Central or State Government. The State Government also provides Rs.1 lakh per annum for paying electricity bills, maintenance of drinking water schemes, rural sanitation and other activities for each Panchayat area.

A Taluk Panchayat has been constituted for every revenue taluk as the intermediate in the panchayati raj system. It consists of elected members at the rate of one member for every 10,000 population or part thereof. However, taluks having a population of not exceeding one lakh have 11 elected members. The Taluk Panchayat is functioning through three standing committees namely General Standing Committee, Finance, Audit and Planning Committee and Social Justice Committee.

At the Taluk Panchayat level an Executive Officer of the SDO level has been appointed apart from the BDO. The Executive Officer not only functions as Secretary of the Taluk Panchayat but also coordinates and supervises implementation of all development activities of Taluk Panchayat. The officers of fisheries department working at Taluk level are, however, borne on the establishment of Zilla Panchayat. Other functionaries who assist the Executive Officer are Junior Engineer, Credit Extension Officer and supporting staff of administration and accounts, etc.

Taluk Panchayats have no powers to raise resources through taxation. There is a mandatory provision in the Act that State Government shall make a grant to every Taluk Panchayat to cover the expenditure of establishment. Apart from discretionary grants for specific purposes, some of them are also deriving income from immovable assets and their additional stamp duty at 3 per cent on the value of the instrument of sale or mortgage of immovable properties collected in the State which is also apportioned between the Taluk Panchayats in proportion to their population.

The Zilla Panchayat consists of elected members at the rate of one member for every 40,000 population and part thereof. In Zilla Panchayat there are 5 standing committees namely General Standing Committee, Finance, Audit and Planning Committee, Social Jutice Committee, Education and Health Committee and Agriculture and Industries Committee.

The senior scale officers of IAS cadre are posted as chief executive officers in all Zilla Panchayats. The Chief Executive Officer of the Zilla Panchayat is assisted by a Council Secretary, Deputy Secretary (Administration), Deputy Secretary (Development), Chief Accounts Officer, a Chief Planning Officer along with other junior officer and supporting staff. A separate Engineering Division is also functioning under the Chief Executive Officer (Zilla Parishad), headed by the Executive Engineer. The district level officers of nearly 28 departments also are functioning under the administrative control of Zilla Panchayat.

The Zilla Panchayats do not have any power to levy taxes and virtually all their resources are received from the government, for meeting establishment expenses, implementing various development programmes under the State or Central sector plan and also for implementation of schemes transferred under various sectors to PRIs. A massive transfer of resources to the district sector has, however, been made by the State Government by making a distinct provision in the State budget while making sectoral allocations. A lump sum is indicated in advance to each Zilla Panchayat as its plan outlay. Zilla Panchayat in turn makes allocation to the Taluk Panchayats and Gram Panchayats

In all PRIs the reservations were provided to the SCs, STs, OBC and women. The SEC was appointed in May 1993. First Elections to all the tiers were conducted in December, 1993. Reservations for the offices of Adhyaksha and Upadhyaksha is on the basis of rotation among different categories. Now there are 5640 Gram Panchayats at the grass-root level, 175 Taluk Panchayats at the middle level and 20 Zilla Panchayats at the district level. There is no separate identity of DRDAs in the State. The functions of DRDAs are being carried out by the Zilla Panchayat itself. The State Government has already constitute District Planning Committees.

Karnataka is known for devolution and transfer of a wide range of State's functions to Zilla Panchayat and Mandal Panchayat as back as in 1987. After the enactment of the new legislation there seems to be a further enhancement in the powers and functions of PRIs in the State. As many as 70 activities of 31 sectors have been assigned to Panchayats under Schedule I (Section 58) of this Act. As regards Taluka Panchayats, Schedule II (Section 145) of this Act provides for 56 activities of 28 sectors whereas for Zilla Panchayats 60 activities of 29 sectors have been assigned under Schedule III (Section 184) of this Act. These provisions for all the three tiers are no doubt mandatory in its nature but again subjected to the condition that such functions shall be performed by these institutions on provision of funds and also in accordance of the guidelines and norms laid down for this purpose. This would mean that these functions can be performed by these institutions only after provision of funds by the Government. The Government has also been authorized by the legislature to prescribe certain guidelines and norms in respect of each of these functions. The State Government have, however, already transferred adequate funds to PRIs in order to enable them to perform almost all the functions of the State in aforesaid Schedules appended to this Act.

The state Act further provides for certain obligatory functions to be performed by all the three tiers of these institutions as per availability of funds at their disposal. The State government has also been authorized under this Act for assignment of certain functions by notification to Gram Panchayats under section 59 of the Act, to Taluk Panchayat under section 146 of the Act and to Zilla Panchayats under section 185 of this Act. In this case the Government has also been authorized to withdraw or modify such functions assigned to PRIs by notification as may be deemed necessary from time to time.

In Karnataka there has been a large devolution of functions, along with commensurate financial resources and personnel. There is better delivery of services, an increase in the number of micro level projects taken up and a greater measure of accountability at the local level. The panchayati raj has given an opportunity to a large number of peoples representatives to participate actively in local programme including substantial numbers from SCs, STs and BCs. The representation of women has gone up sharply at all levels. But the situation can not be considered to be wholly satisfactoriy. The decentralized planning is yet to become a reality. Panchayats at the lower levels do not have staff support needed for meaningful planning. Planning continues to be essentially a top down process.

A Critical Evaluation

In conformity with the constitutional amendment, the states have incorporated, in their panchayati raj legislations, appropriate provisions regarding powers, functions and funds of PRIs. There are, however, wide variations in the actual implementaiton of these statutory provisions. Only few states had given functional and financial autonomy to PRIs where a strong political will was exercised while others had retained most of the powers and functions of 29 subjects.

In Maharashtra a very strong and powerful system of panchayati raj was established and district was accepted as a unit of devolution of powers and panchayat samithis as executive arms of of Zilla Parishad. A wide range of powers, duties and funcitons have been assigned to PRIs in West Bengal. As a result, the PRIs in this state are very strong bodies to funciton as real institutions of self-governance. There was strong panchayati raj system in Karnataka before the constitutional amendment. There is a further enhancement in the powers and functions of PRIs under the new Act of 1993. In Madhya Pradesh, various administrtive and financial powers have been delegated to the District Government instead of PRIs. In Gujarat only 15 out of 29 subjects have been transferred to PRIs. The Rajasthan Government have chosen to delegate only a very few subjects and PRIs are mainly functioning as agencies of state government rather than as institutions of self-governance as mandated by the Constitution.[7] Some states have devolved more power to intermediate or district level PRIs whereas some states have ignored these institutions and transferred powers only to Village Panchayats. The PRIs are not entrusted with the task of developmnt planning and implementaiton. In many states, the state government departments are implementating the functions of PRIs.

An analysis of functioning of panchayati raj in the states clearly indicates that despite several attempts by the government, civil society and other concerned actors, the PRIs could not truly emerge as people's institutions. It was expected that the newly created panchayati raj system, drawing strength from the constitutional provisions, would emerge as an effective tool of local self – governance and would strongly further the primary objectives of economic growth and social justice. Unfortunately these expectations have remained largely unfulfilled.

The state governments claim that most of the subjects included in the eleventh schedule have been devolved to PRIs. However, the findings of research studies reveal that the state governments have not given appropriate functional responsibilities to the PRIs. The State Governments have been willing to hold elections and to respect stipulations governing reservations for scheduled castes, scheduled tribes and women. But they have been unwilling to vest the PRIs with sufficient administrative control over significant functions or fiscal autonomy. Most of the states had satisfied only the basic requirements relating to the transfer of functions, functionaries, funds and financial autonomy to PRIs. Certain provisions of the amendment were mandatory, while on many others, the state legislatures could make its own provisions.

The functions and powers of PRIs have been left to the discretion of the state government. The Art. 243 G is the heart of the whole scheme of decentralization contained in the Act, but it is not mandatory on the part of the States because in this article the word 'may' is used five times. Thus it is at the discretion of the state government that it "may" give or "may not" give powers to the PRIs. The 73rd Constituion Amendment Act, thus, gives the states considerable powers in deciding the nature and scale of devolution of powers to PRIs.

The 'conformity' legislations outline the powers, functions and procedures of local government at village, district and intermediate levels. The conformity Acts also recognize the possibility that changing circumstances will give rise to new regulatory requirements and, therefore, give individual states substantial autonomy to enact rules of 'delegated legisaltion' which emerge through government orders and which in actual fact are the source of state control over the PRIs. States reserve the right to assign or withdraw functions to and from the PRIs by executive fiat. Most of the states have retained powers of appointment, dismissal and review over the PRIs.

The reluctance on the part of state governments to decentralize power and inadequacies in terms of functional devolution have made the PRIs fail as vibrant institutions of self-government.[8] The Union Ministry of Rural Areas and Employment had advised the states several times for devolution of powers to PRIs. The Task Force set up in 2001 as a result of the resolution of the conference of panchayati raj ministers had requested the state governments and union territories to complete the process of devolution of powers to the PRIs by March 2002. However, in many states devolution of powers has been so far very limited. This is constraning effective functioning of the PRIs. It has also been causing disappointment and frustration among the elected representatives. The frequent redefining of the roles and responsibilities of PRIs through amendments and office orders is also a great hindrance.

It is clear from the above discussion efforts have been made by the state governments in devolution of powers, functions and funds to PRIs. But not much improvement has not been noticed in the functioning of the PRIs. There is, therefore, the need to enlarge the functions of the PRIs. In the states where the PRIs are endowed with increasing functions and responsibilities their functional capabilities have to be improved appropriately by adoption of suitable measures. Schedule 11 should be made mandatory on the lines of Union and State lists and this schedule should be enlarged to include all administrative, regulatory and maintenance functions. The comprehensive development of rural areas is possible through the success of PRIs. For their success the constitutional provisions regarding organizational structure, powers and functions must be enforced strictly. The power of dissolving PRIs in an arbitrary manner by state government should be restricted.

One of the most important weaknesses relating to functioning of PRIs is that of revenue generation. The PRIs cannot fulfill their functions without sufficient funds. Many states have not transferred funds to the PRIs for the subjects devolved upon them. Many states have introduced the requirement that the PRIs make matching payments for particular schemes such as irrigation works or drinking water supply. The ability to raise resources to meet such requirements is highly constrained by the size of the local revenue base. The panchayats at all levels have inadequate powers of taxation.

Article 243-G stipulates that the state legislature may authorize the PRIs to levy and collect taxes, duties, tolls and fees. The legislature may also assign to them taxes, etc. levied and collected by the state government as well as may provide for making grants – in- aid to the PRIs from the state consolidated fund. Article 243-I provides for the appointment of State Finance Commission by the Governor in the beginning of enforcement of Amendment Act and later within every five years to review financial position of the PRIs and recommend principles and measures for its improvement. The new or amended state panchayati raj Acts include financial provisions in conformity with the Constitution Amendment Act. The legislatures of many states authorize only village level panchayats to collect taxes. The other two tiers have not been given powers to mobilize their internal resources.

The PRIs cannot plan and implement schemes for economic development and social justice as mandated by the Constitution unless they are given powers to generate resources and statutory entitlement to share the total revenue of the State. The entire tax revenue of the state should become distributable between the State Government and Local Government with mandatory backing and force of law. All plan and non-plan funds related to 29 subjects should be transferred to PRIs. The total amount of land revenue should be assigned to PRIs. The PRIs may be allowed to use local resources such as ponds, forests etc.

The decisions to which taxes, duties, tolls and fees should be assigned to local bodies and which should be shared by the state with them are with the state legislature. The SFCs were established by many states but few states have given mandatory powers to the SFCs.[9] The state governments have been slow and hesitate in accepting the recommendations of the SFCs. The SFC should be given mandatory powers and it should be made mandatory to the state governments to accept and implement the recommendations of SFC. The National Finance Commission and Planning Commission should also come forward to make available regular flow of funds to the PRIs.

Many state governments have not transferred the required staff to the PRIs after the devolution of the powers. Only some states like Gujarat, Karnataka, Kerala, Madhya Pradesh, and Rajasthan have transferred the functionaries and issued instructions to keep them under the control of the PRIs. In many instances the attitude of state official machinery is not favourable to the PRIs. Many government officers are not willing to work under the administrative control of elected PRIs. The state governments should, therefore, keep required staff under the administrative control of PRIs. The PRIs should also have disciplinary control over such staff.

References

1. Sriram Maheswari, *Local Government in India*, Agra, Lakshmi Narain Agarwal, 2005, p. 192.
2. B.S. Khanna, *Rural Local Government in India and South Asia*, New Delhi, Deep & Deep Publications, 1999, p. 43.
3. E.M. Thomas, "Decentralised Planning and Transfer of Development Functions: A Case Study of Four Village Panchayats in Kerala", *Administrtive Change*, Vol. XXXI, No. 2 and Vol.XXXII, No.1, January-December 2004, p. 99.
4. M.R. Biju, "Decentralised Planning Process in Kerala: A Unique Experiment of Participatory Democracy" in M.R. Biju (ed.), *Decemntralisaiton: An Indian Experience*, New Delhi, National Publishing House, 2007, p. 200.
5. K. Chandrashekar (ed.), *Panchayati Raj in India – Status Report 1999*, New Delhi, Rajiv Gandhi Foundaiton, 2000, p. 213.

6. M. Naganathan and K. Jothi Sivagnanam, "Decentralised Governance: Tamil Nadu Experience", in M.R. Biju (ed.), *Decentralisation: An Indian Experience*, New Delhi, Ntional Publishing House, 2007, p. 391.
7. Government of Rjasthan, *Report of the Administrtive Reforms Commission*, Jaipur, 2001, p.195.
8. Aurcliano Fernandes, "Changing Role of Panchayats in the New Millennium", *Kurukshetra*, November 2001, p.16.
9. Mahi Pal, "From Raj Governance to Swaraj Governnce", *Kurukshetra,* August 2004, p. 8.

3

Panchayati Raj in Andhra Pradesh

Andhra Pradesh has a geographical area of 274.40 lakh hectares. The population of the state is 7.57 crores as per 2001 census. It is the fifth largest State in the country accounting for 8.37 per cent of the country's area and also fifth most populous State. The density of the State is 275 persons per square kilometer as against 324 in the country. For the first time the sex ratio in the State has increased and it stood at 978 as against 933 for all India. As per the poverty estimates released by Planning Commission based on modified expert group methodology, the percentage of people below poverty line in the State works out to 15.77 per cent as against 26.10 for all India during 1999-2000. The employment growth in the State is significantly low when compared with that of all India. Unemployment rates in Andhra Pradesh continue to be higher than all India rate.

Agriculture is the main occupation for the rural people in the State. The net area sown is of the order of 97 lakh hectares constituting about 35 per cent of the geographical area. The total surface water of entire river system of the State is estimated at 2764 TMC at 75 per cent dependability. The gross area irrigated during the year 2002-03 is 45.36 lakh hectares. Wells account for a major share of 24.79 lakh hectares (54.65 per cent).[1] The State has about 62 lakh hectares of forest area, accounting for about 23 per cent of the geographical area.

The State has the second largest coastline of 974 km. The State ranks first in coastal aquaculture and fresh water prawn, second in inland fisheries and fifth in marine fish production. It is a potential income generating sector. Sericulture is an agro-based labour industry providing gainful employment mostly to rural people. The State occupies second position in the country in the production of silk. The State is the second largest in mineral resources and production in India. The State stands second in mineral value of production contributing 8 per cent of the country's mineral value of production.

Road transport plays a vital role in the economic development of the State. As on 31-3-2003 the total road network is at 2,00,000 km out of which the State highways constitute 8201 km and major district roads constitute 34605 kms. The remaining length is accounted by other category roads. The road density in the State is 0.73 km per one square kilometer and 293 kms per one lakh population as against the all India average of 1.00 kilometer per one square km and 389 kms per one lakh population.

As on March 2003 there were 16213 post offices in the State of which 13694 branch offices, 2364 sub-post offices and 104 head offices. There were 3140 telephone exchanges and 32.56 lakh telephone connections in the State as at the end of March 2003. There are 5288 bank offices of scheduled commercial banks and the deposits in all the scheduled commercial banks in the State increased to Rs.76763 crores. The advances also increased to Rs.50687 crores by the end of March 2003.

There are 28,914 factories with an employment of 7,07,774 persons in the State.[2] Highest number of 13,545 factories are under the industry group of manufacturing of food products and beverages followed by manufacturing of wood and products of wood and cork. It is observed that highest number of factories is registered in Guntur district followed by Ranga Reddy district. Index of industrial production of Andhra Pradesh reveals that the index has increased from 132.5 in 1999-2000 to 138.8 in 2001-02.

The three-tier system of panchayati raj was introduced in Andhra Pradesh in 1959. It has been introduced in the State mainly with a view to involve the representatives of the people in rural development. It has had its ups and downs during the last 45 years from unqualified eulogy to total condemnation. The history of panchayati raj system in the State is traced briefly in this chapter. This would help us develop a clear perspective in understanding the nature of the local institutions of the past.

Ancient and Medieval Period

Often it is claimed that the panchayati raj of today has descended from the panchayats of ancient India. There is some substance in this contention. Much of the inspiration for the system of rural local government comes from the panchayats that existed in the past. Information on the subject is, however, not easily available. It is from a close study of the inscriptions of the time and of stray references to it found in literature that historians have been able to get some idea of it. We know something of the system of local self government which flourished in villages from the days of the Satavahanas, who ruled Andhra from 271 B.C. to 174 A.D., to the days of the Kakatiyas, from whom power was wrested by the Muslim invaders in 1323 A.D. Althrough this long period villages enjoyed a great deal of autonomy in the sense of freedom from the control of the State. Even though the ruling dynasties changed from time to time, there was not much of a change in the nature and degree of village autonomy, though the internal structure of village government underwent certain modifications.

The village was the lowest unit of settlement and administration in early times. Most of the land in ancient Andhra fromed part of the vast Dandakaranya forest through which Srirama, Sita and Laxmana are said to have wandered in their exile. Efforts were made by the people as well as by their rulers to clear the forest and to make land fit for cultivation. This was regarded as one of the primary functions of Government and several rulers took pride in calling themselves Kadu Vattis, the clearers of forests. On the lands so cleared they founded villages, settled colonies of peasants with a due proportion of craftsman of several kinds in them, constructed tanks and other sources of water supply and exempted the cultivators from the payment of the usual taxes for number of years to start with. It was villages like these that became centres of self-government. Kautilya says in his well known 'Arthasastra' written about 300 B.C. a great deal about the settlement of villages. Many of the precepts laid down by him were followed by rulers in all parts of the country, including Andhra.

The people in each village were divided into a number of castes and professional groups. The principle of mutual duties and obligations was accepted and all worked together in a spirit of harmonious unity. There was little room for caste and personal rivalries which mar the administration today. The spirit of unity was responsible for the construction of many works of public utility – wells, tanks, choultries, schools and hospitals without any consideration as to which caste or class would be benefitted by it. It is to this spirit that we have to attribute the success which village self-government achieved in the past.

Every village had a number of functionaries known as Ayagars or Grama Bhatas. The normal number of Ayagars was twelve (12) but it might be a little less or more according to the size of the village, its population and its prosperity. The twelve Ayagars were (1) Reddi or Peda Kapu, (2) Karanam, (3) Talari, (4) Purohit, (5) Blacksmith, (6) Goldsmith, (7) Carpenter, (8)

Potter, (9) Washerman, (10) Barber, (11) Vetti and (12) Shoe-Maker.

Among the Ayagars the Reddi occupied a position of primacy. He was the Pedda Kapu or the Head Man of the village. He was the successor of the Gramani, the Gramunda, the Gramika, the Gramakuta or the Pabbalika, the names used for the holder of the headship of the village at different times and in different places. In early times the Reddi represented the villagers in their dealings with the State ruler and he also represented the ruler in dealings with the villages. He, thus, served as a link between the two. He was responsible for the collection of all taxes due from the village to the ruler. From the days of the Kakatiyas when Grama Sabhas and their committees fell into a state of decline and even disappeared from many villages he discharged other civil and magisterial duties and was responsible for the defence of the village from all external attacks and for the maintenance of internal peace and order. The duty of the Karanam was to keep all the records relating to the village. All the records which he maintained were collectively known as 'gudi kattu' or Ayakattu. Some of them which were later included in the Mackenzie collection serve as a mine of information about many villages of the past.

The Talari was the policeman of the village working under the Reddi. It was his duty to go on rounds day and night and bring offenders and bad characters to book. In addition to him there was also a Barikapu (corrupt form of Prahari Kapu) the person keeping a watch over the Prahara or boundary wall of the village and over the cultivated fields. He stationed himself in the watch tower and when any hostile raiders approached the village, he proclaimed it by beat of drum. The talari was held responsible for any property stolen from the village and he had to make good all losses if he failed to catch the thieves and recover the stolen goods. Both he and Barikapu were remunerated by fees which were paid to them by all householders on auspicious occasions and at the time of harvest. This was in addition to what they got from their Manyams. The duty of the Purohit was to fix the auspicious days for household ceremonials and festivals, for beginning the agricultural operations of the year, for sowing the seed, for harvesting, for undertaking journeys and for other private and public functions. Every morning he went round the outskirts of the village and recited the sacred mantra with a view to warding of all the evil spirits. The duties of the other functionaries are self-explanatory. The blacksmiths and the carpenters made and repaired agricultural implements. It was the duty of the goldsmith to examine the purity of the coins used as currency and to measure the grain during harvest. The Vetti attended to various menial tasks, kept a watch over the tank bund and regularised the supply of water to the irrigated fields in villages where there was no Nirukattu. In several villages there was a Nirukattu whose duty was to see that water was distributed equitably to all the agricultural lands. In several other villages an astrologer, a Pauronik and a doctor were also included among the functionaries and they also enjoyed Manyams or tax-free lands. The village was, thus, not only a compact economic unit but also an administrative unit with its full complements of public functionaries. They were servants of the village community and not of the Government.

All the villages had a number of institutions of self-government to manage their affairs. The first of them was the Sabha. All the adult residents of the village were its members. The Sabha had within its jurisdiction the management of all the public affairs in the village. No distinction was, in those days, drawn between local affairs on one side and state affairs on the other. The Sabha provided for the defence of the village. It undertook the punishment of criminals. It settled other disputes arising in the village. It managed the communal lands, maintained the sources of irrigation, roads, gardens and other works of public utility. It supervised the proper utilization of endowments made by charitable persons for religious, medical and other purposes. It provided relief in times of famine. It looked after temple management and it made provision for education. It even carried on banking business. There was no affair concerning the village which was beyond the purview of the Sabha. To facilitate the work of day-to-day administration the Sabha appointed an executive committee known in the early days as the committee of Mahattaras or Rashtrakuta Pramukhas. It was to this the name panchayat was given in subsequent times. It is quite possible that as in the Tamil country of the day its members were chosen by lot for one year at a time and that various restrictions were placed against the same man being chosen from year to year. These restrictions applied to the sons, the brothers and other near relations of those who held office in a particular year. The principle accepted was that offices should go by turns to all the qualified residents of the village. There were also rules against resort to corrupt practices which included the obtaining of the recommendations from the State officials in matters concerning the affairs of the village. The powers and functions of the Executive Committee were as wide as those of the Sabha. Besides the Executive Committee, there were committees to look after particular affairs. Among them were the tank committee, the garden committee, the gold committee, the committee of justice and so on. Members were chosen in the same way as those of the executive committee subject to similar restrictions. There were also prescribed rules of debate and voting at the meetings of the Sabha and its various committees. All these supervised the work of the Ayagars. Both sets of institutions worked in complete harmony.

Village self-government was more real in the past and villages enjoyed more autonomy than they do today, under the panchayati raj system. One reason for this is that the present day panchayati raj owes its existence to legislation enacted by the State Government. It is created by the State and can be abolished by the State. This was not the case with village self-government in the past. It owed its existence to custom and tradition and no ruler, however despotic he might be, had the coverage to interfere with what the custom laid down. This gave to the village institutions a unique stability and performance. It was an accepted theory, in ancient India, that all institutions derived their authority from Dharma. Even the State and its rulers were subject to it. Their duty was to uphold it and not to interfere with it. Dharma of which custom was a part, ordained that every village should have its own self-governing institutions and that it was not right for the rulers to interference with them. This resulted in the decentralization of all political authority.

There were many territorial divisions above the village like Nadu, Mahanadu, Vishaya, Seema, Rajya, Sthala, etc. But the information available on these divisions is scanty. In some of the earlier inscriptions there is a mention made of these divisions. The Nadu or Vishaya or Mandala or Sthala as a group of villages from their location, is a popular local body under its head Nadu-Prabhu or Vishayapati. The Nadu was a quasi-independent territorial unit and territorial assembly, managing local affairs and entrusted with certain branches of administration in the local areas. The assembly of Nadu or Vishaya corresponds either to modern Mandala or District. The earliest reference to it appears to be in the Koneki inscription of A.D. 669. The Assembly of the villages of a Nadu was called by the same name. The basis for its formation was the common interests of the villages. The Nadu Assembly met frequently to attend to the needs of all the villages under its jurisdiction. It had the responsibility of the administration of the region and discharges corporate responsibilities connected with taxation, irrigation, public works and justice. The system of dividing territory into units called Nadu or Vishaya for purpose of administration was a popular practise not only in Andhra but also in contemporary Karnataka, Tamil Nadu and Kerala. The Nadu became a popular assembly during the period of the Eastern Chalukyas of Vengi and continued to be so under the Kakatiya, the Reddy and Vijayanagara kings.[3] The Nadu enjoyed similar powers as the village assembly, but that the jurisdiction extended over a wider area.

The biggest local assembly was known as Mahanadu which brought different local corporations under its organization and created common understanding among them in pre-Vijayanagar Andhra. Mahanadu was the largest assembly corresponding to Mahanadu in medieval Karnataka and Periyanadu in Tamil Nadu. G.S. Dikshit says that the Mahanadu was the district assembly,[4] while K.V. Subrahmanya Aiyer calls it the largest provincial organization.[5] The Mahanadu met occasionally. Merchants took initiative in holding its meeting. Thus its leadership remained with them. Information relating to its area, membership and headship is meagre. It does not appear to have had its own establishment. Though it was a regional assembly, it had no responsibility for the administration of the region. However, it performed some of the functions of the local bodies. Some of the local bodies in Telugunadu developed themselves indigenously from the Satavahana period and they enjoyed autonomy in corporate matter. The local bodies in medieval Andhra displayed the spirit of co-operation in corporate matters. They settled their own affairs, looked after matters of public interest and discharged several corporate responsibilities. The local institutions played an active role in the transformation and development of socio-economic, religious and political life of Andhra Desa.

Andhra passed through several political vicissitudes after the fall of Warangal in 1323. Part of the country came under the rule of Muslims, part under that of Vijayanagar, the Gajapatis of Orissa and several other dynasties. In the later days of Kutub Sahis the whole of Andhra came under their control and after their overthrow the rule of Mughals was established. Then came the rule of Nizam-ul-Mulk, who made himself independent of the Mughal Emperor in due course and of his successor Nizams of Hyderabad. But the latter, like many other Indian rulers of the day, proved themselves incapable of defending their territory against the superior military strength of the British with the result that by 1800 a large part of Andhra (coastal area and Rayalaseema) came under the rule of the British. Telangana alone continued to be ruled by the Nizam. During the five centuries following the fall of Warangal there were no changes of any appreciable character in the system of rural local self-government. The situation, however, underwent a change with the establishment and consolidation of British rule.

British Period

During the period of British rule the isolation of the village had completely broken and with that, age long economic self-sufficiency and the community spirit received a serve blow. The administrative policies pursued by the British strengthened the force leading to the disintegration of the village as a community. One prominent feature of British rule was the establishment of direct connection between the Central and Provincial Governments on one side and the individual inhabitants of each village on the other. Much of the work which had for ages been associated with village authorities was taken over and carried out even more efficiently by official agencies from outside. Another feature of British administration which dealt a blow to the community spirit among the villagers was the change which the British brought about in the position of the village officials – the headman, karanam, etc. These public functionaries who had been regarded throughout the ages as the representatives and spokesmen of the village community were now made the salaried officials of the Central Government. The village, at the end of the British rule, was not what it had been in earlier times.

Later, however, the British took a number of steps to introduce institutions of local self-government in the rural areas. Various measures taken during the British period particularly during the later part of the 19th century, and in the 20th century became the precursors of today's panchayati raj. Lord Ripon's resolution of 1882, the Decentralization Commission of 1909 and the subsequent acts laid the foundation for the modern panchayati raj system. Three-tier structure of rural local bodies with the Union Panchayats at the base, the Taluk Boards in the middle, District Boards at the apex was created after the passing of the resolution by Lord Ripon in India.

The structure of rural local self-government created in Andhra region of Madras Presidency was along the lines suggested by Lord Ripon though on a restricted democratic foundations. In the Telangana region of the present state of Andhra Pradesh rural local governments similar to those established in the Andhra region of Madras Presidency were created since the promulgation of the Dastur-Ill-Amal in 1888. However, in Andhra region the members of the local bodies were elected by those who possessed property or education while the local bodies of Telangana consisted of nominated non-officials only. There was considerable official domination over the local bodies in both the regions. Starting from 1920 villages panchayats have come to be established in the Andhra region, while legislation for the creation of similar institutions in Telangana was undertaken only in 1941. A close examination of the political events since the 1930s reveals that with the intensification of the freedom struggle, the issue of local self-government receded completely to the background.[6] However, one important development, viz., the abolition of the Taluq Boards took place in the Andhra region in 1936. At the time of independence the rural local bodies were completely managed by the Government officials with the District Collector directly taking over the charge of the District Board.

Developments after Independence

The normal constitutional government was restored in the provinces of British India in 1946. Prior to the introduction of a new panchayati raj system in the State of Andhra Pradesh in 1959 several concrete developments took place first in Madras (of which Andhra was a part till 1953) and later in Andhra Pradesh. Of these, the most noteworthy are the Firka Development Scheme, the Village Panchayat Act, 1950 and the CD and National Extension Service Blocks. All these had their influence on the subsequent growth of PRIs in the State.

The Firka Development Scheme was originated by Tanguturi Prakasam Pantulu, who became the Chief Minister of Madras Province when constitutional government was restored in 1946. He was one of the most ardent disciples of Gandhiji and the idea of self-sufficient village republics modelled on those which flourished in ancient times was an article of faith with him. Long before he became Chief Minister he held the view that the entire economic life of the country should be village based. He started a weekly entitled Village Republic and with the help of the Andhra Provincial Congress Committee he constituted in 1940 a Village Service Committee (Grama Seva Sangh) with himself as President to experiment with his ideas in Gopannapalem in the West Godavari district. The Firka Development Scheme was a more comprehensive scheme.

The Firka, a revenue administration unit of about 30 villages was the most convenient area for intensive development and it became the real forerunner of the later community development scheme which has several similarities with it. The objective of the Firka Development Scheme was the all-round development of rural life under the joint auspices of trained Government staff and the people in village. The people's participation was stressed in the scheme. It was conceived as a joint enterprise of the salaried government staff supplying direction, guidance and expert knowledge and the people playing a more and more increasing and active part with the advance of years and the gaining of experience. It was on this philosophy that the Community Development Programmes started from 1952 were based.

To execute the scheme an administrative organization was set-up which functioned at all levels – the State, the District and the Firka. At the capital, there was a Firka Development Board consisting of the heads of departments. At the district level the Collector was made primarily responsible for the successful implementation of the scheme in his district. He was advised by the District Rural Welfare Board, consisting of the various heads of the departments in the district and prominent social workers. At the bottom level there was a Rural Welfare Officer, who was incharge of single firka or a group of two or three firkas. He was assisted by a team of technical officers like the works supervisors and agricultural fieldmen and a number of general village workers called Grama Sevaks. Each firka was divided into three to five groups and each group consisted of five to ten villages. Each group was under a Gram Sevak. These officials were advised by a Firka Development Committee made up of officials as well as representatives of villages and social service organizations in the areas.

The scheme was in operation for a period of only six years. It was absorbed in the Community Development Programme in 1953. By that time the scheme was in operation in 108 firkas of the Madras State.[7] The scheme deserves to be regarded as the first organized effort to bring about an all-round improvement in the condition of the people and modernize their economy and their general outlook and implant in them a desire for change.

A new Village Panchayat Act (Madras Act No. X of 1950) was passed and it was brought into effect on April 1, 1951. In several respects it marked an advance on the earlier Acts under which the panchayats were functioning up till then. The panchayats acquired a more democratic character. Their functions and powers were considerably widened. They secured more finances. All this meant progress in a needed direction. The panchayats acquired a more democratic character under the new Act in consequence of the various provisions included in it. It now became obligatory for the Government to confer the benefits of panchayati raj to all the people in rural areas without exception. Every village with a population of 500 and above had to be given a panchayat under the Act. Villages with a population of less than 500 had to be included within the jurisdiction of an adjoining panchayat or grouped with other continguous villages so that there might be a single panchayat for the whole group. This meant that, in future, there should be no village without coming under the jurisdiction of some panchayat or other and enjoying all the advantages of the local self-government. Elections to the panchayat were to be based on adult franchise. All those who were entitled to vote for the Legislative Assembly were to be enrolled as voters for elections to panchayats. Provision was made for voting by secret ballot.

Though the Act of 1950 provided for the compulsory establishment of panchayats in all villages, it took several years for Government to complete the process. Andhra was separated from Madras in 1953-54 and constituted into a new State. It was in October, 1956 that the present Andhra Pradesh, consisting of the two regions of Andhra and Telangana was formed. The panchayats in Andhra continued to function under the Act of 1950, while those in Telangana functioned in accordance with the Act of 1956. In 1964 an integrated Andhra Pradesh Gram Panchayats Act was passed and all the panchayats in the State were governed by it, till it was repealed in 1994.

In pursuance of the philosophy of community development four projects were started in October, 1952 – the Kakinada – Peddapuram and the Kurnool – Cuddapah projects in Andhra and the Nizam Sagar and the Mulug projects in Telangana. Each of these was expected to cover about 300 villages and a population of about 3 lakhs. The expenditure which the

Government proposed to incur on the development of each of them was Rs.65 lakhs spread over 3 years. It was, however, found that the resources available would not permit the working of projects on the scale especially in view of the decision that 1/4th of the States should be covered by the Community Development Programme by the First Five Year Plan.

A survey of the history of local government in Andhra during the last hundred or more years reveals certain significant facts. In the first place, a hundred years ago, there were no statutory local authorities in Andhra region of Madras State.[8] There were here and there voluntary associations constituted by village elders for specific purposes; but they were in a languishing state. At the end of 1950, however, there was a network of local authorities. Further by 1950 all local authorities were democratized and all the members of local authorities were elected by a direct vote.

Three-tier System of Panchayati Raj

The Andhra Pradesh Panchayat Samithi and Zilla Parishads Act, 1959 was an important landmark in the evolution of panchayati raj in Andhra Pradesh. This Act was the outcome of the recommendations made by the Balwantray Mehta Team. The Government of Andhra Pradesh accepted almost all the recommendations of the Mehta Team. A white paper was issued by the State Government in November, 1957 pronouncing their new policy relating to rural local governments. Adhoc panchayat samithis at the rate of one for each district were created in May 1958. Satisfied with the working of the adhoc bodies the Panchayat Samithis and Zilla Parishads Act was adopted on September 15, 1959. According to the provisions of the Act, 235 panchayat samithis started functioning from First November, the State Formation Day, and 20 Zilla Parishads from First December.[9] The powers and functions discharged by the erstwhile District Boards along with their assets and liabilities were vested with the Zilla Parishads and panchayat samithis. By 1962-63, the entire State was covered by the three-tier system of panchayati raj with 448 panchayat samithis and 20 Zilla Parishads. As far as gram panchayats are concerned two separate Acts were in force in Andhra and Telangana regions. They were amalgamated with the passing of the Andhra Pradesh Gram Panchayats Act in 1964.

At the bottom of the structure stood the Gram Panchayat elected by the voters of the village once in five years. The head of the Gram Panchayat is Sarpanch, elected by the members of the panchayat and assisted by a upa-sarpanch in the implementation of the resolutions of the panchayat and its functional committees. The number of members of a Gram Panchayat varies depending upon its population, the smallest panchayat may consist of five and the largest may have as many as seventeen members. For big panchayats the executive officers were appointed by the Government. In all such cases the sarpanch exercised supervision and control over Executive Officer. The law provided for an assembly of all the voters of the village known as Gram Sabha. Meeting twice every year the Sabha could review the activities of the panchayat besides advising it on village affairs.

The Panchayat Samithi, the middle-tier, was the most important body in the three-tier system of panchayati raj. It consisted of the sarpanches of the panchayats of the area (ex-officio), members of the State legislature representing the area (ex-officio) and co-opted members representing scheduled castes and tribes and women. Members of the samithi elected their president who was its political head. Most of decision-making power was exercised by the Standing Committees. The executive authority of the Samithi was vested in the Block Development Officer (BDO) over whom the President exercised supervision and control for the purpose of the implementation of the resolution of the Samithi and its committees. The Block

Development Officer was assisted by a host of subject specialists known as Extension Officers. Besides supervising and coordinating the work of panchayats of the block area, the Samithi performed the important role of a development agency in rural Andhra Pradesh.

The Zilla Parishad was the apex body of the panchayati raj in the State. It comprised the presidents of the Samithis in the district, the State and the central legislators elected from the district and the District Collector, as ex-officio members. Representation to scheduled castes and scheduled tribes as well as women was given through co-option. Though chiefly conceived as a supervisory and coordinating body, the Zilla Parishad exercised executive functions in respect of secondary and vocational education, inter-samithi roads and minor irrigation. The executive authority of the Zilla Parishad was exercised by the Secretary appointed by the State Government over whom the Chairman of the Parishad elected by its members exercised administrative control and supervision. The District Collector was not only made an ex-officio member of the Parishad but also the chairman of all its standing committees.

Reform Measures

Initially, people evinced keen interest in the system and the representatives of the people participated in various development activities, by offering liberal contributions in cash and kind for laying roads, providing drinking water facilities, establishment of primary schools, primary health centres and for provision of various other amenities in the rural areas. The intial euphoria did not really last long. As Professor Ram Reddy, a serious analyst of panchayati raj, notes: "the enthusiasm lasted for about a decade and was then followed by a decade of criticism".[10] The initial enthusiasm and public participation which were in evidence in the earlier period of panchayati raj seem to have gradually diminished on account of politicization of these bodies.

With the emergence of the office of the Zilla Parishad as a rallying point at the district level successive chief ministers found a threat to the hierarchical authority structures. Such a perception was reinforced when factional structures opposed to their authority surfaced in a number of districts in Andhra Pradesh with the Samithi and Zilla Parishad chiefs providing the interface to dissident legislators. The formation of a State level Panchayati Raj Chamber in 1961 under the leadership of J. Vengal Rao (the then Chairman of Khammam Zilla Parishad) seemed to be a source of considerable political embarrassment to Brahmananda Reddy, the then Chief Minister of Andhra Pradesh. The political consolidation of the latter was in a way threatened by the growth of parallel leadership under the dispensation of panchayati raj. Around this time several bureaucrats of the top and middle echelons who had all along been irked by the erosion of their authority, seized the opportunity to convey to the political chiefs about the need for reform. Accordingly, a scheme envisaging the formation of Zilla Development Boards was introduced in 1967.[11] Under the scheme a Zilla or District Development Board (ZDB) was constituted with the District Collector as Chairman and the Chairman of the Zilla Parishad as a member. The Zilla Development Board was made responsible for the formulation and implementation of policies relating to the agricultural and industrial growth of the district. This measure went contrary to the country-wide trend of devolution of development functions to elected rural local bodies. To that extent, it subordinated the Zilla Parishad to the Zilla Development Board. The substance of the structural innovation marked a departure from the democratic philosophy of the statute enacted in 1959. The introduction of ZDB scheme had the effect of diluting the authority of the Zilla Parishad. This instance of reform indicates that leadership struggles, factional politics and the bureaucracy's orientations had much to do with efforts to tinker with the panchayati raj structure.

There was disenchantment with the structure and functioning of panchayati raj in Andhra Pradesh for quite sometime, particularly after the introduction of ZDB Scheme. So there has been a growing concern for reform of rural local government. Perhaps, the attempts at reform and their fruition are characterized by a high frequency. Several steps were taken to improve the functioning of the rural local bodies and attempts were made to remove the structural bottlenecks in the functioning of these bodies since the early 1960s.

Committees were appointed to go into the working of these institutions and suggest changes in their organizational structure. The important committees which expressed views on various aspects of the panchayati raj are the Vengal Rao Committee (1968)[12] and the Narasimham Committee (1972 and 1981). While reiterating their faith in the panchayati raj these committees had suggested structural changes to make the panchayati raj institutions more democratic and also more effective as instruments of rural development. The Ashoka Mehta Committee had also submitted its proposals for re-organization of panchayati raj so as to equip it to play a larger role in planning and implementation in the field of rural development. Keeping the recommendations of these committees and also the views of the panchayati raj functionaries the State Government amended the Panchayat Samithis and Zilla Parishads Act of 1959 and Gram Panchayats Act of 1964 several times from 1976 till the elections were held in 1981. The important reforms, among others, in rural local government made prior to these elections were noted below:

1. The voting age for the purpose of election of panchayati raj institutions had been reduced from 21 to 18 years. However, the minimum age of a candidate contesting for an office was kept at 21 years.
2. Provision had been made for direct elections for all important elected functionaries of PRIs. The Sarpanch and the members of the Gram Panchayat and President

of Panchayat Samithi had to be elected directly and the Chairman of Zilla Parishad indirectly.

3. Provision was made for reservation of elected posts for persons belonging to weaker sections, viz., scheduled castes and scheduled tribes. Fourteen per cent of the offices of the Presidents of Panchayat Samithis in each district were reserved for scheduled castes. Further, all the offices of President of Panchayat Samithis in scheduled areas and a certain proportion of offices of the president of panchayat samithis in non-scheduled areas with a high proportion of scheduled tribes were reserved for them. Similarly, the office of the Chairman of three Zilla Parishads were reserved for scheduled castes and one for scheduled tribes.
4. Three persons belonging to backward classes, one from minorities (religious or linguistic) and two women had to be coopted by the elected members of each panchayat samithi and zilla parishad.

Mandal System

The efforts of the Government of Andhra Pradesh to reform the rural local government and to streamline the panchayati raj administration had not stopped after the 1981 elections. The successive chief ministers had tried to bring minor amendments to the rural local government acts. But the major task was undertaken by the Telugu Desam Government to introduce mandal panchayats. The Telugu Desam Government felt that the development programmes and other welfare schemes had not been forthcoming in adequate measure in the three-tier structure of panchayati raj. The developmental programmes were not being implemented effectively as the people's participation was not forthcoming in adequate measure. The panchayat samithi with a population of 80,000 or more had grown unwieldy for giving the people a sense of participation.

The government, therefore, felt it necessary to involve the people more closely in the administration of developmental and other government programmes at lower spatial levels, and create mandal parishad in the state.

When the proposals for the introduction of Mandal Parishads in the place of Panchayat Samithis was first mooted in 1983 there was an uproar from the Congress (I) elites. Besides raising a serious political controversy the proposal also opened up the possibility of protracted litigation. The State Congress (I) leaders swung into action by organizing the Panchayati Raj Convention to which all the elected functionaries of rural local bodies were invited. The convention provided a major rallying point for mobilising the elected functionaries of Panchayat Samithis who faced the prospect of being unseated from positions of power in the event of the introduction of mandals. Sensing the intensity of political opposition and the possibility of the court injunctions in favour of the continuance of the elected functionaries the Telugu Desam Government dragged its feet. The possibility of the elected functionaries of panchayat samithis taking the issue to the courts was very much talked about. In such an event there was every likelihood of adverse judicial verdicts against the State Government's move because the Samithi Presidents were elected in June 1981 for a full five-year term under the statute. In this context, it preferred to go ahead with the implementation of the scheme of revenue mandals, a less controversial issue.[13] This was thought to be a prelude to the introduction of mandal parishads. The posts of part-time village officers were abolished and village assistants were appointed as full-time government servants in March, 1983. An ordinance was promulgated on 11th January, 1984 amending sections 2 and 3 of the Districts (Formation) Act, 1974 enabling the introduction of Revenue Mandals. However, the implementation of revenue mandals was delayed as the ruling party suffered a setback in August, 1984. Although the party returned to power after a break of one month it took a few months to complete the legal formalities. Finally 1104 revenue mandals started functioning from 25th May, 1985.[14] The Government also reiterated its resolve to introduce mandal panchayats which would be coterminous with the revenue mandals.[15] The State Government had gone ahead with the preparatory work connected with the introduction of mandal panchayats by planning for the location of schools, hospitals and provision of other infrastructural arrangements during the Seventh Five Year Plan.[16]

Andhra Pradesh Mandala Praja Parishads, Zilla Praja Parishads and Zilla Pranalika Abhivrudhi Mandals Act, 1986

A Cabinet Sub-Committee was set-up by the TDP Government to suggest measures to reorganize the PRIs in the State. The Cabinet Sub-Committee examined the mandal system, recommended by the Asoka Mehta Committee, and also the functioning of the panchayati raj administration in Andhra Pradesh and other states and made its recommendations. Based on the recommendations of the committee, the Andhra Pradesh Maṇdal Praja Parishads, Zilla Praja Parishads and Zilla Pranalika Abhvrudhi Mandals Act was enacted and the Andhra Pradesh Panchayat Samithis and Zilla Parishads Act, 1959, was repealed in July, 1986.[17] Under the provisions of the Act eleven hundred and four Mandala Praja Parishads (MPPs) came into existence on 15th January 1987, the pongal day of Sankranti in the place of 330 panchayat samithis. In other words, there are 3 or 4 MPPs in the place of one panchayat samithi. The MPPs were constituted for a population of 35,000 to 55,000 covering 20 – 25 villages with certain relaxation in tribal areas.[18] Rangareddi District bordering State Capital has the minimum number of 33 MPPs while the maximum number of 65 are n the southern district of Chittoor closely followed by Mahaboobnagar district in Telangana with 64 MPPs.

Mandala Praja Parishad

The Mandala Praja Parishad consisted of the sarpanches of all the gram panchayats in the mandal area and Member of the Legislative Assembly representing the concerned mandal area. Members of Parliament were also ex-officio members of the mandal parishads but they had to opt for one mandal within their constituency of the district. Besides, there was one elected member belonging to minorities whether based on religion or language. Each mandal parishad had a President and Vice-President. Their tenure of office was five years. President was elected directly in a manner similar to that of an MLA. The Vice-President was elected indirectly by the members of the MPP among themselves. Fifteen per cent of the mandal presidentships in each district were reserved for the members of scheduled castes, 6 per cent for scheduled tribes, 9 per cent for women, and 20 per cent for backward classes.

The President was the head of the Mandala Praja Parishad. He had to convene, preside over and conduct the meetings of Mandala Praja Parishad. In case of emergency he was authorized to execute any work which is, in his opinion, necessary for the service of general public. The Vice-President was authorised to exercise the powers and perform the functions of the President, if the latter was absent from the mandal or incapacitated continuously for more than 15 days. The post of Mandal Development Officer was specifically created and so designated under Section 28 of the 1986 Act. He is the Chief Executive Officer and Member-Secretary of the Mandala Praja Parishad. He was responsible for implementing the resolutions of the Mandala Praja Parishad, attended its meetings without right to vote and supervises the staff working in the Mandala

Praja Parishad. The Mandala Praja Parishad was entrusted with a wide range of functions including the execution of all developmental programmes.

Zilla Praja Parishad

The Zilla Praja Parishad consisted of Presidents of Mandala Praja Parishads, MLAs representing rural areas of the district, Members of Parliament and one person belonging to minorities based on religion or language.[19] There should be a Chairman and a Vice-Chairman. While the Chairman was directly elected by the entire electorate of the district, the Vice-Chairman was elected indirectly by the members of Zilla Praja Parishad from among themselves. Out of 22 ZPPs three (15 per cent) were reserved for SCs, and one (6 per cent) for STs, two (9 per cent) for women and five (20 pr cent) for BCs.

The District Collector was the Secretary and the District Development Officer was the Chief Executive Officer of the Zilla Praja Parishad. There were six standing committees in the Zilla Praja Parishad. Each committee was entrusted with one subject such as development, education, social welfare, women welfare, finance and works. Every Standing Committee consisted of the Chairman of Zilla Praja Parishad and the District Collector who were ex-officio members, and such number of members as may be arrived at by dividing the total number of members by five. The Chairman of Zilla Praja Parishad was the Chairman of every Standing Committee. In his absence the District Collector and in the absence of both a member chosen by the members present was to preside over the meeting. All the powers, functions and finances of the existing Zilla Parishad were transferred to the Zilla Praja Parishad.

Zilla Pranalika Abhivrudhi Mandal

The Act also empowered the Government to constitute the Zilla Pranalika Abhivrudhi Mandal (District Planning and

Development Board) at district level. The Chairman of ZPP, MLAs and Members of Parliament and District Collector constituted it. It was headed by a minister nominated by the Chief Minister as Chairman with District Collector as its Member-Secretary. The Chairman of ZPP was its Vice-Chairman. The District Planning and Development Boards (DPDBs) were empowered to formulate and execute annual district plans and distribute funds. These powers were, however, transferred to the elected Zilla Praja Parishads by an amendment to the 1986 Act. The District Development Review Board empowered to review all the regulatory and development activities in the district but devoid of 'sanction authority' had replaced the existing DPDBs. The decision to dilute the authority of DPDBs was taken in order to strengthen the hands of the democratically elected ZPPs since the rural voters had not been able to appreciate the government's policy of imposing the nominated DPDBs over the elected ZPPs. The sanctioning authority was restored to the ZPs and District Collectors. The review boards were entrusted the task of only review the activities. It was, however, decided to entrust DDRBs at a later date, the powers enjoyed earlier by the District Planning Boards. This had reversed the earlier amendment to the 1986 Act and gave powers to the MLAs as desired by them.

Merits of Mandal System

Taking the administration closer to the people is the credo of all those who believe in grassroots democracy and planning. The creation of MPPs has made decentralization of authority meaningful as these bodies are proximate to the people. The block, as a unit of planning and implementation of rural development programmes was found unwieldy and the common man found it difficult to reach the Samithi headquarters frequently for getting the services whereas the MPPs are situated within a radius of 10 kilometres from the population covered by them. The new measure has, thus, paved the way for creating a smaller unit of administration facilitating better access to people at least in geographical terms. Most of the government functionaries of revenue and development agencies are available at the mandal headquarters. Further each MPP has a primary health centre, a veterinary hospital, a hostel for students of weaker sections and a junior college. The mandal complexes to house all the offices of the mandal have also been constructed in a phased manner. It is hoped that under the mandal administration, the basic amenities and facilities of day-to-day life of the rural population will be met while at the same time ensuring autonomy to the local units in their functioning.

There can be no two opinions about the importance of the structural changes in panchayati raj sought to be achieved through the formation of mandal panchayats. The concept of mandal is not identical with that of any PRI in vogue. In fact, it may be considered as a revolutionary one in some respects. Andhra Pradesh again got the distinction of being one of the two states (Karnataka being the other State) to introduce mandal system as recommended by the Asoka Mehta Committee. The mandal systems in Karnataka and Andhra Pradesh indicate a trend of revival of interest in PRIs.[20] The increase in percentage of reservations for scheduled castes and scheduled tribes and the introduction of reservations for backward classes have facilitated the sharing of power and status by more number of people from the respective communities in Andhra Pradesh. Normally, the key positions of panchayati raj institutions are occupied by the rich and vested interests. The mandal system of Andhra Pradesh and Karnataka provides adequate safeguards in this regard. Another welcome aspect of the reform is the extension of the principle of party based contest to the political executive at the level of MPP and ZPP. The party based contests would minimize the possibilities for caste and communal oriented voter mobilization. The election by direct method to the key positions in PRIs is also a step in the direction of greater democratization. This mode of election would help in reducing the effects of the prevalence of unhealthy practices associated with indirect election to these positions.

Andhra Pradesh Panchayati Raj Act, 1994

The Congress (I) which came to power in November, 1989 had tried to change the mandal system. In fact the Congress (I) Government in the State attempted to abolish the mandal system and restore the pre-mandal set-up with some minor alterations. By that time, the mandal system had already taken deep roots and there was wide-spread resistance from the rural people. The government's move was also severely opposed in circles within ruling party and the opposition. The State Government felt, therefore, it was worthwhile to continue the system. Thus, the Government had not succeeded in its efforts to abolish the system. It had, however, tried to bring some changes in the system. The word Praja was removed and the MPPs and ZPPs were renamed as Mandal Parishads and Zilla Parishads. The Government proposed to have Mandal Parishad and Zilla Parishad elections on non-party lines. It brought out a new Act namely the Andhra Pradesh Local Bodies Electoral Reforms Act, 1989. An Expert Committee on Panchayati Raj headed by B.P.R. Vithal, a retired I.A.S. Officer, was appointed to examine and submit a report on the reorganization of panchayati raj and also on the re-organization of revenue set-up below the district. The Expert Committee had submitted two separate reports to the Government. The Government had, thereupon, appointed a Cabinet Sub-Committee with the then Minister for Panchayati Raj, D.K. Samarasimha Reddy, as Chairman to examine and make suitable recommendations on the Expert Committee report. Meanwhile, the 73rd Constitution Amendment Act was enacted by the Parliament. The Cabinet Sub-Committee considered the report of the Expert Committee as also the provisions of the Constitution Amendment Act and submitted its reports to the Government.

The Government accepted the report of the Cabinet Sub-Committee and declared to enact a comprehensive law on all PRIs in the State. Accordingly and in conformity with the Constitution (Seventy-Third Amendment) Act, 1992 the Andhra Pradesh Legislature repealed three of its earlier Acts relating to PRIs in the State,viz., Andhra Pradesh Gram Panchayats Act, 1964, Andhra Pradesh Mandala Praja Parishads, Zilla Praja Parishads and Zilla Pranalika and Abhivrudhi Mandals Act, 1986 and Andhra Pradesh Local Bodies Electoral Reforms Act, 1989, and enacted a new Act namely, the Andhra Pradesh Panchayati Raj Act, 1994. The provisions of this Act came into force on 30th day of May, 1994.

References

1. Government of Andhra Pradesh, *Economic Survey 2003-2004*, A.P. Secretariat, Planning Department, Hyderabad, 2004, p. 2.
2. Government of Andhra Pradesh, *Statistical Abstracts of Andhra Pradesh 2003,* Directorate of Economics and Statistics, Hyderabad, 2003, p.159.
3. T.V. Mahalingam, *Administration and Social Life Under Vijayanagara,* Madras, 1940, pp. 215-216.
4. G.S. Dikshit, *Local Self-Government in Medieval Karnataka*, Dharwar, 1964, p. 29.
5. K.V. Subramanya Aiyar, "The Largest Provincial Organizations in India", *QJMS*, Vol. XLV, p. 29.
6. S.P. Ranga Rao and M. Tukaram, "Rural Local Government" in M.A. Aleem and Shamim Aleem (eds), *State Administration in Andhra Pradesh*, Allied Publishers, Hyderabad, 1988, pp. 270-282.
7. M. Venkatarangaiya and G. Ram Reddi, *Panchayati Raj in Andhra Pradesh*, Andhra Pradesh State Chamber of Panchayati Raj, Hyderabad, 1967, p. 68.

8. V. Venkata Rao, "A Hundred Years of Local Government in Andhra and Madras", *Quarterly Journal of Local Self-Government"*, Vol. XXVIII, No. 4, April, 1958, pp. 675-730.
9. For a detailed discussion on the introduction of three-tier system of panchayati raj, see P.A. James, "Democratic Decentralization in Andhra Pradesh", *Quarterly Journal of Local Self-Government"*, Vol. XXXI, No. 3, January 1961, pp. 452-464.
10. G. Ram Reddy, "Panchayati Raj Proposals", *Seminar,* February, 1979.
11. *Report on the Reorganization of District Administration,* (Chairman: M.T. Raju), Board of Revenue, Government of Andhra Pradesh, April, 1967.
12. *Report of the Committee on Panchayati Raj* (Chairman: J. Vengala Rao), Andhra Pradesh Congress Legislative Party, Hyderabad, 1967.
13. See Government of Andhra Pradesh, *White Paper on Revenue Mandals,* Department of Revenue, Hyderabad,1984.
14. 305 Taluks and 1,084 Firkas were substituted with 1,104 Revenue Mandals, see *Indian Express,* Vijayawada, May 26, 1985.
15. See the Statement of the Chief Minister, *The Hindu,* Hyderabad, June 9, 1985.
16. G.O.Ms.No.185, dt. 30-3-1984, Panchayati Raj Department, Government of Andhra Pradesh, Hyderabad, and the *Report of the Working Group on Panchayati Raj for the formulation of Seventh Five Year Plan* (1985-1990).
17. Government of Andhra Pradesh, *Andhra Pradesh Mandala Praja Parishads, Zilla Praja Parishad and Zilla Pranalika Abhivrudhi Mandals Act, 1986*, Government Press, Hyderabad,1986.
18. For a detailed discussion of Mandal System, see C.V. Raghavulu and E.A. Narayana, "The Mandal System in Andhra Pradesh: An Appraisal", *ISDA Journal*, Vol.2, No.2, April-June, 1992, pp. 149-162.

19. For a detailed discussion on Zilla Praja Parishad, please see "The Role of Zilla Praja Parishad in Rural Development" in G. Vidyasagar et al. (eds.), *Rural Development and Local Participation*, Anmol Publications, New Delhi, 1992, pp.65-73.
20. C.V. Raghavulu and E.A. Narayana, "Reforms in Panchayati Raj: A Comparative Analysis of Andhra Pradesh, Karnataka and West Bengal", *The Indian Journal of Public Administration*, Vol. XXXVIII, No. 1, January-March, 1991, pp. 34-36.

4

Profile of the Study Areas

The enactment of the 73rd Constitution Amendment Act had brought to frontline the significance of panchayati raj system. The panchayati raj institutions (PRIs) have been in existence in India for a long time. These institutions have, however, not been able to acquire the status and dignity of a viable and responsive people's bodies due to a number of reasons including absence of regular elections, prolonged suppressions, insufficient representation of weaker sections, inadequate devolution of powers and lack of financial resources. In view of these short-comings and in the light of past experience, it is considered that there is an imperative need to enshrine in the constitution certain basic and essential features of PRIs. Therefore, the subject of panchayati raj has acquired greater significance with the enactment of 73rd Constitution Amendment Act, 1992.

The Constitution Amendment Act conferring constitutional status to PRIs is a land mark in the history of democratic decentralization. One of the basic features of the constitutional status is to recognize these institutions as an institution of self-government. Those concerned with the earlier experience saw in it a ray of hope for revival and rejuvenation of the panchayati raj system. A lot of enthusiasm was evinced for the new system and the advocates of grassroots democracy thought that it would usher in a new era in the annals of Indian democracy and sooner or later lead to, what came to be popularly known as the third tier of government below the state level, and thereby ensure true self-government.

The Act provides a basic framework of decentralization of powers and authorities to the PRIs at different levels. However, responsibility for giving it a practical shape in the field rests with the states. The states are expected to act in consonance with spirit with which the Government of India has embarked upon the major task of laying down a constitutional framework for establishing a strong and viable panchayati raj system. In other words, the success of these institutions depends upon, to a greater extent, the commitment of the state governments in allowing the provisions of the Amendment Act to take material shape.

Based on the framework provided in the Amendment, the state governments initiated measures and gave shape to the concept of local governance through legislations and rules. The Government of Andhra Pradesh joined the company of other state governments in giving effect to the implementation of Amendment Act. A new legislation was enacted in 1994 according to which the PRIs in the state are functioning at present. In this context, a study was undertaken to examine the panchayati raj system in Andhra Pradesh.

Studies on Panchayati Raj

The panchayati raj is a fascinating area of research for students and teachers in political science and public administration. As observed by Iqbal Narain, the panchayati raj is an important potential area of research.[1] There are several hundreds of studies on various aspects of panchayati raj. These studies throw light on conceptual, organizational, political, administrative, functional, financial and many other aspects. There have been historical studies, general studies, and micro studies. Some studies have all India character and some studies concentrate on state, district and panchayat level units. There has been a plethora of study team reports on the working of panchayati raj. Finally, there are a number of important unpublished theses in the field of panchayati raj. A brief review of studies on panchayati raj is done in this section of the chapter.

Jathar, in his work, examines the historical background of village panchayats in ancient India and also discusses the history of local self-government under the British rule.[2] Khanna (1966) attempts to study the structure, functions, finances and working of panchayati raj in Punjab and Haryana.[3] He has also made suggestions for improving the working of panchayati raj through democratic measures.

The study done for the Andhra Pradesh Chamber of Panchayati Raj by M. Venkata Rangaiya and G. Ram Reddy entitled "Panchayati Raj in Andhra Pradesh", surveys the panchayati raj scene in the state from the earliest period of traceable record of events, i.e. ancient, medieval, British and post-independence developments in the rural local government institutions in the state.[4] The data reveal not only a gratifying degree of enthusiasm for panchayati raj elections among illiterate villagers but also considerable attention to the quality of leadership in so far as it is reflected in educational background. The book of Venkatarangaiah and Pattabhiram on "Local Government in India" is a historical study of the evolution of local self-government in the modern India.[5]

Narain, et al (1970) have covered the panchayati raj institutions in Madras, Rajasthan and Maharastra.[6] Various functional spheres, economic, social, political and administrative and their way to strengthening their roots in the soil of rural India have also been discussed.

Inamdar (1970) has attempted to study the functioning of four village panchayats namely Dehu, Rahatwade, Khadakwasla and Damini panchayats in Maharastra state.[7] He has dealt with the working of this basic unit of government and administration in all its varied aspects: elections, personnel (elected and appointed), functions, finances, gram sabha and most important its leadership. The four case studies examine how far the purpose underlying the Village Panchayat Act of 1958 of Maharastra state is realised in practice.

In a study on "Panchayats in Baroda District" Chokshi finds neither that the panchayats are functioning satisfactorily nor that the resources are adequate for these bodies.[8] He points out that each and every panchayat should follow the broad principles of programme budgeting and accordingly should have a properly worked out demand schedule of different types of resources. So also the government should have a properly planned supply schedules of resources. The study points out that unless the resource position of these bodies improved, panchayats could not justify their existence as developmental units. He comes to the conclusion that there is popular reluctance towards local taxation.

There is one in-depth study by B.C. Muthayya on panchayat taxes with particular reference to a few panchayats in Andhra Pradesh.[9] He reveals the truth that, for funds these bodies depend heavily on grants from the government. But taxation is also conceived of as one of the sources of revenue for these bodies and this understanding, he concludes, may be one of the influencing factors in their tax payment.

Grover et al (1972) have inquired into the nature and extent of supervision and control which the Government of Rajasthan had been exercising over the panchayati raj bodies through both formal and informal media with special reference to their efficacy and utility.[10]

Kumar and Venkataraman (1974) have examined the administrative, financial and technical aspect of supervision and control in Tamil Nadu.[11] It has been realized that the way in which control is exercised depends very much on the linkages of officials and non-officials who are concerned in the panchayati raj movement.

Sharma (1976) has attempted to study the reforms in panchayati raj in the country since independence.[12] The author has summed up analytically the major findings of the reports of the different committees, study teams, etc., having a bearing on the problem of the democratic decentralization and panchayati raj institutions.

Samiuddin (1976), in her study, has highlighted importance of democratic institutions of panchayati raj, with special reference to Uttar Pradesh.[13] Basically she attempted to evaluate the system of democratic decentralization and studied its impact on various socio-economic activities in Uttar Pradesh.

Dubey and Murdia (1976) study the influence of particular consideration like those of caste, kinship, patron-client relationship, party and political affiliations and decision-making by panchayati raj leaders in the districts of Manar and Shripur in Maharastra.[14] They have selected administrative situations in which locational and distributive decisions are involved and attempted to identify the attributes of all the significant actors in the decision making process and the strategies employed by these actors in trying to influence the final decisions. While discussing politico-administrative dynamics in the panchayati raj system, Bhargava's study (1978), based on Jhunjhunu district in Rajasthan, emphasizes the behavioural aspects of the political (non-officials) and administrative (officials) factors in day-to-day concrete situations.[15]

Nandekar has examined the role of Zilla Parishads as local governments and development bodies with special reference to the Nasik Zilla Parishad in Maharastra.[16] He has discussed the social, civil and economic functions of the body and looks at the organization of Zilla Parishad in Maharastra as the fusion of the traditional local government organization and new development organization. While emphasizing the unity between the two, he concludes that the Zilla Parishads are the units of development and administration should be provided with more resources.

Darshankar (1979) discusses the interaction between caste and politics, role of money, education and social rank in the working of panchayati raj institutions in Marathwada region of Maharastra state.[17] Prasad has critically analyzed the organization and functioning of panchayats in Andhra Pradesh. He has focussed on the administrative aspects of the village panchayat with particular reference to "operational dynamics in achieving the objectives of rural development".[18] The structural factors such as the organs of panchayat, supervision, control and guidance mechanism and vertical and horizontal relations have been examined in detail. The author has also brought out very clearly the financial problems of the panchayats. The author concludes that the structure of the panchayat tends to be feeble because of inadequacy of powers and resources, lack of trained and competent staff, concentration of power in the hands of sarpanch, ineffective linkages and channels of communication, improper supervision and lack of guidance, insensitive bureaucracy and the absence of proper priorities.

Harichandran has examined the role of the PRIs in rural development with particular reference to Tamil Nadu.[19] An in-depth analysis has been made with regard to the economic aspects, i.e. expenditure, revenue and physical achievements. The study has also highlighted the fact that the panchayats can handle effectively the developmental activities, e.g., health, election, supply of water, etc.

Singh (1987) has discussed the three-tier structure of panchayati raj institutions and their functioning in the State of Himachala Pradesh.[20] He has also discussed the development activities of panchayats. He concludes that panchayati raj has brought an awakening among the rural masses and with little finances at their disposal the panchayats have very successfully implemented small schemes.

The study of Mishra and Singh (1993) is an attempt to highlight the alternative roads for the success of the panchayati raj institutions.[21] but the whole discussion boils down to giving constitutional status to these institutions. Several suggestions, as a result of field experience and interactions with the official and general public, have been made in the study.

The study of Palanithurai on the new panchayati raj system gives a comprehensive picture about the historical evolution of the institutions, nature of new system, operational devices of the new system and its implications in the socio-economic life of the rural people.[22] Kailash C. Sharma finds from his study on panchayati raj leadership in a district of Rajasthan that the emerging leaders of panchayati raj possess the full knowledge and are aware of the objectives of the panchayati raj and the impediments coming in the way of rural development.[23]

The National Institute of Rural Development has conducted immediately after the introduction of 73rd Constitution Amendment Act in states, an analytical study in five states namely Andhra Pradesh, Gujarat, Karnataka, Maharastra and West Bengal regarding the existing patterns of devolution of powers and functions to the PRIs.[24] The study has clearly brought out large variations in the pattern of operationalization of the 73rd Constitutional Amendment.

The study of Shakuntala Sharma on the profile of leadership and rural power structure throws a new light on the working of panchayat system.[25] It investigates and analyzes various aspects of grass-root democracy and politics in terms of performance of panchayats, pattern of rural power structure and links of rural leaders with higher political leadership.

The study of A.C. Jena on "Panchayati Raj Finances in West Bengal" covers a broad scenario of panchayat finances in the country, financial resources of panchayats and devolution of resources at various levels:[26] The tax administration, problems and revenue prospects and financial administration involving budgeting accounting and auditing of PRIs and suggests measures for their improvement besides reviewing the SFC Report of West Bengal.

In his study on needs and resources of Kshetra Panchayats and Village Panchayats in Saharanpur district in Meerut region of western Uttar Pradesh, Mahipal has assessed the gap in the availability and requirements of basic services and suggests measures to mobilize additional resources for panchayats to enable them effectively provide the basic services to the rural population.[27]

From the above review of studies, it is clear that a lot of work has been done on the pattern of panchayati raj and functioning of PRIs at different levels at all India level, state level and local level. But a little work has been done on working of PRIs after the introduction of 73rd Constitution Amendment Act. There is no study on the panchayati raj system in Andhra Pradesh. The present study fills this knowledge gap in the existing literature on the subject.

Objectives of the Study

The main objectives of the study are as follows:

1. To examine the Panchayati Raj System in Andhra Pradesh before and after 73rd Constitution Amendment Act;
2. To examine how the 73rd Constitution Amendment Act and its conformity state legislation are implemented;
3. To examine organizational structure, powers, functions, personnel and financial resources of PRIs in the State;
4. To find out the working of PRIs; and
5. To ascertain the views of the officials, non-officials and the people on the functioning of the PRIs.

Research Methodology

To examine the above objectives of the study a critical evaluation has been made on the working of Panchayati Raj system in Andhra Pradesh since 1995. The research methodology used in the study is historical, case study method and survey research methods. For the study the data have been collected from primary and secondary sources.

The libraries of the universities and the institutes, research papers, books and journals having a direct bearing on the subject constitute the secondary sources of information. The main burden of the study is, however, on the primary data. The primary sources for data collection for the study include the field, relevant documents, reports and guidelines, issued by the Government of India and Government of Andhra Pradesh. The information has also been collected from the statements, reports, and records of selected panchayati raj institutions (PRIs). The field data have been collected through three structured interview schedules. These interview schedules have been administered to the officials, peoples representatives and the people to elicit their views on the panchayati raj system in Andhra Pradesh. The data collected have been processed by using simple arithmetic techniques and also by using computer.

Study Areas

The main purpose of this study is to examine the Panchayati Raj system in Andhra Pradesh. The districts of West Godavari (from Andhra region), Cuddapah (from Rayalaseema region) and Warangal (from Telangana region) were selected for an intensive study. Two Mandal Parishads from each of these districts and two grama panchayats from each of 6 Mandal Parishads were also identified for the intensive study. A brief profile of the districts, mandals, and villages selected for the study is given in this chapter.

West Godavari District

The district of West Godavari was carved out of the Godavari district in 1925. As the western delta of the river Godavari lies in the district, it was appropriately named West Godavari and the headquarters of the district is located at Eluru. According to 2001 census, the total population of West Godavari district is 37,96,144 comprising 19,06,104 males and 18,90,040 females.[28] The West Godavari district is a densily-populated district. In fact, it has the highest density of population of all the districts except Hyderabad. Against the State average of 242 persons per sq. km., West Godavari has 454 persons per sq. km. The district has 85 inhabited villages, 35 uninhabited villages and 10 towns. Out of the total population in the district rural population accounts for 30.07 lakhs (79.20 per cent) and urban population for 7.89 lakhs (20.80 per cent). In terms of agricultural development and industrial growth and communication, health and educational facilities, West Godavari is one of the most advanced districts in the State of Andhra Pradesh.

West Godavari district is popularly known as "grannery of Andhra Pradesh" and "rice-bowl of Andhra Pradesh". Paddy is grown extensively in both kharif and rabi seasons in almost all mandals. The wet paddy crop is popular and is raised in all phases where irrigation facilities are available. The net area cultivated forms about 57.44 per cent of the total geographical area of the district. Out of the net area shown a large portion of the area is irrigated by the network of irrigation canals from Godavari and Krishna rivers. The other predominant crops raised in this district are banana, sugarcane, chillies, coconut, tobacco and oil palm.

There are many medium and large-scale industries in the district. Sri Krishna Jute Mills Limited, Eluru; Andhra Sugars Limited, Mandapaka; Jaipur Sugar Company Limited, Chagallu; Messers Foods, Fats, and Fertilizers Limited, Tadepalligudem;

Sri Akkamamba Textiles Limited, Mandapaka; Sri Satyanarayana Spinning Mills Limited, Mandapaka; etc., are worth-mentioning. The investment in all these industries is approximately 350 crores providing employment nearly 50,000 workers. All these industries are concentrated in delta area and most of them are agro based. The industries in the small scale sector are also agro-based as agricultural commodities support nearly one-third of the total industrial units now functioning in the district. As a whole the small scale sector has been providing employment to 27,520 persons. The industries both in the large and small scale employed significant number of people. Consequently there is an inflow of migrants from the neighboring districts and also from outside the State. Handloom weaving is an important cottage industry of the district. The main products of this industry are coarse cloth of hand-spun yarn and fine cloth woven with mill yarn. The carpets of Eluru are known through out the world for their gaiety and workmanship. The Crochet laces are exported to U.K., U.S.A., Canada, France and Australia. The annual turnover from this industry is about 10.56 crores.

All the towns and villages in the district are covered with good communication systems. The telephone facility is available even in small inhabited villages. The district has a satisfactory network of road and rail communications. All the 10 towns in the district are well connected by buses. The national highway No. 5 connecting Madras with Calcutta goes through the district. The district is served by a total length of about 169 km of railway track. The most important railway line is one which connecting Madras in the south with Calcutta in the east.

There are good medical and health services available in this district. A big hospital is functioning at district headquarters, Eluru, with 372 beds. Four government hospitals, 5 government dispensaries, 3 postmortem centres, 60 primary health centres and 544 sub-medical centres are functioning at present in the district. All the villages and towns of the district were electrified. In other words, cent per cent electrification was done in this district. In the district nearly 112 protected drinking water supply schemes are in operation and 2971 hand pumps are working to provide drinking water to the people in 1573 inhabited areas.

There are 2,342 primary schools, 234 upper primary schools, 299 high schools, 27 junior colleges, 17 degree colleges, 22 professional colleges, 5 post-graduate colleges and 26 residential colleges. The total number of students enrolled in the district is 1,21,637 out of which 68,417 are boys and 53,220 are girls.

Attili Mandal

Attili is one of the 46 mandals in the West Godavari district. According to 2001 census the total population of the Attili mandal is 68,252. It includes 34,339 males and 33,913 females. Out of the total population of the mandal 48,188 are literates, which includes 25,512 males and 22,676 females. The literacy rate in the mandal is 70.60 per cent. This mandal has an area of 85.90 sq. kms. The percentage of cultivable area to total land is 84.58 and irrigated area to total cultivable area is 90.90.

There is no dearth of educational, medical, water supply, postal and tele-communication and power supply facilities in the mandal. There are 53 primary schools, 13 upper schools, 8 high schools, 1 junior college and 1 degree college in the mandal. There are 6 dispensaries, one primary health centre, one family planning centre and 20 private medical centres in the mandal. The drinking water from different sources is available to all the villages in the mandal. The sources include taps, canal, tank and wells. There are 11 post offices with phone in the mandal. The mandal is well connected with road and rail network. There are 3 railway stations namely (1) Atiili, (2) Manchili and (3) Aravalli in the mandal. All the villages in the mandal have pucca approach roads. The R.T.C. buses pass through all the villages in the mandal. All the villages in the mandal are electrified.

Kommara Village

The Kommara village is 5 km away from mandal headquarters in Attili. The area of the village is 1854.53 acres and the population is 2776 as per the 2001 census. It includes 1379 males and 1397 females. Kommara is a small village. It is an agricultural village. The main crop of this village is paddy. This village has good irrigation water facilities. Main source of water for agriculture here is Godavari canal. It goes through this village. In addition to this, there are tanks, wells and bore wells are also in usage. This village is mainly a paddy producer.

This village has a connecting road to national highway No.5. In this village there are at present 4 primary schools and 1 high school. One branch post office with a public telephone is working in this village. There is also one public telephone booth in the village. The village is a electrified village. The Andhra Pradesh State Road Transport Corporation buses go through this village. There are two small scale rice mills and one flour mill in the village. They give employment to about 20 members.

Gummampadu Village

The Gummampadu is a small village in Attili mandal 3 km away from mandal headquarters. The area of the village is 383.22 acres and the population is 3080 as per the 2001 census. It includes 1505 males and 1575 females. The people of this village totally depend upon agriculture. The main crop of this village is paddy. A canal from Godavari is going through this village. Canal water is useful for both drinking and irrigation purposes. This village has a connecting road to national high way No.5 in a distance of 8 km. The village is completely electrified. There are two primary schools in the village.

Lingapalem Mandal

Lingapalem is one of the 16 mandals in the revenue division of Eluru in West Godavari district. According to 2001 census the total population of the Lingapalem mandal is 56399. It includes 28,624 males and 27,775 females. The literacy rate in the mandal is 61.15 per cent. This mandal has an area of 23.9 sq. kms. The major crops grown in the mandal are paddy, maize, blackgram, chillies, etc. In some parts of the mandal greengram, redgram, cotton, groundnut, jowar, tobacco, vegetables, sunflower, etc. are grown. In addition to this in some areas coconut, mango, cashew and oil palm are also grown.

Theer is no dearth of facilities in the mandal. The facilities available in the mandal include educational, medical, water supply, postal and telecommunication, and power supply facilities. There are 68 primary schools, 6 upper primary middle schools, 6 high schools, and 1 junior college in the mandal. There are 2 primary health centres and 4 medical sub-centres in the mandal. Two veterinary hospitals are working in the mandal, one at Lingapalem and another at another village named Dharmajigudem. All the villages in the mandal are provided postal, telegraphic and telephone facilities. The mandal is well connected with road network. All the villages in the mandal have pucca approach roads. The Road Transport Corporation buses pass through all the villages in the mandal. All the villages in the mandal are electrified. Two branches one each of the State Bank of India and Andhra Bank are functioning in the mandal. In the mandal there are 4 primary agriculture credit co-operative societies.

Dharmajigudem

The population of Dharmajigudem, an important village in Lingapalem mandal, is 8,247, which includes 4158 males and 4089 females as per the 2001 census. It is 2 km from Mandal headquarters. The main occupation of the villagers is cultivation.

The main crops grown in this area are paddy, chillies, cotton and maize. Mahatma Gandhi visited this village in 1921. This village is completely electrified. The educational facilities in the village include a primary school, a high school and a junior college. Postal, telegraph and telephone facilities are available to the villagers. The Andhra Pradesh State Road Transport Corporation buses ply to district and mandal headquarters from this village. There is a veterinary hospital in the village. State Bank of India has a branch in this village. A primary agricultural credit co-operative society is also functioning in the village.

Mathamgudem

The Mathamgudem village is located in upland and backward area of Lingapalem mandal. The population of the village is 3463 as per the 2001 census. It includes 1768 males and 1695 females. The village is 8 km from mandal headquarters. The main occupation of this village is agriculture. The main crops of this village are paddy, maize, chillies and cotton. Mathamgudem is a electrified village. There is only one primary school being maintaining by the Mandal Parishad in the village. The Andhra Pradesh State Road Transport Corporation buses run through this village, connecting mandal as well as district headquarters. A branch post office is working with a telephone in the village.

Cuddapah District

Cuddapah district is the 8th largest district in Andhra Pradesh in respect of area. The district is spread over to 15,359.59 sq. kms. The district was first formed in the year 1808 with Siddavatham as its headquarters, which was later shifted to Cuddapah in 1812. Cuddapah district is the heart of Rayalaseema region of Andhra Pradesh lying between 30^0 43 and 15^0 14N and 79^0 55 and 70^0 29E. It is bound by Kurnool district on the North, Nellore district on the East, Chittoor district on the south and Ananthapur district on the west.

The total population of the district, according to 2001 census, is 25,92,048 out of which 13,13,256 are males and 12,78,792 are females. There are 956 females for every 1000 males. The density of population of the district is 147.

The predominant soils of the district are black clay (26 per cent), black loam (18 per cent), red loam (26 per cent) and red sandy (30 per cent). Black clay mainly found in Jammalamadugu, Pulivendla, Proddatur, and Kamalapuram mandals and to a small extent on the western side of Cuddapah mandal. Black loam is an alluvial soil varying in the texture and colour and occurring in almost all the mandals. It is the richest in western plains region and responds well for well-irrigation. Red loam soil is found very extensively over the areas of Rajampet and Badvel mandals. The eastern portion of Cuddapah district has extensive areas containing red loam. This soil is of the high agricultural value and all varieties of crops can be grown in the lands. Red sandy is considered to be the most treacherous and unproductive and we find it mostly in Rayachoti Mandal.

Based on the agro climate conditions the district falls both in southern zone and also scare rainfall zone. All the 16 mandals of Proddatur division and 6 Mandals of Rajampet Division fell into scare rainfall zone. The annual normal rainfall of the district is 692.2 mms., which is 230 mms less than the state average of the total normal rainfall of 925 mms. During khariff, generally crops like paddy, sajja, jowar, ragi, groundnut, korra, redgram, etc., are raised besides sugarcane, turmeric, etc., which are one year crops. Garden crops like citrus, mangoes and other cash crops are raised. Paddy, ragi and sajja are staple food crops of the district. During rabi season the high yielding varieties of paddy, cash crops like groundnut, gingily, onion, coriander, sunflower, etc., are raised. Sericulture started in the district during 1976-77 and the area under Mulbary is about 11,372 acres by the end of the 1986-87 with the production of 13.63 lakhs kgs of cocoons. The district occupies 3rd place in the state. Anantapur and Chittoor districts are in the first and second places respectively.

The total forest area in the district is 5,05,495 hectares which constitutes 32.87% of the total geographical area of the district. Among the forest produces 'Prerocarpus Santalinurs' otherwise known as Red Sander is the foremost product. Softwood useful for the manufacture of woden combs and toys is also available. The minor forest produce consists of beedi leaves, Thangedu and Relabarks, Tooki leaves, Nux-vomica seed, soap nuts, etc. The forest wealth has helped to establish many number of saw mills, wooden furniture manufacturing and bamboo basket making industries in the district. The district with its vast and valuable resources of agricultural, forestry and livestock, offers adequate opportunities for development of a good number of industries. The Cuddapah district has an agricultural oriented economy with a vast scope for the promotion of agro-based industries.

Cuddapah district is endowed with rich mineral resources particularly, barytes, asbestos, lime stone and clay. The barytes deposits in Mangampet area are considered to be the best and largest in the world and the availability of superior quality of asbestos deposits in Pulivendula area is a monopoly of the state. Based on the mineral resources available in the district, three cement factories, one barium chemicals unit, one asbestos minerals processing and grading unit under large and medium sector besides many number of small scale industries like pulverizing and slab polishing, barium chemical, asbestos mineral processing and grading stones crushing units and china clay levigation have came up in the district. As on date the district has 13 large scale and medium scale industries with an investment of Rs.5517.85 lakhs and employing 7606 persons.[29] The district has 5,694 small scale units employing 41,142 persons with an investment of Rs.4703.58 lakhs.

One of the Most important prerequisites for development of industries is effective transport or communication. The district has not only road transport but also rail. The district has 25 railway stations connecting Madras and Bombay broad gauge railway line. The district has also got a good network of road communication connecting all the important places both within and outside the state. The district has 640 kms of highway. The district has good telegraphic communication facilities. The All India Radio has set up a medium wave transmitting station in Cuddapah. The Cuddapah district has become one of the major power generation centers in the state with the establishment of Muddanur Thermal Power Station with an installing capacity of 420 KWS.

There are good educational facilities in the district and the percentage of literacy is around 41. The district has been served by 2,616 primary schools and 226 upper primary schools. It has 282 high schools, 39 junior colleges, 19 degree colleges and one SVUPG centre for general education.[30] For the technical education the district has four polytechnics, three engineering colleges and four industrial training institutes. The district has nine residential schools and one Navodaya School.

The district has one Government General Hospital and one Government T.B. Hospital at district headquarters with requisite specialists. There are 50 mandal primary health centers in mandal headquarters. The total number of private hospitals in the district around 110. About twenty financial institutions are working in the district with a network 111 branches. The district is divided into three revenue divisions i.e. Cuddapah, Rajampet and Jammalamadugu. There are 50 mandal parishads in Cuddapah district. The mandal Parishads of Chennur and Sidhavatam were selected for a detailed study.

Chennur Mandal

Chenur village in Cuddapah district is situated on Cuddapah – Kurnool highway, It is the headquarters of the mandal. The area of the Chennur mandal is spread over 123.62 sq. kms., with 15 revenue villages and 18 inhabitations. As per 2001 census the population of the mandal is 36,567. Out of the total population, 18,887 are males and 17,680 are females.

The mandal consists of two types of soil-blacky and sandy soils. The blacky soil is well suited for paddy cultivation and sand soils are better suited for dry crops like papaya and varieties of vegetables. The land of this mandal area is being irrigated with Krishna canal water. Paddy is the main food crop. The important commercial crops are betal leaves and sunflower. The average rainfall in the mandal is 53.75 mm.

There are 38 primary schools, 7 upper primary schools, 5 high schools and one government junior college in the mandal. There are 13 post offices and 12 telephone exchanges in the mandal. In this mandal one primary health centre with 7 sub-centres, and three private hospitals are working for public health. Communication facilities are provided to all the villages in this mandal. Mandal headquarters has been linked with main roads of the State. There are 18 gram panchayats in Chennur mandal. Ramanapalle and Sivallapalle gram panchayats were selected for a detailed study.

Ramanapalle

The village Ramanapalle came into existence by Cuddapah District Collector's orders in 1963 and it is now a major panchayat in Chenur mandal of the district. This village is 12 kms. away from the district headquarters and 2 kms. to the mandal headquarters. The total population of the village according to 2001 census figures is 3420 out of which males are 1740 and females are 1650. The total voters in the village are 2,754. The percentage of literates in the village is 66 which is more than the literacy rate of the mandal. The village is well connected with road. There are postal and telephone facilities in the village. There are 4 elementary schools and one zilla parishad high school in the village. The Kurnool-Cuddapah (KC) canal is the main source of the village for cultivation of land. The crops of paddy, palm leaves and groundnut are cultivated in the village.

Sivallapalle

The village Sivallapalle came into existence by Cuddapah District Collector's orders in 1969 and it is a minor gram panchayat in Chennur mandal of the district. This village is 36 kms., away from the district headquarters and 16 kms to the mandal headquarters. The total population of the village, according to 2001 census figures is 1135 out of which males are 573 and females are 562. There are 856 voters in the villages out of which males are 458 and females are 398. The percentage of literates in the village is 54 which is less than the literacy rate of the mandal. The village is well connected with road. There are postal and telephone facilities in the village. In the village, there are two high schools and three elementary schools. The Kurnool-Cuddapah canal is the main source for the cultivation of the land. The main crops in the village are paddy and palm leaves.

Sidhavatam Mandal

Sidhavatam village in Cuddapah district is the headquarters of the mandal. The mandal is spread over an area of 122.26 sq. kms., with 7 revenue villages and 18 habitations. As per 2001 census the population of the mandal is 35,101. Out of which, 17,301 are males and 17,800 are females. The literacy rate of the mandal is 54.30 per cent. There are 36 primary schools, one upper primary school, 10 high schools and two junior colleges in the mandal. Three primary health centers with 8 sub-centres, and one veterinary hospital are working for public health. Mandal headquarters has been linked with main roads of the State. There are 13 revenue villages and 9 gram panchayats in the mandal. The gram panchayats for the villages of Madhavaram and Rajampeta were selected for a detailed study.

Madhavaram

The village Madhavaram came into existence by Cuddapah District Collector's orders in 1994 and now it is a major panchayat in Sidhavatam mandal of the district. This village is 45 kms. away from the district headquarters and 9 kms. to the mandal headquarters. The total population of the village, according to 2001 census figures is 5,411, out of which 2513 are males and females are 2898. In this village the total voters are 3945 out of this male are 1863 and females are 2082. The percentage of literates in the village is 72.36 which is higher than the literacy rate of the mandal. The village is well connected with road and rail. There are postal and telephone facilities in the village.

Rajampet

The village came into existence by Cuddapah District Collector's orders in 1978 and it is a minor panchayat in Sidhavatam mandal. This village is 18 kms. away from the district headquarters and 3 kms. to the mandal headquarters. The total population of the village, according to 2001 census figures is 513; out of which 262 are males and 251 are females. The total voters are 463 out of which males voters are 236 and females voters are 227. The percentage of literates in the village is 54.36 which is less than the literacy rate of the mandal. The village is well connected with road. There are postal and telephone facilities in the village. In the village there are 3 elementary schools. The Kurnool- Cuddapah canal is the main source of water for the cultivation of land. The crops of paddy and sunflower are cultivated in the village.

Warangal District

The Warangal District is one of 10 districts in Telangana region. The District lies between the latitude of $17^0 - 19^0$ and

$18^0 – 36^0$ north and longitude of $78\text{-}69^0$ and $80^0\text{-}43$ East, and is above mid sea level by 870 ft. It is bounded on the north by Karimnagar district, on the west by Medak district, on the south by Nalgonda district and by Khammam district on east and south-east. The geographical area of the district is 12840 sq.kms. The entire area is studded with isolated hills, hill streams, rainfed tanks and large lakes. The district possesses interesting pictures of geographical formations and contains minerals of economic importance. The soils of the district comprise of sandy loams with patches of shallow black cotton soils, and at places even medium and deep black cotton soil. The district is generally tends to be dry. It gets quite warm during the summer months of April, May and June and also continues to be warm in the rest of the year except during the December and January, when the temperature drops slightly. The maximum and minimum temperature have been recorded as $50^0.5$ and $13^0.5$ centigrades respectively.

With a total population of 28.18 lakhs (2001 census), the district occupies 13th place in the State of Andhra Pradesh in its population and 12th place in regards to its area. There are 219 persons per sq. km. in the district as against 242 in the State. The percentage of literacy in the district is 32.6 as against the State figures of 44.9. The scheduled caste population in the district is 4.84 lakhs and the scheduled tribes population is 3.8 lakhs which forms 17.2 and 13.7 per cent respectively of the district population.

Out of 1098 revenue villages of the district 1003 villages are inhabited and the rest of the villages are deserted. The total rural population of the district is 22.7 lakhs. There are three revenue divisions i.e. 1. Warangal, 2. Mahabubabad, 3. Jangam and 50 mandal parishads. The total urban population is 5.5 lakhs (i.e. 18 per cent). Warangal city is classified as Municipal Corporation. The working class population in the district is 13.47 lakhs (47.8 per cent of the total population).

The workers in agricultural sector are 9.05 lakhs forming 32.1 per cent of the total population. The remaining 4.42 lakhs are the workers engaged in non-agricultural sectors comprising of 15.7 per cent of the total population of the district.

The principal cereal crops grown in the district are rice and maize. In production of rice the district occupies 4th place in Telangana region and 11th place in Andhra Pradesh. Ninety per cent of the people of the district are rice-eaters. The important irrigation sources in the district are Ramappa, Ghanpur (M), Parkhal and Lakhavaram tanks and Salivagu project under which considerable area is irrigated. The other sources of irrigation in the district are rainfed tanks, wells and hill-streams which require good showers in the season. The rainy season sets in the district with the on set of south-west monsoon in the later part of the June month, and ends with the month of September with the closure of the south-west monsoons. The normal annual rainfall of the district is 1048.1 mm. The maximum of it occurs in the months of July, August, September and the highest rainfall occurs in Mulug, Parkal, Mahabubabad and Narasampet mandals.

The Warangal city has considerably developed during the past three decades. The establishment of many new educational institutions like Kakatiya University, Regional Engineering College, Kakatiya Institution of Teaching and Service, (KITS), Government Polytechnic, Kakatiya Medical College, Industrial Training Institute, Law College, Women's College, College of Education, Music and Dance School have added to the growth of education and culture in a wide circle covering large section of population attracting even beyond the district and state boundaries.

Warangal district has large number of small and medium size industries. The Azam Jahi Textile Mills is major industry (which employs nearly 900 persons). The tanning, light engineering, rice mills, wood works, saw mills, cottage and village industries, industrial cooperatives are the other important industries in the district, employing a major portion of the working population in the industrial sector. There are three industrial estates in the district one is in middle of the city another at Correkunta and third one at Rampur. With the starting of various educational institutions and industrial establishments, construction works in the city have gained considerable momentum.

Warangal occupies importance in trade next to Hyderabad in Telangana. The entire district is covered with regulated markets which attracts produce even from other neighbouring districts. The district is traversed by the Madras – Delhi (Broad-Guage) railway line starting from Dornakal in the south to Hasanparthi road in the North, over a total length of 70 kms. Another railway line connects Kazipet to Hyderabad with a total lengths of 38 kms., forming part of south central railway. Dornakal junction connect the Singareni coal mines from where the coal is supplied to all over the country.

The infrastructure facilities available to the area plays a vital role in the development of local economy. Above 65.36 per cent villages had been electrified so far. There are 2,318 schools of all types i.e. elementary, upper primary and high schools, where 3,19,675 students are enrolled. There are 63 junior colleges, 36 degree colleges with an intake of 56,363 students. There are also professional and technical institutes in the district. The Kakatiya University is located at Hanamkonda. There are 6 head post offices, 126 sub-post offices, 563 branch offices, 13 telegraph offices and 123 telephone exchanges. There are 12 general hospitals and 3 dispensaries with 236 doctors. Fifty four primary health centers, 29 ayurvedic dispensaries and 9 homeopathic dispensaries are also working in the district. The Gandhi Medical Hospital, Warangal, is one of the premier institution in health care in the State.

Hasanparthy Mandal

Hasanparthy is a village in Warangal district. It is the headquarters of the mandal. The Hasanparthy mandal is spread in the area of 135.36 sq. kms., with 18 villages and 13 hamlets. This mandal come into existence with effect from 15.1.1987 when mandal system was introduced in the state. Prior to formation of the mandal it was a part of the erstwhile panchayat samithi of Hanmkonda. As per 2001 census the population of the mandal is 64,724. Out of the total population 32,156 are males and 33,568 are females. The literacy rate of the mandal is 65.13 per cent. There are 36 primary schools, two upper primary schools, 14 high schools and three junior colleges in the mandal. In this mandal one primary health centre with 6 sub-centres, and one veterinary hospital are working for public health. Communication facilities are provided to all the villages in the mandal. The mandal headquarters has been linked with main roads of the State. There are 23 gram panchayats in the Hasanparthy mandal. The gram panchayats of Chintagattu and Ganturpalle were selectd for a detailed study.

Chintagattu

The village Chintagattu came into existence by Warangal District Collector's orders in 1964 and it is a major gram panchayat in Hasanparthy mandal. This village is 27 kms., away from the district headquarters and 9 kms., away from the mandal headquarters. The total population of the village, according to 2001 census figures is 3379, out of which males are 1687 and females are 1692. The total voters in the village are 2551. Out of this male voters are 1249 and female voters are 1302. The percentage of literates in the village is 70.23 which is the highest literacy rate in the mandal. The village is well connected with road and rail. There are postal and telephone facilities in the village. In the village, there are one zilla parishad high school, one upper primary school and two primary schools.

Ganturpalli

The village Ganturpalli came into existence by Warangal District Collector's orders in 1981 and it is a minor Gram

Panchayat in Hasanparthy mandal. This village is 36 kms. away from the district headquarters and 5 kms. to the mandal headquarters. The total population is 1355 out of which males are 684 and females are 671. The total voters in this village are 677. Out of this male voters are 345 and 332 are females voters. The percentage of literates in the village is 63.27 which is average literacy rate in the mandal. There are two primary schools and one post office in the village.

Kuravi Mandal

Kuravi is a big village in Warangal District. It is the headquarters of the mandal. The Kuravi mandal is spread over the area of 153.63 sq.kms., with 14 revenue villages and 23 Gram Panchayats. As per 2001 census, the population of the mandal is 64,169. Out of the total population, 32.211 are males and 31,958 are females. The literacy rate of the mandal is 52.36 per cent. The mandal consists of two types of soil, the blacky and red cloany soils. The blacky soil is well suited for paddy cultivation and red soils are better suited for dry crops like cotton and chilies. The land of this mandal area is being irrigated with Sriramsagar canal water. Paddy is the main food crop. The average rainfall in the mandal is 58.54 mm.

There are 32 primary schools, 10 upper primary school, and 5 high schools in the mandal. There are 12 post offices and one telephone exchange in the mandal. In this mandal one primary health centre with 5 sub-centres, and one veterinary hospital are working for public health. Communication facilities are provided to all the villages in this mandal. Mandal headquarters has been linked with main roads of the State. Out of the 23 gram panchayats in the mandal two gram panchayats namely Nallela and Chintalapalli were selected for a detailed study.

Nallela

The village Nallela came into existence by Warangal District Collector's orders in 1963 and it is a major gram panchayat in Kuravi mandal of the Warangal district. This village is 72 kms away from the district headquarters and 5 kms to the mandal headquarters. The total population of the village, according to 2001 census figures, is 3,414, out of which males are 1767 and 1647 are females. The total voters in this village is 2,776, out of which 1414 are male voters 1362 are women voters. The percentage of literacy rate in the village is 60.27 which is the average literacy rate of this mandal. The village is well connected with road. There are postal and telephone facilities in the village. In the village there are 4 primary schools and one primary health sub-centre.

Chintalapalli

The village Chintalapalli came into existence by Warangal District Collector's orders in 1981. This village is 79 kms. away from the district headquarters and 7 kms. to the mandal headquarters. The total population of the village, according to 2001 census figures is 1746, out of which 933 are males 813 are females. The total voters in this village are 1286, out of this male voters are 651 and female voters are 635. The percentage of literacy rate in this village is 54.27 which is the lowest literacy rate in this mandal. There are postal and telephone facilities in the village. There are one zilla parishad high school and two primary schools in the village. The Sriramsagar canal is the main source of the village for the cultivation of land. The crops of paddy and cotton are cultivated in the village.

References

1. Iqbal Narain, "A Perspective on Research in Panchayati Raj" in S.L. Verma (ed.), *Panchayati Raj, Gram Swaraj and Federal Polity,* Rawat, Jaipur, 1990, p. 51.
2. R.V. Jathar, *Evolution of Panchayati Raj in India*, J.S.S. Institute of Economic Research, Dharwad, 1964.

3. R.L. Khanna, Panchayati Raj in Punjab and Harayana, Mohindra Capital Publishers, Chandigarh, 1966.
4. M. Venkatarangaiah and G. Ram Reddy, *Panchayati Raj in Andhra Pradesh,* Andhra Pradesh Chamber of Panchayati Raj, Hyderabad, 1967.
5. M. Venkatarangaiya and M. Pattabhiram (eds.), *Local Government in India: Select Readings*, Applied Publishers, Calcutta, 1969.
6 Iqbal Narian, Susil Kumar and M.V. Mathur, *Panchayati Raj Administration*, Indian Institute of Public Administraiton, New Delhi, 1970.
7. N.R. Inamdar, *Functioning of Village Panchayats*, Popular Prakashan, New Delhi, 1970.
8. H.P. Chokshi, *A Study of Mobilisation of Resources for Village Panchayats in Baroda District*, Planning Commission, New Delhi, 1971.
9. B.C. Muthaya, *Panchayat Taxes: Factors Influencing their Mobilisation: A Study in three Panchayats in East Godavari, Andhra Pradesh*, National Institute of Community Department, Hyderabad, 1972.
10. V.P. Grover, et al., *Panchayati Raj Administration in Rajasthan*, Lakshmi Narayan Aggarwal, Delhi, 1972.
11. Sushil Kumar and K. Venkataraman, *State - Panchayati Raj Relations: A Study of Supervision and Control in Tamil Nadu,* Asia Publshing House, Bombay, 1974.
12. Sudesh Kumar Sharma, *Panchayati Raj in India*, Trimurti Publications, New Delhi, 1976.
13. Abida Samiuddin, *A Critique of Panchayati Raj with special reference to Uttar Pradesh*, Sahitya Bhawan, Agra,1976.
14. S.N. Dubey and Ratna Murdia, *Structure and Process of Decision Making in Panchayati Raj Institutions*, Somiya Publications, Bombay, 1976.

15. B.S. Bhargava, *Politico-Administrative Dynamics in Panchayati Raj System*, Ashish Publishing House, New Delhi, 1978.
16. V.G. Nandekar *Local Government: Its Role in Development Administration*, Concept Publishing Co., Delhi, 1979.
17. Arjun Y. Darshankar, *Leadership in Panchayati Raj: A Studyof Beed District of Maharastra*, Panchsheel Prakashan, Jaipur, 1979.
18. V. Sivalinga Prasad, *Panchayats and Development*, Light & Life Publishers, New Delhi,1981.
19. C. Harichandran, *Panchayati Raj and Rural Development: A Study of Tamil Nadu*, Concept Publishing Co., New Delhi, 1986.
20. Surat Singh, "Functioning of Panchayati Raj Institutions in Himachal Pradesh", *Kurukshetra*, Vol.XXXVI, No.3, December 1987.
21. S.N. Misra and S.S. Singh, *Roads to Model Panchayati Raj*, Mittal Publications, New Delhi, 1993.
22. G. Palanithurai, *Empowering People for Prosperity: A Study in New Panchayati Raj System,* Kanishka Publisher, Delhi, 1994.
23. Kailash C. Sharma, *Leadership in Panchayati Raj: A Study of Chitturgarh District*, Printwell, Jaipur, 1996.
24. National Institute of Rural Development, *Panchayati Raj Institutions in Select States: An Analytical Study*, NIRD, Hyderabad, 1995.
25. Shakuntala Sharma, *Grassroots Politics and Panchayati Raj,* Deep & Deep Publications, New Delhi, 1997.
26. A.C. Jana, *Panchati Raj Finances in West Bengal – A Status Study*, National Institute of Rural Development, Hyderabad, 1999.
27. Mahipal, *Gap Between Needs and Resources of Panchayats in India*, Mittal Publications, New Delhi, 2003.
28. *Census of India 2001,* Series-29, Andhra Pradesh, Provisional Population Totals, Paper-2 of 2001, Director of Census Operations, Andhra Pradesh.

29. *Progress Report on Industries*, District Industries Centre, Cuddapah, 1998, p.15.

30. *The Hand Book of Statistics* – Cuddapah District, 1996-97, p.7.

5

Organizational Structure, Powers and Functions of Panchayati Raj Institutions

The system of panchayati raj organized in conformity with Seventy- third Constitution Amendment Act and Andhra Pradesh Panchayati Raj Act, 1994 comprises Gram Panchayat, Mandal Parishad and Zilla Parishad. At the village level, there is Gram Panchayat. There are 21,943 gram panchayats in the State. At the intermediate level, i.e. mandal level there is mandal parishad. There are 1096 mandal parishads in the State. At the district level, there is a Zilla Parishad. It is the apex body at the district level as far as developmental works concerned. The zilla parishads have been organized for 22 districts in the State.

The first ordinary elections to PRIs in the state, after the implementtion of 73rd Constitution Amendment Act, were held in 1995. Elections to the Mandal Parishads and Zilla Parishads were held in March 1995 and to the Gram Panchayats in June 1995. Election to 14,647 MPTCs each with a population of 3,000 to 3,500 and 1092 ZPTCs each with a population ranging from 35,000 to 50,000 were conducted during 6th and 10th March 1995. The elections to 21,743 sarpanch positions and 2,60,000 ward members were held in June 1995. Elections to the PRIs in the scheduled areas in the state were also held in 1995. But the election results were not announced for them.

The second ordinary elections to PRIs were due by May 2000. Elections had been postponed several times and finally conducted in 2001. Elections to the panchayati raj bodies in Andhra Pradesh were held in two phases during July-August 2001. Elections to 14,590 MPTCs, 1094 ZPTCs were held in July 2001. The elections to 21,434 Gram Panchayats and 2,08,291 wards in the Gram Panchayats were held in August 2001.

In both the elections the members of ZPTCs and MPTCs were elected directly by the voters in rural areas. The Chief of ZPs and MPs were elected among the members of ZPTCs and MPTCs respectively. Both the sarpanch and ward memebrs of the Gram Panchayat were directly elected by the people. Election to the MPTC and ZPTC members and chief of MPs and ZPs were held on party basis, while the elections to gram panchayats were held on non-party basis.

The State legislation provides for reservation of various offices as well as seats in PRIs. The ratio of reservations provided to various categories is 34 percent to Backward Classes (BCs), 18 per cent for Scheduled Castes (SCs) and 8 percent for Scheduled Tribes (STs). One-third of the offices and seats including General Category were reserved for women. The reservation formula covered all the offices or chair-persons of Gram Panchayat, MP and ZP and Panchayat ward, MPTC and ZPTC memebrs. The major political parties namely Telug Desam, Congress, Bharatiya Janata Party, Communist Party of India and Communist Party of India (Marxist) contested the elections. The newly formed Telangana Rashtra Samiti also fielded their candidates in the elections held in July 2001.

The elections to the PRIs in the State were held under the supervision and control of the State Election Commission. The first State Election Commission was appointd in September 1994. Sri Kasipandyan, a retired IAS officer, was the first State

Election Commissioner. The second State Election Commission was apointed in June 1999. Sri K. Madhava Rao, the former Chief Secretary of the Government of Andhra Pradesh, was the Election Commissioner. Both the first and second State Election Commissions performed a stupendous task in conducting the elections. The organizational structure, powers and functions of all these three institutions have been examined in this chapter. The actual functioning of these institutions has also been analyzed in this chapter.

Gram Panchayat

A Gram Panchayat consists of members ranging from 5 to 21 depending upon its population. The members of the Gram Panchayat are elected by the voters of the village from the wards. The chairperson of the Gram Panchayat is elected by all the registered voters and continues in office for a period of 5 years unless or otherwise removed from office. The up-sarpanch of a Gram Panchayat is, however, elected by the ward members. The Gram Panchayat shall meet once every month. The meeting of the Gram Panchayat is presided over by the sarpanch.

Gram Sabha

The Gram Sabha is constituted in each Gram Panchayat and it consists of all the voters within that Gram Panchayat as its members. The gram sabha shall meet at least twice in a year for considering the following matters.

(a) Annual statement of accounts and audit reports,

(b) Report on the administration of the preceding years,

(c) Programme of works for the year or any new programmes not covered by the budgets at the annual programme,

(d) Proposals for fresh taxation as for enhancement of existing taxes,

(e) Selection of schemes, beneficiaries and location, and

(f) Such other matters as may be prescribed.

All the meetings of the Gram Sabha are convened by the sarpanch or panchayat secretary and will be presided over by the sarpanch.

Committees

The Act provides for a Beneficiary Committee for execution of the work of the Gram Panchayat. The composition of the committee, including cooption of the members to it, its powers or functions and related matters shall be such as may be prescribed. The Act also provides for setting up of functional committees of Gram Panchayat on various subjects like water supply, family planning, education, agriculture, public health, sanitation and communication. Andhra Pradesh is the only State which has provided for such committees in the Act. These committees are expected to play a vital role in effectively discharging the functions of the Gram Panchayat.

Powers and Functions

A number of functions relating to development, maintenance, regulating and civic amenities are to be performed by the gram panchayats. Apart from the functions mentioned in the eleventh schedule of the Constitution (73rd Amendment) Act, the State Panchayati Raj Act listed out a wide array of functions of Gram Panchayat. They included 12 obligatory functions and 27 optional functions. The obligatory functions include the construction, repair and maintenance of roads and culverts, lighting of public places, cleaning of streets, opening and maintenance of cremation and burial grounds, sinking and repairing of wells, the registration of births and deaths, establishment and maintenance of cattle ponds, etc. The optional functions of the gram panchayat range from construction and maintenance of dharmasalas to setting up of organizations to promote goodwill and social harmony between different communities.

One of the important functions entrusted to the gram panchayats is the planning of resources (section 45 (3)). The panchayats shall prepare an inventory of the physical, human, financial, natural and other aspects available in their jurisdiction and reports on issues and matters related to them such as their level of exploitation and how their full potential can be harnessed. This resource planning will help the gram panchayat in preparation of its development plan. The membership varies from the gram panchayat to gram panchayat. The number of ward members of the 12 selected gram panchayats was given below:

Table 5.1
Ward Members in Gram Panchayats

Sl.No.	*Name of the Gram Panchayat*	*No. of Members*
1.	Kommara	16
2.	Gummampadu	13
3.	Dharmajigudam	12
4.	Mathamgudem	8
5.	Ramanapalle	9
6.	Sivalapalle	8
7.	Madhavaram	12
8.	Rajampeta	8
9.	Chintagattu	10
10.	Ganturpalli	8
11.	Nallela	10
12.	Chintalapalli	10

The number of ward members in the Gram Panchayats of Mathamgudem (West Godavari District), Rajampeta and Sivalapalle (Cuddapah) and Ganturupalli (Warangal) was 8 while this number was 10 in the Gram Panchayats of Chintagattu, Nallela, and Chintalapalli (Warangal) and 12 in Madhavaram (Cuddapah) and Dharmajigudem (West Godavari). The Gram Panchayat of Gummamupadu consisted of 13 ward members and Ramanapalle Gram Panchayat had 9 members. There were 16 ward members in the Kommara Gram Panchayat. Each Gram Panchayat is required to meet atleast once in a month. The Gram Panchayats under study met more than the prescribed member of times in the year 2002. The number of meetings held by each of the 12 Gram Panchayats was given below:

Table 5.2
Meetings held by Gram Panchayats

Sl.No.	Name of the Gram Panchayat	No. of Meetings
1.	Kommara	17
2.	Gummampadu	16
3.	Dharmajigudam	14
4.	Mathamgudem	13
5.	Ramanapalle	12
6.	Sivalapalle	13
7.	Madhavaram	15
8.	Rajampeta	15
9.	Chintagattu	18
10.	Ganturpalli	16
11.	Nallela	14
12.	Chintalapalli	13

The highest number of panchayat meetings i.e. 18 were held in Chintagattu village (Warangal), while the minimum required meetings i.e. 12 in Ramanapalle village. The number of meetings held by other 10 Gram Panchayats varied from 13 to 17.

The activities undertaken by the gram panchayats during a period of 7 years from 1995-96 to 2001-02, are more or less similar. The supply of drinking water was received utmost attention by the gram panchayats. Street lighting and cleaning streets were undertaken by all the GPs. Laying and maintenance of roads and culverts in the village is another important function of the gram panchayat. The gram panchayats participated actively in the implementation of various programmes like DWCRA, CMEY, Old Age Pension Scheme, Girl Child Protection Scheme, Deepam, etc. The gram panchayats had also implemented Janmabhoomi, Food for Work, Jawahar Rojgaryojana, Swarna Jayanti Samarudhi Yojana (SJSY) and Neeru-Meeru programmes. Issuance of birth, death and nativity certificates is being performed by all the Gram Panchayats.

Mandal Parishad

A Mandal Parishad is constituted for a revenue mandal in rural areas, as such, both the Mandal Parishads and the revenue mandals are coterminous. The Mandal Parishad consists of the following members:

(i) Mandal Parishad Territorial Constituency Members.

(ii) Members of the Legislative Assembly having jurisdiction over the mandal.

(iii) Members of house of people having jurisdiction over the mandal.

(iv) Members of the council of states who are voters in the mandal.

(v) One co-opted member, belonging to minorities (relegious or linguistic).

The District Collector, Sarpanches of Gram Panchayats and the Presidents of agricultural marketing committees in the mandal are the permanent invitees to the Mandal Parishad meetings.

The Mandal Parishad Territorial Constituency (MPTC) members are directly elected by the voters. For the purpose of election of members from territorial constituencies, each constituency consists of population between 3000 – 4000. The members are elected for a term of five years. Only directly elected members of the Mandal Parishad are eligible either to contest or vote in the election to the offices of President and Vice-President of Mandal Parishad. The President and Vice-President are elected by the members of MPTCs. Their term of office is for five years. Any vacancy arising in the office of the President or Vice-President has to be filled within a period of six months by fresh election and a person elected against the vacancy shall continue for the remaining period. The Act provides for constituting a joint committee for 2 or 3 Mandal Parishads if required by the State Government. There is, however, no provision in it for constituting subject committees. The joint committees or subject committees are not constituted in the State.

Powers and Functions

(1) The Mandal Parishad shall exercise all the powers conferred on, and perform all the functions entrusted to it by or under the Andhra Pradesh Panchayati Raj Act, 1994.

(2) Every Mandal Parishad may levy a duty in the form of surcharge on any tax by a Gram Panchayat on land cess or local cess levied within its jurisdiction in such manner and subject to such maximum as may be prescribed.

The development administration is vested in the Mandal Parishad. It shall perform a number of functions ranging from community development to self-help programmes and management of trusts. A detailed list containing the functions to be performed by the Mandal Parishad is given in schedules I and II of the State Act. Schedule I is a reproduction of the Eleventh Schedule of the Constitution. The functions under schedule II are classified under broad categories of (1) community development, (2) agriculture, (3) animal husbandry and fisheries, and (4) health and rural sanitation. In this way a wide range of subjects have been entrusted to the Mandal Parishads. The Mandal Parishads also undertake extension and review functions at mandal level. Six Mandal Parishads, two from each district, were selected for detailed study. They are Attili and Lingapalem in West Godavari district, Chennuru and Sidhavatam in Cuddapah district and Hasanparthi and Kuravi in Warangal district.

According to the provisions of the Andhra Pradesh Panchayati Raj Act, 1994, a Mandal Parishads is supposed to hold one ordinary meeting every month. It can also convene special meetings. The number of meetings conducted by 6 Mandal Parishads in the year 2002 were given below:

Table 5.3

Meetings held by Mandal Parishads

S.No.	*Name of the Mandal Parishad*	*Number of Meetings*		
		Ordinary	*Special*	*Total*
1.	Attili	12	6	18
2.	Lingapalem	12	7	19
3.	Chennuru	12	8	20
4.	Siddhavatam	12	4	16
5.	Hasanaparthi	12	5	17
6.	Kuravi	12	6	18

On an average, the six Mandal Parishads, convened 12 ordinary and 6 special meetings in the year 2002. Many resolutions were passed by the Mandal Parishads in these meetings. As many as 144 resolutions were passed by the Hasanparthy Mandal Parishad (Warangal District) in its 18 meetings in the year 2002. More than half of the resolutions of the Mandal Parishads are on agriculture. The resolutions are on construction and repair of water channels, procurement of seeds, fertilizers and tools, disbursement of agricultural loans and subsidies, laying out of demonstration plots and seed farms, carrying on production campaigns, etc. The Mandal Parishads had also devoted much time to the subject of the supply of drinking water supply.

The meetings of Mandal Parishad have also devoted considerable time to the problem of roads and communications. Quite a large number of resolutions have been adopted to request the State Government to construct roads. More than one-fourth of the resolutions have been passed on staff problems, like regularization of the service of temporary employees, the provident fund scheme, distribution of grant-in-aid, constitution of committees, adoption and amendment of variety of by-laws, rules and regulations, etc. Thus a wide range of subjects have been discussed in Mandal Parishad meetings and passed resolutions.

All the six Mandal Parishads reported that they had undertaken many rural development programmes like Swarnajayanti Gram Samruddhi Yogana, Janmabhoomi, Food for Work, Clean and Green, Neeru-Meeru, Adarana, etc., during the last 7 years. Construction of primary school buildings were undertaken by the Lingapalem Mandal Parishad (West Godavari District). Haranparthi Mandal Parishad (Warangal District) spent an amount of Rs. 46,65,369 sanctioned under the JGSY/SGSY during 1997-2002 for construction of village roads and primary school buildings. During the same period, the Chennuru Mandal Parishad in Cuddapah district utilized an amount of Rs. 36,28,324 released under the JGSY/SGSY for construction of village roads.

Zilla Parishad

The Zilla Parishad is the apex panchayati raj institution. It is constituted by the Government for a district. Zilla Parishad is composed of following members.

(i) Zilla Parishad Territorial Constituency members.

(ii) Members of the Legislative Assembly having jurisdiction in the district.

(iii) Members of the house of people having jurisdiction in the district.

(iv) Members of the council of states who are registered voter in the district.

(v) Two persons belonging to minorities who are to be co-opted.

For the purpose of election of ZPTC members each Mandal Parishad is demarcated as a ZPTC. In other words, each directly elected member of Zilla Parishad represents a Mandal Parishad. The members of ZPTCs are directly elected for a term of five years. The Chairman and Vice-Chairman of Zilla Parishad are elected by the and from among the ZPTC members. Zilla Parishad shall meet atleast once in a month. The following are the permanent invitees to the meetings of the Zilla Parishad.

(i) Chairman, District Co-operative Marketing Society,

(ii) Chairman, Zilla Grandhalaya Samastha,

(iii) Chairman, District Co-operative Central Bank,

(iv) District Collector; and

(v) All Presidents of Mandal Parishads in the District.

All permanent invitees are entitled to participate in the meeting of the Zilla Parishad without the right to vote.

Standing Committees

There are seven standing committees of the Zilla Parishad. They are:

(1) Standing Committee for Planning and Finance

(2) Standing Committee for Rural Development

(3) Standing Committee for Agriculture

(4) Standing Committee for Education and Medical Services

(5) Standing Committee for Women's Welfare

(6) Standing Committee for Social Welfare; and

(7) Standing Committee for Works.

All the Standing Committees barring the one on agriculture and two other committees are headed by the Zilla Parishad Chairman. The Chairman, Zilla Parishad is the ex-officio member of all the standing committees. The members of different standing committees are nominated by the Zilla Parishad Chairman.

Powers and Functions:

The powers and functions of the Zilla Parishad are mentioned under Section 192 of the Act. Two categories of functions are described in this section. One category is those functions that can be entrusted to the Zilla Parishad by the State Government from Schedule-I. The second category of functions are the 16 functions specifically listed for performing by the Zilla Parishad in the section itself. These functions are mainly coordinating, advisory and supervisory in nature. Some of the important powers and functions are given below:

The Zilla Parishad shall have the power to

(i) Examine and approve the budgets of Mandal Parishads in the district,

(ii) Distribute the funds allotted to the district by the Central or State Government among the Mandal Parishads,

(iii) Co-ordinate and consolidate the plans approved in respect of the Mandal Parishads in the district and prepare plans in respect of the entire district,

(iv) Secure the execution of plans projects, schemes or other works either solely relating to the individual Mandal Parishads or common to two or more mandal parishads in the district,

(v) Supervise generally the activities of the Mandal Parishads,

(vi) Advise Government on all matters relating to development activities and maintenance of services in the district,

(vii) Advise Government on the allocation of work among Gram Panchayats and Mandal Parishads and co-ordination of work between the said bodies and various departments,

(viii) Advise Government on matters concerning the implementation of any statutory or executive order specially referred by the Government to the Zilla Parishads,

(ix) Collect and publish statistics or other information relating to the activities of the local authorities, and

(x) Establish, maintain, or expand secondary, vocational and industrial schools.

The Zilla Parishads in the State including the Zilla Parishads in the districts of West Godavari, Cuddapah and Warangal adhered to the schedule laid down by the statute for holding meetings and held some more ordinary as well as special meetings. The meetings held by the West Godavari, Cuddapah and Warangal Zilla Parishads are 23, 26 and 21 respectively. These meetings had been quite well attended. The percentage of the attendance is different from one Zilla Parishad to another Zilla Parishad and from among the members of one category to another category. The percentage of attendance varies from 60 (Cuddapah) to 75 (Warangal). It was found that the elected and coopted members were more active and their attendance in the meetings was more than that of other members. The participation of ex-officio members (MLAs and MPs) ranges from 40 per cent (Cuddapah District) to 50 per cent (Warangal District).

A study of the minutes books of the Zilla Parishads gives an idea about the concern of the members on the problems of the people in their respective districts. The Zilla Parishad of West Godavari District passed 138 resolutions, Cuddapah Zilla Parishad 117 resolutions and Warangal Zilla Parishad 145 resolutions during 2002-2003 on various aspects. The important items on which discussions were held and resolutions passed are administration of primary health centres, veterinary hospitals, sanitation in rural areas, drinking water supply, measures to check epidemics, expansion of educational facilities, etc. The resolutions on developmental activities include agriculture and rural roads. The minutes book also reveals that the Zilla Parishads are concerned with many issues of people. However, the programmes undertaken by these are very few and very limited activities are being undertaken by them.

The major programmes implemented by the these Zilla Parishads are drinking water supply, education and minor irrigation. The Zilla Parishads had undertaken the supply of drinking water to the people living in rural areas of the districts with the grants given by the central and state governments under different schemes. The Zilla Parishads have been maintaining secondary schools in their respective districts. Provision of water to agricultural lands is another important function of the Zilla Parishads. Construction and maintenance of tanks and wells which provide water to agricultural lands are being undertaken by the Zilla Parishads.

The West Godavari (District) Zilla Parishad completed during the period of study 1347 works under Comprehensive Protected Water Scheme (CPWS). It has provided 3066 hand pumps in the remaining villages for the purpose of drinking water. At present West Godavari Zilla Parishad is maintaining 240 high schools covering the entire district. Nearly 2,636 teachers are working in these scholars with a student strength of 1,04,030. All the schools in the district are provided with own buildings. The Zilla Parishad, West Godavari has been undertaking the maintenance of tanks and wells, which provides irrigation facility. At present under this minor irrigation schemes nearly 97,522 acres of land is under irrigation. For this, there are 216 irrigation water societies and 23 ayakatta committees in force.

There are at present 195 secondary schools under management of Cuddapah Zilla Parishad. The total strength of students studying different classes (VI to X) in these schools is 56,316. All the schools have own buildings. There are 2639 different categories of teaching staff working in these schools. The Cuddapah Zilla Parishad completed during the period under study 364 works under the protected under supply schemes, for supply of drinking water in 658 villages. The Cuddapah Zilla Parishad completed 3661 irrigation works and developed new ayacut in 1,16,985 acres. Similarly, the Warangal Zilla Parishad had undertaken the supply of drinking water, maintenance of secondary schools and construction and maintenance of minor irrigation works.

6

Panchayati Raj Personnel

When the community development programme was taken up, the extension organization was superimposed on the traditional district administration without adequate connecting links. The consequence is that in many districts different organizations – revenue administration, development departments and community development organization – were working on parallel lines with their activities largely unco-ordinated. The establishment of democratic institutions at the district and block levels and the role assigned to the gram sabha and the village panchayat constitute fundamental and far reaching changes in the structure of district administration and in the pattern of rural development. Their significance lies in the fact that subject to guidance and supervision by the State Government, the responsibility for the implementation of rural development programmes is now belong to the PRIs thus form part of a larger administrative and technical network.

There is a significant measure of diversity in personnel practices in different states. However, the administrative personnel working in PRIs in various states belongs to broadly two categories.[1] One category is of those deputed or transferred by the State Government to occupy posts created for PRIs and also posts transferred by the State Government to the PRIs due to delegation of certain functions to them. Usually this category of personnel comprises senior and middle level officers. The senior personnel in the PRIs in all the states are members of the state services and the State Government concerned deputes them by rotation to work in these bodies. After spending a spell of time in the rural local government, these civil servants are expected to go back to the state services. These vacancies are again filled up by civil servants nominated by the State Government. The ultimate control of the personnel rests with the original employer i.e. the State Government which alone has the authority to punish, transfer and promote them. The PRI under which a particular officer happens to serve has to be content with the exercise of only day to day control over him. There are, however, some states which have constituted a separate service from which alone they are drawn for posting in the PRIs.

The second category of the personnel comprises those occupying posts created for the PRIs and recruited and controlled by PRIs. This category includes generalist employees and junior technical or semi-skilled employees, office staff and manual workers. Rules, regulations and general terms of employment for this category of personnel are prescribed usually by the State Government with or without consultation with the PRIs. Appointment to some of these posts require also approval of the State Government. Numerical strength, specialization and status of the panchayati raj personnel have been recently changing in various states, depending upon nature and extent of devolution and delegation of functions along with finances to the PRIs.

Andhra Pradesh has created three cadres for the panchayatai raj personnel – state cadre, district cadre and mandal cadre. The state cadre comprises chief executive officer of zilla parishad, mandal parishad development officer and extension officers or technical and professional officers. The district cadre consists of the clerical staff in the zilla parishad and mandal parishad. The lower level class IV staff have been placed in the mandal cadre. The details of the personnel of all the three tiers in this state are presented in the following table.

Table 6.1
Panchayati Raj Personnel in Andhra Pradesh

S.No.	*Designation*	*No*
1.	Chief Executive Officers	22
2.	Deputy Executive Officers	22
3.	Accounts Officers	22
4.	Parishad Education Officers	22
5.	Mandal Parishad Development Officers	1096
6.	Mandal Education Officers	1096
7.	Mandal Engineering Officers	1096
8.	Extension Officers (Panchayati Raj and Rural Development)	1096
9.	Superintendents	1281
10.	Senior Assistants	1433
11.	Junior Assistants	1659
12.	Typists	1296
13.	Panchayat Secretaries	20624
14.	Attenders, Drivers and Record Assistants and others	5568

Gram Panchayat Personnel

The gram panchayat is the base and sustaining force of the panchayati raj system of rural local government. In the beginning the village panchayat had a secretary who provided secretaria assistance to it and also maintaining panchayat records. The panchayat secretary was a full-time employee. The panchayat secretary was later designated as executive officer in Andhra Pradesh. He was appointed for all major gram panchayats.[2] In case of small or minor gram panchayats, the executive officer was appointed for a group of 3 or 4 gram panchayats. He was popularly known as group executive officer. However, there were many gram panchayats in the state which have no full time functionary to assist the sarpanch. In these gram panchayats the functions of the executive officer were also discharged by the sarpanch.

Panchayat Secretary

There is substantial devolution of funds to gram panchayats under various schemes of the Government of India. The State Government is also devolving substantial funds in terms of assigned revenues, per capita grant, etc. It may not be possible for the sarpanch to take care of the administrative functions as well and it is felt desirable to create an administrative post to work under the sarpanch to provide the necessary administrative assistance. The Government also felt that if a post is created which can look after revenue aspects in the village as well, that would facilitate clubbing of revenue and panchayat functions in a single functionary. The Government accordingly created the post of Panchayat Secretary combining all the functions of village administrative officer, executive officer and also village development officer in one official functionary who will work under the control of sarpanch.[4]

The category of major and minor, the notified and non-notified gram panchayats was dispensed with the introduction of panchayat secretary system. All the executive officers of gram panchayats were redesigned as panchayat secretaries and were asked to function with new designation. The Grade-III VDOs, Junior Assistants, Bill Collectors of Panchayati Raj Department and Junior Assistants of Revenue Department were appointed as Panchayat Secretaries and deployed to remaining gram panchayats. These Panchayat Secretaries were directed to perform both revenue and panchayat functions. The Panchayat Secretary is under the administrative control of M.P.D.O., but he is responsible to the M.R.O. on the revenue side and to the M.P.D.O. on the developmental side.

The Panchayat Secretary shall perform functions relating to panchayat administration as well as general administration. He has also police, community welfare, and development functions. He shall coordinate all revenue, development, and welfare activities in the village. He shall also attend to other duties as assigned by the government and district administration from time to time. The panchayat secretary provides necessary assistance to the sarpanch in the matter of gram panchayat administration.

The creation of post of village secretary in each gram panchayat for looking after the revenue and panchayat functions is a historical decision to strengthen local bodies. The government announced that reorganized village administrative system, better known as Grama Sachivalayam, headed by Panchayat Secretary, would fulfil a long felt need for a proper executive support to the elected sarpanch. The new system would ensure government presence in every panchayat. The government was optimistic that the introduction of the new system would bring a new revolution in the village administration and it would pave way for devolving more functions and funds to villages in accordance with the 73rd Constitutional Amendment.

In addition to Panchayat Secretary, there are officials like sanitary inspector, bill collectors and office and sanitary staff in larger panchayats. The following is the list of officials of Kommara Gram Panchayat in Attili Mandal, West Godavari District.

Panchayat Secretary	-	1
Sanitary Inspector	-	1
Junior Assistant	-	1
Bill Collectors	-	2
Night Watcher	-	1
Park Watcher	-	1
Bore Watcher	-	1
Drain Cleaner	-	1
Sanitary Mastry	-	1
Sweepers	-	12
Thoti	-	1

The above list of officials applies only to a few gram panchayats in the state. The appointment of these officials depends upon the revenue and requirements of the panchayat.

Mandal Parishad Personnel

The Mandal Parishad is equipped with an administrative machinery which is spearheaded by an officer called the Mandal Parishad Development Officer (MPDO). The Mandal Parishad Development Officer is the chief executive of Mandal Parishad. He is appointed by the State Government. His powers and functions are as follows :

(1) The MPDO convenes the meetings of the Mandal Parishad and attends the same.

(2) He is responsible for implementing the resolutions of Mandal Parishad.

(3) He exercises powers of supervision over gram panchayats in the mandal.

(4) The staff borne on the establishment of the Mandal Parishad and the staff working in institutions and schemes transferred by the government to the Mandal Parishad are under the control and supervision of MPDO.

He is supported by the personnel at the Mandal Parishad level. The Mandal Parishad personnel include Mandal Engineering Officer, Mandal Education Officer, Extension Officer (Panchayati Raj and Rural Development), Senior Assistant, Junior Assistants, Works Inspector, Typist, etc. The MPDO is the leader of a team of officers in the fields of education, cooperation, rural development, etc. The MPDO is an area officer and officers in his team are specialists in their respective fields. In addition to these officers, there are the office and field personnel, under the jurisdiction of Mandal Parishad. The details of personnel of Chennur Mandal Parishad in Cuddapah district are given below:

Mandal Parishad Development Officer	-	1
Mandal Education Officer	-	1
Mandal Engineering Officer	-	1

E.O. (Panchayati Raj and Rural Development)	-	1
Superintendent	-	1
Senior Assistant	-	1
Junior Assistant	-	1
Attenders	-	4
Watchmen	-	2

There is no difference in the staffing pattern of other 5 Mandal Parishads selected for the study. There is, however, variation in the number of lower level staff. There are 4 Junior Assistants in Attili Mandal Parishad and 3 in Lingapalli Mandal Parishad. There is a post of Typist for all Mandal Parishads. This post is vacant in Chennuru and Siddhavatam Mandal Parishads of Cuddapah District.

Zilla Parishad Personnel

The execution of policies and decisions made by Zilla Parishad constitute the responsibility of the administrative machinery. The administrative machinery is headed by an officer now called the Chief Executive Officer (CEO).[5] He has to oversee the administration of Zilla Parishad. He has the following powers and functions:

1. He executes all powers and performs the functions specially conferred or imposed upon him by or under the Andhra Pradesh Panchayati Raj Act.
2. He convenes the meetings of the Zilla Parishad.
3. He is entitled to attend the meetings of the Zilla Parishad or any of its Standing Committees.
4. He is responsible for implementing the resolutions of the Zilla Parishad and of Standing Committees.
5. He supervises and control the execution of all activities of the Zilla Parishad.
6. He lays down the duties of all officers and servants of, or holding office under Zilla Parishad.
7. He exercises supervision and control over the acts of the officers and servants of Zilla Parishad.

The CEO of the Zilla Parishad is supported by the Deputy CEO, Accounts Officer, and Zilla Parishad Education Officer. The subordinate staff at the Zilla Parishad level include Superintendents, Senior Assistants, Junior Assistants, Typists, Record Assistants, etc. The following officials are working at present in the Zilla Parishads of West Godavari, Cuddapah and Warangal Districts.[6]

Table 6.2
Officials of Zilla Parishads

S.No.	*Designation*	*West Godavari*	*Cuddapah*	*Warangal*
1.	Chief Executive Officer	1	1	1
2.	Deputy Chief Executive Officer	1	1	1
3.	Accounts Officer	1	1	1
4.	Zilla Parishad Education Officer	1	1	1
5.	Superintendents	13	9	8
6.	Senior Assistants	34	13	3
7.	Junior Assistants	51	20	31
8.	Stenos	4	2	2
9.	Record Assistants	2	6	2
10.	Typists	13	10	6
11.	Drivers	3	2	4
12.	Attendars	32	11	16
13.	Malis	1	1	5
14.	Sweepers	9	5	3
15	Night Watchmen	-	1	7
	Grand Total	166	84	91

In addition to the above mentioned staff members, the officers and employees working in the Mandal Parishads are under the management of Zilla Parishads. The Chief Executive Officer is drawn from the I.A.S. or State Cadre. All the officers of the Zilla Parishad including the Chief Executive Officer are under the administrative control of the district collector. The number of district level officers under the control of Zilla Parishad is declining day-by-day. The engineers, planners and district level programme officers had been given status independent of the Zilla Parishad. So very few officers are now under control of Zilla Parishad today.

Officers of Panchayati Raj Department

The above description of personnel relating to the officials working in the PRIs. There are some other important officials working in the panchayati raj department. They include the Commissioner, District Panchayat Officer and Divisional Panchayat Officer. The Commissioner, is required to supervise the working of 22 Zilla Parishads, 1096 Mandal Parishads and 21,943 gram panchayats. The Commissioner is the Government's agent for implementing the A.P.P.R. Act, 1994. To assist him as also the District Collectors there are departmental officers, viz., District Panchayat Officer at district level, and Divisional Panchayat Officer at divisional level. At the district level, the department organization has one District Panchayat Officer. There are 22 District Panchayat Officers and each District Panchayat Officer has about 900 to 1000 gram panchayats in his jurisidiction. At the Revenue Division level, there is a Divisional Panchayat Officer to supervise the work of about 300 – 400 panchayats. There are 70 Divisional Panchayat Officers in the State. The powers and functions of these officers are given in the following pages.

Commissioner, Panchayati Raj

The Commissioner, Panchayati Raj, is the Head of the Department for the Panchayati Raj Institutions. The Commissioner, Panchayati Raj, has the following duties to attend to:

1. Distribute the funds allotted to State by the Government of India and the Government of Andhra Pradesh among the Zilla Parishads, Mandal Parishads and Gram Panchayats.
2. Co-ordinate and consolidate the plans prepared in respect of the Zilla Parishads, Mandal Parishads and Gram Panchayats.
3. Supervise and review the activities of Zilla Parishads, Mandal Parishads and Gram Panchayats.
4. Monitor the powers and functions in relating to any development programme taken up or conferred on the Zilla Parishads, Mandal Parishads and Gram Panchayats.
5. Advise and assist the government on all matters relating to development activities and maintenance of services in the State, whether undertaken by Panchayati Raj Institutions or the Government.
6. Advise and assist the Government on the allocation of work among Zilla Parishads, Mandal Parishads and Gram Panchayats and co-ordinate the work between the said bodies.
7. Advise and assist the Government on maters concerning the implementation of statutory or executive duties, matters relating to training plan for officials and non-officials, and matters relating to rural employment and rural environment.
8. Monitor the conduct of training on rural development, rural employment, rural environment, role and functions of Panchayati Raj Institutions, democratic decentralization, etc.
9. Collect, compile and publish the statistical and other information regarding PRI.
10. Conduct elections to Panchayati Raj Institutions under the supervision of the State Election Commission.

District Panchayat Officer

The administration of Gram Panchayats at the district level is under the supervision of District Panchayat Officer who has to

(a) exercise supervision and control over the Divisional Panchayat Officers, Extension Officers (PR & RD) and their offices within his jurisdiction;

(b) exercise supervision and provide guidance to Gram Panchayats and their executives in his jurisdiction in the administration of Gram Panchayats;

(c) visit as many Gram Panchayats as possible for the purpose of inspection, superintendence, conducting of enquiries, etc., and shall inspect all the Gram Panchayats atleast once between one ordinary elections and another ordinary election.

(d) Visit the offices of the Divisional Panchayat Officers and Extension Officers (PR & RD) as often as necessary and atleast once a year for the purpose of inspection;

(e) Hold enquiries and submit reports to the higher authorities on complaints of mal – administration of Gram Panchayats;

(f) Maintain necessary statistics about the working of Gram Panchayats within his jurisdiction;

(g) Maintain personal files of Panchayat Secretaries and Divisional Panchayat Officers within his jurisdiction, and

(h) Monitor resources of Gram Panchayats.

Divisional Panchayat Officer

Administration of Gram Panchayats at the Divisional level is under the supervision of Divisional Panchayat Officer who has to

(a) exercise supervision and provide guidance to the Gram Panchayats and their executive in his jurisdiction in the administration of Gram Panchayats;

(b) visit all the Gram Panchayats in his jurisdiction atleast once a year for the purposes of inspection and superintendency, irrespective of his visits for the holding enquiries, etc;

(c) visit offices of the Extension Officers (PR & RD) as often as necessary and not less than twice a year for the purpose of inspection.

(d) hold enquiries and submit reports to higher authorities on complaints of mal-administration of Gram Panchayats, and

(e) maintain necessary statistics about the working of Gram Panchayats in his jurisdiction and submit periodical reports on progress of works of various departmental programmes.

Recruitment

In Andhra Pradesh there are three ways in which the Panchayati Raj Institutions get the employees working with them. They are:

1. By deputation from State Government.
2. On the basis of selection by the Andhra Pradesh Public Service Commission, and
3. By selection by the District Selection Committee.

Deputation by the State Government

From the inception of Panchayati Raj and its predecessor community development programme, all the gazetted rank officials have been sent on deputation to the rural local bodies. Though there have been a number of changes, modifications, and alterations in the Panchayati Raj, the system of deputation of key officials did not undergo any change, even today it remains intact. The Chief Executive Officer, the Deputy Chief Executive Officer, the Zilla Parishad Accounts Officer, and the Zilla Parishad Education Officer are deputed to the Panchayati Raj Institutions from the government departments. There is also the practice of appointing IAS officers as the CEOs to some Zilla Parishads. For instance, the Chief Executive Officer of Warangal Zilla Parishad is an IAS Officer.

These officers are entitled to increments and promotions in their parent cadre as would have accrued to them if they were not deputed. These deputed officials remain under the technical control of their respective Heads of the Departments during their tenure with the Panchayati Raj Institutions. Administrative control is being exercised by the District Collector at Zilla Parishad level and the Mandal Parishad Development Officer at the mandal level. In case of promotion, they can be withdrawn by the State Government. On other grounds also they can be withdrawn by the parent department at any time.

Selection by the Andhra Pradesh Public Service Commission

The following posts in Panchayati Raj have come under the purview of Andhra Pradesh Public Service Commission for the purpose of direct recruitment.

(1) Junior Assistant
(2) Typist and Steno-Typist
(3) Village Development Officer
(4) Mandal Parishad Development Officer

Whenever the vacancies arise in the above four categories of employees, the Zilla Parishad writes to the Panchayati Raj Department. The Panchayati Raj Department furnishes the details of the vacancies to the State Public Service Commission. The Public Service Commission advertises these vacancies as in the case of other competitive examinations. It will conduct written examination and interviews to the candidates who succeed in the written examination. After the completion of these formalities, it will send the list of selected candidates for different categories to the Panchayati Raj Department for appointment.

The Village Development Officers (now the Panchayat Secretaries), the Stenos and Junior Assistants work under the administrative control of Mandal Parishad Development Officer and are liable to be transferred by Chief Executive Officer within the district. In the case of inter-district transfers, the Commissioner of Panchayati Raj is the competent authority. The Junior Assistants, Typists and Steno-Typists working in the Zilla Parishad function under the direct control of Zilla Parishad Chief Executive Officer.

Selection by the District Selection Committee

The Government have constituted the District Selection Committee for the selection of the lower level personnel in rural local bodies.[7] The following categories of employees at present are directly recruited by the District Selection Committee.

1. School Assistants
2. Language Pandits
3. Craft Teachers
4. Physical Education Teachers
5. Drawing Teachers
6. Music Teachers
7. Record Assistants
8. Bill Collectors
9. Attenders
10. Drivers
11. Sanitary Maistrys
12. Maternity Assistants
13. Health Assistants
14. Electricians
15. Sweepers, Watchmen and Scavengers

The District Selection Committee prepares the panels for the appointment in accordance with the Government orders. The panel of candidates is sent to the Commissioner of Panchayati Raj for the necessary approval. After the approval of the panel by the Commissioner of Panchayati Raj, the Chief Executive Officer allots the selected candidates for various mandal parishads according to the existing vacancies.

Training

The quality of personnel of an agency-governmental or non-governmental-can be improved only by necessary orientation in their responsibilities and in modern methods and procedures of management. A number of studies – both by independent scholars and expert panels – conducted on training of personnel in Government have been generally critical of the training facilities.[8] All the studies were unanimous in emphasizing the importance of the training. In the light of the importance of training for Government functionaries we now examine the system of training of Panchayati Raj personnel in Andhra Pradesh.

The personnel of Panchayati Raj in the State has been called upon to discharge a large number of responsibilities. It has to act as a relentless agent of social change to initiate and implement rural development programmes. The responsibilities of Panchayati Raj officials call for a wide variety of specialized skills and knowledge of extension work. Besides, it must learn to work in active collaboration with the subordination to elected peoples representatives. Permanent functionaries, unlike most of their counterparts at other levels of Government, have face-to-face contact with the consumer of their services being exposed to both political and local pressures. Hence, necessary training to meet the environmental needs assumes great importance. The elected and permanent functionaries unlike their counterparts at higher levels of Government continuously function as a team in the council and its committees. This necessitates to evolve a special pattern of relationship. Training will go a long way in appreciating each other's work.[9] The senior personnel must improve managerial capability to guide, supervise and control the lower staff.

To develop these diverse competency of personnel of Panchayati Raj Institutions training programmes have been organized by the Government of Andhra Pradesh. The training programmes had been conducted in the National Institute of Rural Development (NIRD), the MCR Institute of HRD and Andhra Pradesh Academy of Rural Development – all located in Hyderabad, the State capital. Besides, the training programmes for lower level staff were organized at district levels. When the attention of the officials of the Panchayati Raj Institutions was drawn to their training needs and the actual training they received all observed that the training has a must for them to discharge their duties effectively. All the administrative staff expressed the view that training would improve their job performance. Training also helps in knowing work and accounting procedures and the ways to dealing with people. They also reported that all had received training of different durations. The duration of training varies from one week to six months. It is, however, noted from the study that there is no direct recruitment for some posts in Panchayati Raj Institutions. The MPDOs are promoted as Dy CEOs. The Executive Officers are promoted as MPDOs. The persons promoted to higher positions are not being exposed to any training programme to enable them to understand their new responsibilities and the ways of discharging them.

References

1. B.S. Khanna, *Rural Local Government in India and South Asia*, Deep and Deep Publications, Delhi, 1999, p.78.
2. Gram Panchayats were devided into notified and non-notified Gram Panchayats on the basis of their annual income. Gram Panchayats whose annual income was not less than Rs.40,000/- were declared as notified Panchayats and for each of these a full-time Executive officer was appointed by the Government. Notified Panchayats constituted about 15 per cent of the total number of Panchayats in the state. In respect of non-notified Panchayats, the village development officer acted as Group Executive Officer for a group of 3 or 4 gram panchayats.

3. There are 28,260 revenue villages, more than the village Panchayats in the state. For each revenue village there is a part-time village administrative officer.
4. G.O. M.S. No.369, Panchayati Raj and Rural Development (Mdl-II) Department Dt. 12-12-01 and G.O. Ms.No.384 Panchayati Raj and Rural Development (Estt. – IX) Department, Dt. 22-12-01. Government of Andhra Pradesh, Hyderabad.
5. Earlier the Chief Executive Officer was called the Secretary and later designated as the District Development Officer.
6. The information on Personnel was collected from the offices of the respective Zilla Parishads.
7. The District Selection Committee, constituted by the Government from time to time for each District, normally consists of District Collector, Z.P. Chairperson, Z.P. C.E.O and the district officer of the concerned Department.
8. For details of the studies on training see V.A. Pai Panandiker, *Personnel System for Development Administration*, Popular Prakashan, Bombay, 1966; S.K. Chand, *Training of State Administrative Officers in India*, Indian Institute of Public Administration, New Delhi, 1971; and United Nations, *Handbook of Training in Public Service*, New York, 1966.
9. M.A. Muttalib and Mohd Akbar Ali Khan, *Theory of Local Government*, Sterling Publishers, New Delhi, p.221.

7

Financial Resources of Panchayati Raj Institutions

The significance of finance is too obvious to need any elaboration as no organization can exist, much less achieve its objectives without atleast a minimum of finances. That is why Kautilya, the great Indian philosopher, remarked "all undertakings depend upon finance, hence foremost attention should be paid to the treasury".[1] Every administrative act has its financial implications, either creating a charge on or making a contribution to treasury. The importance of finance is so great in administration that Llyod George is said to have once remarked that Government is said to have once remarked that 'Government is finance'.[2] In fact, finance constitutes the backbone, the life and blood of Government; it provides fuel to the administrative machinery.

The local self government institutions have their own course of action , planning for it and funding it independently and hiring and firing their own staff under their own conditions of service. For these essential objectives to be realized, it is necessary that they should have their own sources of finance which should be assured of sources and not depend on donations like grants-in-aid. The local government system in India had, however, been weakened mainly because of financial inadequacy and lack of financial autonomy.

The Taxation Enquiry Committee (1953-54) observed that in most of the states a village within its jurisdiction overlaps with higher bodies functionally as well as financially; and suggested that functions, finances and taxation powers of the higher body should be coordinated with those of the village panchayats to safeguard its growth and efficiency.[3] The Santhanam Team (1963) after a careful consideration of the local resources pleaded that financial resources should be made available to these local bodies.[4] The G.V.K. Rao Committee (1983) while looking into the role of Panchayati Raj Institutions in rural development, pointed out the weak financial position of Panchayati Raj Institutions.[5] Hence, making available and transfer of substantial and growing resources of income to these bodies was accepted as an essential concomitant for the stability and grwoth of these bodies.

The Panchayati Raj bodies now shoulder a wide range of responsibilities. There are about 29 functions enlisted in the Eleventh Schedule for which the responsibility has been given to the Panchayati Raj Institutions. Out of these, 21 functions are mainly devoted to the developmental activities and social responsibilities. For efficient discharge of these responsibilities, the Panchayati Raj Institutions should be given adequate financial resources. The Amendment Act provides for financial powers given to the Panchayati Raj Institutions. Article 243 H envisages that the legislature of a State may by law :

(a) authorize a panchayat to levy, collect and appropriate such taxes, duties tolls and fees in accordance with such procedure and subject to such limits;

(b) assign to panchayat such taxes, duties, tools and fees levied and collected by the State Government for such purpose and subject to such conditions and limits;

(c) provide for working such grants-in-aid to the panchayats from the consolidated fund of the State; and

(d) provide for constitution of such funds for crediting all money received, by or on behalf of the panchayats and also for the withdrawal of such money therefrom, as may be specified in the law.

The section (I) of the same article requires the constitution of State Finance Commission (SFC) by the State Governments to review the financial position in their respective states and for the sharing of resources between the State Government and the Panchayati Raj Institutions. Almost all the State Governments had appointed State Finance Commissions. In most of the States, including Andhra Pradesh, these Commissions had already submitted their reports.

The 73rd Constitutional Amendment added a new dimension to Indian federal finance system as there is a need for better sense of direction and clear evolution of objective criteria and norms for inter-governmental transfer of resources. It is also expected that the Panchayati Raj finance system will undergo massive change in the wake of constitution of State Finance Commissions (243I) and their recommendations as intended by the policy makers. The purpose of this chapter is to examine the financial resources of Panchayati Raj Institutions in the State of Andhra Pradesh. The study of financial position of Panchayati Raj Institutions is likely to give an idea as to how far these institutions serve as effective units of local self-governments in rural areas.

Financial Resources of Gram Panchayat

In the three-tier Panchayati Raj system, only Gram Panchayats are empowered to levy taxes. Two types of taxation powers are given to the Gram Panchayats by the Andhra Pradesh Panchayati Raj Act, 1994 - obligatory and optional taxes.

Taxation Powers of Gram Panchayats

It is obligatory on the part of Gram panchayats to levy the following taxes, viz.,

(a) House Tax;

(b) Kolagaram or Katarusum, that is to say a tax on the village produce sold in the village by weight, measurement or number;

(c) Such other tax as the government may direct any Gram Panchayat or class of Gram Panchayat;

(d) Duty on transfer of Property;

(e) Advertisement Tax;

(f) Special Tax on houses for expenses connected with the construction, maintenance and repairs of water or drainage works or lighting up of public streets and public places or other similar works.

The Gram Panchayats may also levy the following optional taxes:

(a) Vehicle Tax;

(b) A Tax on Agricultural Land for a specific purpose;

(c) A Land Cess at the rate of two paise in the rupee on the annual rental value of all occupied lands which are not occupied by or adjacent and appurtenant to buildings;

(d) Fees for the use of Porambokes or communal lands under the control of the Gram Panchayat;

(e) Fees for the use of Buildings including Chavadies and Sarais; and

(f) A Duty in the form of a surcharge on the Seignorage Fees collected by the government on minerals other than minor minerals quarried in the village.

The House Tax continues to be a main source of income for gram panchayats. The Government framed the rules governing the assessment and collection of the house tax. Panchayats are at liberty to levy the tax either on the capital value or on the annual rental value of the property. But in practice gram panchayats are reluctant to levy tax on maximum rates for fear of antagonizing the electorate. The Kolagaram tax is levied on various items of village produce like paddy, groundnut, etc. There is also a proposal to levy this tax on the items like sugarcane, coffee and black pepper.

Among the optional taxes that are being levied by Gram Panchayats tax on bicycles and carts is one, from which the income derived by gram panchayats is negligible. Thus, it indicates that the vehicle tax is more in the nature of regulatory measure and not a revenue-yielding source. A gram panchayat shall levy a special tax on houses at such rates as may be prescribed, to provide for expenses connected with the construction, maintenance, repair, extension and improvement of water or drainage works or the lighting of the public streets and public places and other similar works.

The gram panchayats will also derive income from remunerative enterprises such as shopping complexes. The gram panchayats receive income from assigned revenues such as entertainment tax, profession tax and surcharge on stamp duty. Per capita grant of Rs.4 and salary grant for the provincialized panchayats employees in the districts and JRY grants are some of the grants which are sanctioned to Gram Panchayats. The grants provided by the Central Government under JRY have significantly enhanced the status of gram panchayats.

An examination of the second State Finance Commission Report reveals that the gram panchayats in the State receive income from the following sources:

1. House tax
2. Vehicle tax
3. Special tax
4. Tax on immovable property
5. Rents
6. Income from remunerative enterprises
7. Miscellaneous sources
8. Property tax compensation
9. Land cess

10. Entertainment tax
11. Seigniorage fee
12. Surcharge on stamp duty
13. Grant-in-aid
14. SFC grant
15. TFC grant
16. JRY grant

The total income of the GPs in the years from 1996-77 to 2000-01 is given in the following table.

Total Income of Gram Panchayats

Year	*Total Income (Rs. In Lakhs)*
1996-97	39652.89
1997-98	32988.02
1998-99	45346.12
1999-2000	50646.17
2000-01	48017.51

Source: Report of the Second State Finance Commission.

It may be observed from the table that there are fluctuations in the income of the gram panchayats. The total income of the gram panchayats during 1996-97 is Rs. 39652.89 lakhs which had came down to Rs. 32.988.02 lakhs in the next year i.e. 1997-98. There is however, a significant increase in their income i.e. from 32988.02 lakhs to Rs. 45346.12 lakhs in 1998-99. The income of Gram Panchayats durnig 1999-2000 is Rs. 50646.77 lakhs which was, of course, reduced to Rs. 48017.51 in 2000-01.

After examining the statutory provisions and sources identified by the State Finance Commission we now attempt to know the actual sources of income of 12 gram panchayats covered in the study. The financial resources of these gram panchayats can be broadly classified into :

(a) own sources;

(b) assigned revenues; and

(c) grants-in-aid

The own sources include, taxes (obligatory and optional), fees, levies and duties, and income from remunerative enterprises. The Assigned revenues include land cess; surcharge on stamp duty; entertainment tax; compensation for loss of income from profession tax; and per capita grant; salary grant for provincialised staff; grant for honorarium payable to sarpanches and matching grants for impressive tax collections. The developmental grants such as JRY and SGRY can be included in the source category of grants-in-aid.

The information on income from different resources shows that there are wide variations in the gram panchayats and also in the annual income of the gram panchayats from year to year. The lowest annual income of Kommara Gram Panchayat is Rs.3,19,923 during 1999-2000 and the highest income is Rs.8,95,660 during 2001-02 which reveals a variation of Rs.5,75,737 (Table - 7.1). It may be observed from the data that the Gram Panchayat of Mathamgudem in Lingapalem Mandal (West Godavari district) received only an amount of Rs.18,959 during 1997-98. Its highest annual income was Ra.1,78,526 during 2001-02 (Table- 7.4). The total income for Gummampadu Gram Panchayat during 7 years i.e. from 1995-96 to 2001-02 was Rs.1.83 lakh, Rs.1.15 lakh, Rs.0.88 lakh, Rs.1.85 lakh, Rs.1.10 lakh, Rs.1.73 lakh and Rs.1.41 lakh (Table – 7.2). Similarly, the total income for Ramapalle Gram Panchayat in Chennuru Mandal (Cuddapah District) during the 7 year period of 1995-96 to 2001-02 was: Rs. 377 lakh; Rs. 3.81 lakh; Rs. 3.95 lakh; Rs. 4.57 lakh; Rs.5.02 lakh; Rs.5.07 lakh and Rs.5.20 lakh (Table – 7.5).

The year-wise income of gram panchayats does not reveal any trend-either increase or decrease. Normally the annual income of an institution would be increased from year to year.[6] This general expectation or increase in income was not noticed in the income of 9 gram panchayats (out of 12 gram panchayats). The annual income of Kommara gram panchayat during 1995-96 was Rs.4,57,909 (Table - 7.1). The income for the next two years was Rs.3,70,726 and Rs.3,44,018, which means there was a reduction in the income of Kommara Gram Panchayat from the year 1995-96 to 1996-97 and from the year 1996-97 to 1997-98. The same pattern may be noticed in other 8 gram panchayats (Table 7.2, 7.3, 7.4, 7.7, 7.9 to 7.12). The year-wise income of the Gram Panchayats of Ramanapalle (Table 7.5), Sivalalapalle (Table 7.6) and Rajampeta (Table - 7.8) all in Cuddapah district shows a steady increase. The pattern of income was thoroughly probed and it was found that the variation or reduction in annual income is due to late release of funds or grants to the gram panchayats.

The assigned revenues like surcharge on stamp duty, profession tax compensation and per capita grant are very lucrative source of revenue for some gram panchayats. But the Government will not release the amount due to gram panchayats on time. The release may be postponed to next year. Hence, there is an abnormal increase in the income of the Gram Panchayat from the previous year. For instance, the annual income of Chintagattu Gram Panchayat for the year 1998-99 was Rs.1,82,509. This income was almost doubled in the next year i.e. Rs.3,60,878 during 1999-2000 (Table - 7.9) due to increase in the income under assigned revenue item of surcharge on stamp duty. The income from surcharge on stamp duty for the year 1998-99 was Rs.91,578 while it was Rs.2,62,355 for the year 1999-2000.

The tables for financial resources of gram panchayat also reveal that there is no uniform pattern in the percentage of income under each category of source of income. Out of the total revenue, the income from own sources during 2001-02 accounted for 7.57 per cent for Chintalapalli Gram Panchayat (Table - 7.12) and 58.27 per cent for Gummampadu Gram

Panchayat (Table 7.2). The income from assigned revenue accounted for 16.35 per cent for Mathamgudem Gram Panchayat (Table 7.3) and 81.72 per cent for Nallela Gram Panchayat (Table 7.11). The income from grants-in-aid accounted for only 5.33 per cent for Gummampadu Gram Panchayat (Table 2) and 80 per cent for Madhavaram Gram Panchayat (Table 7.7). Thus, there is wide variation in the income pattern of Gram Panchayats. Hence, we cannot say that the Gram Panchayats are dependent on Government grants. It was also not found that a substantial proportion of income of Gram Panchayats was drawn from own sources or assigned revenue, which is quite contrary to the earlier studies.[7]

Resources of Mandal Parishads

The Mandal Parishads have no taxation powers. However, they have been permitted to impose surcharge on the taxes levied by the gram panchayats. According to the Section 172(1) of the State Panchayati Raj Act, the sources of income of Mandal Parishad consist of

(i) funds relating to institutions and schemes transferred by the Government or Heads or Departments of the Government to the Mandal Parishad;

(ii) funds relating to the community development programmes;

(iii) central and state aid and aid received from the all India bodies and institutions for the development of cottage, and village industries, khadi, silk, coir, handicrafts, and the like;

(iv) donations and contributions received by the Mandal Parishad from gram panchayats or from the public in any in form;

(v) such income of the Zilla Parishad as the Government may, by order, allocate to it;

(vi) such share of the land revenue, state taxes or fees as may be prescribed;

(vii) proceeds from taxes, surcharge or fee which the Mandal Parishad is empowered to levy under this Act or any other law;

(viii) such contributions as the Mandal Parishad may levy from gram panchayats;

(ix) any other income from remunerative enterprises and the like; and

(x) Government grants.

The Mandal Parishads receive income from many sources. These sources of income may be classified into own sources, assigned revenues and grants. The own sources include the rents on shops, fees, fines and income from auction of fruit bearing trees and fish ponds. Under the assigned revenues the Mandal Parishads receive income from land or local cess, surcharge on stamp duty, entertainment tax, seigniorage fee, mineral cess and per capita grant. The grants are released to the Mandal Parishads for the purposes of salaries, social welfare, community development, minor irrigation, roads and bridges and rural water supply. The income from different resources of 6 Mandal Parishads has been presented in this section of this chapter in the Tables 7.13 to 7.18.

The source-wise revenue income of 6 Mandal Parishads for the years 1995-96 to 2001-02 shows that the Mandal Parishads are more dependent on Government grants than on their own sources and assigned revenues. The Attili Mandal Parishad received an amount of Rs.2,04,08,900 as grant out of its income of Rs.2,18,28,900 during the year 2001-02 (Table - 7.13). It is evident from the data that the other Mandal Parishads also depend heavily on Government grants. The quantum of grants is, of course, varied from one Mandal Parishad to other. But the percentage of income from grants is very high for all the Mandal Parishads. For example, during the year 2001-02, the annual income of Lingapalem Mandal Parishad (West Godavari District) was Rs.1,22,95,803 of which Government grant constitute more than 92 per cent (Table - 7.14). The income from own sources of Chennuru and Siddhavatam Mandal Parishads in Cuddapah district and Hasanparthi and Kuravi Mandal Parishads in Warangal district is negligible (Tables - 7.15 to 7.18). The virtual absence of own revenue for the Mandal Parishads indicate their total dependence on the Government grants. The Mandal Parishads in West Godavari district had, however, been able to earn some income from auction of fish ponds, fruit bearing trees and fees and fines.

It is also evident from the data that there were fluctuations from year to year in the income of Mandal Parishads. The total income for Attili Mandal Parishad during 7 years was Rs.1.42 crores, Rs.1.42 crores, Rs.1.43 cores, Rs.2.64 crores, Rs.1.52 crores, Rs.1.99 crores and Rs.2.18 crores, showing a difference in Rs.1.22 crores income. In the case of Lingapalem the difference in income is as high as Rs.1.24 crores. The difference in income of other Mandal Parishads is, of course, marginal.

Resources of Zilla Parishads

The Zilla Parishads in the State also have no powers of taxation. The financial powers of Zilla Parishad are more or less in conformity with those of Mandal Parishads. Under Section 198 of the State Act, the Zilla Parishads receive income from a variety of sources. They are :

(i) The Central or State Government funds allotted to the Zilla Parishad,

(ii) Grants from All India bodies and institutions for the development of cottage, village and small scale industries and the like;

(iii) Proceeds from taxes or fees which the Zilla Parishad may under any law, levy;

(iv) Income from endowments or trusts administered by the Zilla Parishad;

(v) Donations and contributions from the Mandal Parishads or from the public in any form;

(vi) Such contributions as the Zilla Parishad may levy from the Mandal Parishad with previous approval of the Government;

(vii) Income from remunerative enterprises, and

(viii) Per capita annual grant

The Zilla Parishads receive income from many sources. These sources may be grouped into 3 categories. They are own sources, assigned revenues and grants. The own sources are obtained from rents on buildings, guest houses, quarters, tools and plants, commercial complexes, fee from markets, ferries, and revenue from auctions of fish ponds, fruit bearing trees and land leases. The assigned revenues consist of surcharge on stamp duty, tax on minor minerals, entertainment tax, land cess, seignorage cess, profession tax compensation and per capita grant. The per capita grant is paid by the Government to the Zilla Parishads at Rs.4. Salary grant for provincialized staff of the Zilla Parishad including salaries of teachers in secondary schools is another important grant among the grants. Grants are released for developmental works under various programmes such as construction of roads and bridges, social welfare, minor irrigation, rural water supply, rural sanitation, etc. Grants towards honorarium of Chairman, Vice-Chairman, ZPTC members and travelling and daily allowance to non-official members of Zilla Parishad are also provided by the Government. The JRY/SGSY, TFC and SFC are other important grants released to Zilla Parishads. The revenue of the 3 Zilla Parishads have been given in Tables – 7.19 to 7.21.

The income of Zilla Parishads varies from year to year. The annual income from different sources for West Godavari Zilla Parishad for the year 1995-96 was Rs.37,93,38,870 while it was Rs.119,61,31,200 for the year 2001-02 (Table- 7.19). Similarly the annual income of Cuddapah Zilla Parishad was Rs.46,38,73,372 and Rs.130,17,81,000 for the years 1995-96 and 2001-02 respectively (Table – 7.20). The annual income for the

Warangal Zilla Parishad during 7 years was: Rs.88.30 crores; Rs.83.15 crores; Rs.103.88 crores; Rs.116.74 crores; Rs.96.4 crores; Rs.80.59 crores; and Rs.117.59 crores (Table - 7.21). The annual income also varies from Zilla Parishad to Zilla Parishad. For instance, the income for the year 2000-01 of the Zilla Parishads of West Godavari, Cuddapah and Warangal districts was: Rs.117.14 crores; Rs.194.22 crores; and Rs.80.59 crores (Tables – 7.19, 7.20, 7.21).

The Zilla Parishads are mostly financed by Government grants. The data presented in the Tables – 7.19, 7.20 and 7.21 show that the Government grants constituted, in the year 2001-02, 95 per cent, 96 per cent and 98 per cent for the Zilla Parishads of Warangal, West Godavari and Cuddapah districts respectively.

The next important sources of revenue for Zilla Parishads are under the assigned revenue category. For instances, the West Godavari Zilla Parishad received an amount of Rs.1,94,05,380 under assigned revenue during 1995-96 and Rs.3,78,45,700 during 2001-02 (Table 7.19) whereas Cuddapah Zilla Parishad received an amount of Rs.1,10,81,248 and Rs.1,35,22,000 during 1995-96 and 2001-02 respectively (Table - 7.20) and Warangal Zilla Parishad received an amount of Rs.70,40,000 during 1995-96 and Rs.5,04,47,680 during 2001-02 (Table - 7.21). The income through assigned revenue constituted less than 5 per cent of the total income. The Zilla Parishads revenue income shows that their own sources of revenue was less than one per cent. The respective percentages of grants, assigned revenue and own sources clearly indicate that the Zilla Parishads heavily depend on the Government grants.

The above analysis of the data on sources of income indicates that the revenues of Panchayati Raj bodies are derived from their own resources comprising income from taxes, fees, fines, rents, etc., statutory grants and assigned revenues. Revenue is also derived from a variety of grant provided by the government for specified purposes. In the case of Gram

Panchayats, a considerable amount of income is derived from their own resources along with assigned revenues. But in the case of other two levels more than 90 per cent of the revenue is derived from grants provided by the government. This is in conformity with an earlier study on financial resources of PRIs in Andhra Pradesh.[8] The own resources of the Mandal Parishads and Zilla Parishads come from rents from commercial complexes and buildings, fee from market, ferries, fees from inspection bungalows and other miscellaneous sources.

State Finance Commission

The centre-state financial relations in India have been governed by the constitutional provisions which allocate functions and resources, between the Central and State governments. Whereas the financial relations between the State governments and the local governments were governed by the State laws and descretions for a long time. Now the constitution amendments have provided constitutional foundation for the financial relations between the state govenrments and local governments. This is a significant development in the evolution of local self-government in India.[9]

The Seventy-third and Seventy-fourth Constitution Amendment Acts provided for constitution of independent State Finance Commissions at State level. In Andhra Pradesh, the State Finance Commission was constituted as a sequel to the Constitution amendments. The Governor was required under Article 243-I of the Constitution[10] and Section 235 (1) and (2) of the Andhra Pradesh Panchayati Raj Act, 1994[11] to constitute within one year from the date of commencement of the Constitution (seventy-third) Amendment Act 1992 and thereafter on the expiry of every fifth year, a Finance Commission consisting of a chairman and four other members of whom one shall be the member secretary. By an order dated 21st June,

1994, the Government of Andhra Pradesh constituted the First State Finance Commission with the following chairman, member secretary and members. [12]

1.	Sri G. Lakshmana Swamy Former Registrar Dr. B.R. Ambedkar Open University	Chairman
2.	Sri K. Pitchaiah Former Financial Commissioner Panchayati Raj, Rural Development and Relief Department Government of Andhra Pradesh	Member Secretary
3.	Sri T. Srinivasachary Mahabubnagar Town	Member
4.	Sri Chandra Venkata Narayana Rao Sarpanch, Mukkellapadu Nujendla Mandal Guntur District	Member
5.	Dr. O. Chandramma, MBBS Srikalahasti, Chittoor District	Member

Terms of Reference

The State Finance Commission shall review the financial position of gram panchayats, mandal parishads, zilla parishads, municipal corporations and municipal councils in the State and make recommendations to the Government on the following:[13]

1. The principles which should govern
   (a) The distribution between the State and local bodies of the proceeds of taxes, duties, tolls and fees leviable by the State;
   (b) Determination of taxes, duties, tolls and fees which may be assigned to or apportioned by the Panchayati Raj institutions and municipal bodies; and

(c) grants-in-aid to the local bodies

2. The measures needed to improve the financial position of local bodies.

The Commission had made ardent efforts by visiting nine districts and contacting various officials and non-officials. The team met 450 Mandal Parishad presidents, 450 sarpanches, 9 Zilla Parishad chairmen, and 9 district collectors. The Commission also elicited the opinion of the people and the officials through a questionnaire. This apart a massive data related to the Panchayati Raj and municipal finances over a period of 7 years had been collected and analyzed by the Commission before they prepared their report along with the recommendations. The Commission submitted its report to the State Governor on 31st May 1997.

Recommendations of First State Finance Commission

Some of the important recommendations made by the First State Commission relating to Panchayati Raj Institutions are given below.[14]

1. The rate of surcharge on stamp duty may be increased from 5 per cent to 10 per cent and distributed among the gram panchayats, mandal parishads and zilla parishads in the ratio of 6:2:2.
2. The existing rate of land / local cess (18 per cent in Andhra area and 25 per cent in Telangana area) may be increased to 50 per cent of land revenue and an additional amount of Rs.127.75 crores may be transferred to the Panchayati Raj Institutions.
3. The existing per capita grant of the Panchayati Raj Institutions may be revised from Re.1.00 to Rs.4.00 for the Gram Panchayats, from Rs.5.00 to Rs.8.00 for the Mandal Parishads and from Rs.2.00 to Rs.4.00 for the Zilla Parishads.

4. The existing share of local bodies in the profession tax collections may be increased from 90 per cent to 95 per cent on population basis.
5. The local bodies are entitled to 39.24 per cent of state's revenue, both tax and non-tax, and it may be given statutory effect by suitable enactment.
6. Grants should be released for maintenance of the assets of Mandal Parishad roads, Zilla Parishad and Mandal Parishad buildings, offices and guest houses, and minor irrigation.
7. Kolagaram tax or Katarusumu should be levied on the entire village produce whether sold or not and on all items including paddy, cotton, etc.
8. Whenever exemptions or concessions are granted by the Government in entertainment tax, local bodies should be given compensation to that extent.
9. Provisions relating to the percentage of devolution may be incorporated in the State Local Bodies Acts.
10. A total amount of Rs.979.16 crores per annum was recommended as additional devolution to rural and urban local bodies.

The First State Finance Commission made 84 recommendations both financial and non-financial. These recommendations were for three years from 1997-98 to 1999-2000. The Government appointed a Committee of Secretaries to Government to study the recommendations and suggest measures for implementation. A cabinet sub-committee was also appointed.[15] Based on the recommendations of both these committee the cabinet approved certain devolutions recommended by the State Finance Commission.

Out of 84 recommendations the Government had accepted 54 recommendations.[16] While 11 recommendations were accepted with some modifications, 19 were not accepted at all. Necessary provisions have been made in the budget for 1998-99 to the extent of devolutions accepted by the Government and grants were released. Provision was made in the budget for 1999-2000 for release of amounts. The State Government also initiated measures to implement the non-financial recommendations of the First State Finance Commission. The non-financial recommendations accepted by the Government relate to the formula for release of grants to gram panchayats on 'backwardness index', penalties on minor mineral tax, preparation of model plans for towns and villages, computerization in local bodies, training to the panchayati raj officials, regular inspection of offices, transfer of functions to the local bodies, introduction of social audit, etc.

Second State Finance Commission

The Second State Finance Commission was constituted in December 1998 with the following as Chairma, Member Secretary and Members.[17]

1.	Professor D.L. Narayana Retired Professor of Economics Sri Venkateswara University	Chairman
2.	Sri K. Pichayya Retetired Financial Commissioner of Panchayati Raj and Rural Development Department, Former Member Secretary First State Finance Commission	Member
3.	Dr. A. Damodar Chairperson, Wanaparthy Municipality Mahaboobnagar District	Member
4.	Sri J. Krishna Rao Sarpanch, Duggirala Gram Panchayat, Guntur District	Member
5.	Sri M. Venkataramaiah Formerly Deputy Secretary First State Finance Commission	Member

4. The existing share of local bodies in the profession tax collections may be increased from 90 per cent to 95 per cent on population basis.
5. The local bodies are entitled to 39.24 per cent of state's revenue, both tax and non-tax, and it may be given statutory effect by suitable enactment.
6. Grants should be released for maintenance of the assets of Mandal Parishad roads, Zilla Parishad and Mandal Parishad buildings, offices and guest houses, and minor irrigation.
7. Kolagaram tax or Katarusumu should be levied on the entire village produce whether sold or not and on all items including paddy, cotton, etc.
8. Whenever exemptions or concessions are granted by the Government in entertainment tax, local bodies should be given compensation to that extent.
9. Provisions relating to the percentage of devolution may be incorporated in the State Local Bodies Acts.
10. A total amount of Rs.979.16 crores per annum was recommended as additional devolution to rural and urban local bodies.

The First State Finance Commission made 84 recommendations both financial and non-financial. These recommendations were for three years from 1997-98 to 1999-2000. The Government appointed a Committee of Secretaries to Government to study the recommendations and suggest measures for implementation. A cabinet sub-committee was also appointed.[15] Based on the recommendations of both these committee the cabinet approved certain devolutions recommended by the State Finance Commission.

Out of 84 recommendations the Government had accepted 54 recommendations.[16] While 11 recommendations were accepted with some modifications, 19 were not accepted at all. Necessary provisions have been made in the budget for 1998-99 to the extent of devolutions accepted by the Government and grants were released. Provision was made in the budget for 1999-2000 for release of amounts. The State Government also initiated measures to implement the non-financial recommendations of the First State Finance Commission. The non-financial recommendations accepted by the Government relate to the formula for release of grants to gram panchayats on 'backwardness index', penalties on minor mineral tax, preparation of model plans for towns and villages, computerization in local bodies, training to the panchayati raj officials, regular inspection of offices, transfer of functions to the local bodies, introduction of social audit, etc.

Second State Finance Commission

The Second State Finance Commission was constituted in December 1998 with the following as Chairma, Member Secretary and Members.[17]

1.	Professor D.L. Narayana Retired Professor of Economics Sri Venkateswara University	Chairman
2.	Sri K. Pichayya Retetired Financial Commissioner of Panchayati Raj and Rural Development Department, Former Member Secretary First State Finance Commission	Member
3.	Dr. A. Damodar Chairperson, Wanaparthy Municipality Mahaboobnagar District	Member
4.	Sri J. Krishna Rao Sarpanch, Duggirala Gram Panchayat, Guntur District	Member
5.	Sri M. Venkataramaiah Formerly Deputy Secretary First State Finance Commission	Member

The Second State Finance Commission reviewed the financial position of gram panchayats, mandal parishads, zilla parishads, nagar panchayats, municipal councils and municipal corporations in the State and made 82 recommendations to the Government on issues of devolution of funds to Panchayati Raj Institutions and urban local bodies.[18] The State Finance Commission made recommendations also on the aspects of functions and personnel of local bodies. The Commission submitted its report on 19th August 2002. The recommendations are for 5 years from 2000-01 to 2004-05. Important financial recommendations are given below:

1. Some of the gram panchayats are not levying taxes on vehicles (other than motor vehicles) and fruit bearing trees on panchayat lands, etc. Instructions may be issued to the gram panchayats to levy the said taxes.
2. The items of sugarcane, coffee and black pepper may be included in the list of items of the village produce that are proposed to be taxed.
3. Instructions may be issued to the gram panchayats to levy the special tax on houses at the rates indicated in the rules so as to augment their revenues.
4. Special grant may be given for strengthening of small panchayats on population criteria.
5. The revenue foregone by the Panchayati Raj Institutions due to abolition of land cess should be given to them as compensation.
6. Effective steps should be taken to adjust the arrears of land cess already collected, to the Panchayati Raj Institutions by fixing time frame, say 6 months.
7. In respect of major and medium sectors of irrigation, allocation to gram panchayats may be fixed at 10 per cent of the water charges per acre instead of Rs.10 per acre. With a view to consider the development of all areas in the district, the amount collected in the district towards water tax may be allocated among all the Gram Panchayats on population basis.
8. An amount of Rs.367.94 crores required for core civic amenities may be provided and distributed on population basis.

9. An additional amount of Rs.168.60 crores per annum may be provided to the Panchayati Raj Institutions for R.W.S. Schemes.
10. An amount of Rs.130 crores per annum may be provided additionally for maintenance of rural roads under Panchayati Raj Institutions over and above to the existing provision of Rs.100 crores in the budget.
11. An amount of Rs.11.30 crores per annum shall be released to maintain the minor irrigation sources under the Panchayati Raj Institutions.
12. Rs.4.88 crores per annum may be released for maintenance of office buildings of gram panchayats, mandal parishads, and zilla parishads.
13. Release of grants may be linked up to performance of the local bodies in the matter of collection of taxes and non-taxes.
14. Cable tax is not being collected by some of the gram panchayats. Government may direct the District Panchayat Officers to issue instructions to Panchayat Secretaries to collect the cable tax regularly.
15. Gram Panchayats may be allowed to auction fish ponds, retain 70 per cent of the auction proceeds of fish ponds, distribute 15 per cent to fisherman co-operative societies and the remaining 15 per cent to the Mandal Parishads for distribution among other gram panchayats in the Mandal.
16. A surcharge of 5 per cent be levyed on the market cess and passed on to the local bodies viz., 20 per cent of the amount may be passed on to the Gram Panchayats or municipalities where the Market Committee is located and the remaining 80 per cent be allocated to other municipalities and Gram Panchayats within the jurisdiction of the Market Committee.

Table – 7.1

Financial Resources of Kommara Gram Panchayat, Attili Mandal, West Godavari District

S.No.	*Item*	*1995-96*	*1996-97*	*1997-98*	*1998-99*	*1999-2000*	*2000-01*	*2001-02*
1.	Own sources	2,12,627	1,36,565	1,39,243	1,83,830	86,141	1,48,098	3,07,348
2.	Assigned Revenues	54,493	68,464	47,476	85,000	34,494	34,497	2,91,412
3.	Grants	1,90,789	1,65,697	1,57,299	2,35,000	1,99,285	1,94,014	2,96,400
	Total	**4,57,909**	**3,70,726**	**3,44,018**	**5,03,830**	**3,19,923**	**3,76,609**	**8,95,660**

Table – 7.2

Financial Resources of Gummampadu Gram Panchayat, Attili Mandal, West Godavari District

S.No.	*Item*	*1995-96*	*1996-97*	*1997-98*	*1998-99*	*1999-2000*	*2000-01*	*2001-02*
1.	Own sources	76,602	65,225	48,003	96,791	84,667	88,980	82,501
2.	Assigned Revenues	23,467	14,306	32,133	56,936	23,142	79,000	51,561
3.	Grants	83,481	35,803	8,880	31,920	2,880	5,760	7,552
	Total	**1.83,550**	**1,15,334**	**88,966**	**1,85,647**	**1,10,689**	**1,73,740**	**1,41,614**

Table – 7.3
Financial Resources of Dharmajigudam Gram Panchayat, Lingapalem Mandal, West Godavari District

S.No.	*Item*	*1995-96*	*1996-97*	*1997-98*	*1998-99*	*1999-2000*	*2000-01*	*2001-02*
1.	Own sources	1,48,365	2,29,477	1,94,120	3,70,989	3,28,690	4,15,926	4,58,547
2.	Assigned Revenues	1,61,818	97,738	1,56,186	1,24,647	1,17,784	2,64,223	1,33,108
3.	Grants	2,50,197	2,31,052	3,94,668	2,29,285	96,978	1,96,909	2,22,409
	Total	**5,60,380**	**5,58,267**	**7,44,974**	**7,24,921**	**5,43,452**	**8,77,058**	**8,14,064**

Table – 7.4

Financial Resources of Mathamgudem Gram Panchayat, Lingapalem Mandal, West Godavari District

S.No.	*Item*	*1995-96*	*1996-97*	*1997-98*	*1998-99*	*1999-2000*	*2000-01*	*2001-02*
1.	Own sources	NA	12,160	1,528	750	9,478	3,445	90,316
2.	Assigned Revenues	NA	5,852	15,452	32,721	29,802	23,450	45,158
3.	Grants	NA	47,190	1,979	7,356	17,062	1,18,046	43,052
	Total	**NA**	**65,202**	**18,959**	**40,827**	**56,342**	**1,44,941**	**1,78,526**

Table – 7.5
Financial Resources of Ramanapalle Gram Panchayat, Chennuru Mandal, Cuddapah District

S.No.	*Item*	*1995-96*	*1996-97*	*1997-98*	*1998-99*	*1999-2000*	*2000-01*	*2001-02*
1.	Own sources	70,209	73,418	71,594	75,978	84,383	91,816	93,317
2.	Assigned Revenues	88,148	86,467	89,642	91,143	90,545	85,781	87,633
3.	Grants	2,19,243	2,21,594	2,34,310	2,90,699	3,27,326	3,30,075	3,39,342
	Total	**3,77,600**	**3,81,479**	**3,95,546**	**4,57,820**	**5,02,254**	**5,07,672**	**5,20,292**

Table – 7.6

Financial Resources of Sivilapalle Gram Panchayat, Chennuru Mandal, Cuddapah District

S.No.	*Item*	*1995-96*	*1996-97*	*1997-98*	*1998-99*	*1999-2000*	*2000-01*	*2001-02*
1.	Own sources	11,698	11,880	12,340	12,818	13,114	13,687	14,071
2.	Assigned Revenues	32,513	36,435	33,654	35,471	30,723	26,892	37,966
3.	Grants	80,442	82,142	86,837	89,368	91,299	92,497	95,362
	Total	**1,24,653**	**1,30,457**	**1,32,831**	**1,37,657**	**1,35,136**	**1,33,076**	**1,47,399**

Table – 7.7

Financial Resources of Madhavaram Gram Panchayat, Siddhavatam Mandal, Cuddapah District

S.No.	*Item*	*1995-96*	*1996-97*	*1997-98*	*1998-99*	*1999-2000*	*2000-01*	*2001-02*
1.	Own sources	84,072	85,363	88,863	88,084	86,948	89,382	91,690
2.	Assigned Revenues	95,648	96,750	98,613	94,533	-	1,93,853	-
3.	Grants	2,89,204	3,04,399	2,34,630	3,08,092	3,50,798	2,76,824	3,66,880
	Total	**4,68,924**	**4,86,512**	**4,22,106**	**4,90,709**	**4,37,746**	**5,60,054**	**4,58,570**

Table – 7.8
Financial Resources of Rajampeta Gram Panchayat, Siddhavatam Mandal, Cuddapah District

S.No.	*Item*	*1995-96*	*1996-97*	*1997-98*	*1998-99*	*1999-2000*	*2000-01*	*2001-02*
1.	Own sources	84,072	85,363	88,863	88,084	86,948	89,382	91,690
2.	Assigned Revenues	95,648	96,750	98,613	94,533	-	1,93,853	-
3.	Grants	2,89,204	3,04,399	2,34,630	3,08,092	3,50,798	2,76,824	3,66,880
	Total	**4,68,924**	**4,86,512**	**4,22,106**	**4,90,709**	**4,37,746**	**5,60,054**	**4,58,570**

Table – 7.9

Financial Resources of Chintagattu Gram Panchayat, Hasanparthy Mandal, Warangal District

S.No.	*Item*	*1995-96*	*1996-97*	*1997-98*	*1998-99*	*1999-2000*	*2000-01*	*2001-02*
1.	Own sources	1,39,909	75,011	1,10,442	80,872	84,573	81,238	91,181
2.	Assigned Revenues	19,350	39,219	67,983	91,578	2,62,355	1,73,394	2,64,875
3.	Grants	-	-	13,979	10,059	13,950	-	-
	Total	**1,59,259**	**1,14,230**	**1,92,404**	**1,82,509**	**3,60,878**	**2,54,632**	**3,59,056**

Table – 7.10
Financial Resources of Ganturpalli Gram Panchayat, Hasanparthy Mandal, Warangal District

S.No.	*Item*	*1995-96*	*1996-97*	*1997-98*	*1998-99*	*1999-2000*	*2000-01*	*2001-02*
1.	Own sources	20,559	21,482	22,019	26,166	26,935	28,535	28,287
2.	Assigned Revenues	25,468	24,125	25,244	24,341	23,671	24,274	21,482
3.	Grants	-	-	12,862	8,877	9,737	-	-
	Total	**46,027**	**45,607**	**60,125**	**59,384**	**60,343**	**52,809**	**49,769**

Table – 7.11
Financial Resources of Nallela Gram Panchayat, Kuravi Mandal, Warangal District

S.No.	*Item*	*1995-96*	*1996-97*	*1997-98*	*1998-99*	*1999-2000*	*2000-01*	*2001-02*
1.	Own sources	42,632	45,030	44,805	47,557	47,220	45,355	47,214
2.	Assigned Revenues	1,00,472	1,35,929	1,57,734	1,60,474	2,32,372	2,96,397	2,11,095
3.	Grants	-	-	15,580	12,615	14,561	-	-
	Total	**1,43,104**	**1,80,959**	**2,18,119**	**2,20,646**	**2,84,159**	**3,41,752**	**2,58,309**

Table – 7.12
Financial Resources of Chintalapalli Gram Panchayat, Kuravi Mandal, Warangal District

S.No.	*Item*	*1995-96*	*1996-97*	*1997-98*	*1998-99*	*1999-2000*	*2000-01*	*2001-02*
1.	Own sources	11,806	13,679	13,866	13,775	12,098	17,412	20,797
2.	Assigned Revenues	20,642	-	35,410	19,124	21,558	-	36,815
3.	Grants	73,451	80,182	1,37,286	1,89,036	1,80,523	2,44,720	2,03,855
	Total	**1,05,899**	**93,861**	**1,86,562**	**2,21,935**	**2,14,179**	**2,62,132**	**2,61,467**

Table – 7.13

Financial Resources of Attili Mandal Parishad, West Godavari District

S.No.	*Item*	*1995-96*	*1996-97*	*1997-98*	*1998-99*	*1999-2000*	*2000-01*	*2001-02*
1.	Own sources	2,00,500	2,00,500	3,20,263	3,20,000	3,10,000	17,000	6,70,000
2.	Assigned Revenues	7,80,000	7,80,000	6,14,338	7,10,000	7,50,000	6,55,000	7,50,000
3.	Grants	1,32,77,800	1,32,62,800	1,34,07,482	2,54,47,280	1,41,80,400	1,92,50,700	2,04,08,900
	Total	**1,42,58,300**	**1,42,43,300**	**1,43,42,083**	**2,64,77,280**	**1,52,40,400**	**1,99,22,700**	**2,18,28,900**

Table – 7.14

Financial Resources of Lingapalem Mandal Parishad, West Godavari District

S.No.	*Item*	*1995-96*	*1996-97*	*1997-98*	*1998-99*	*1999-2000*	*2000-01*	*2001-02*
1.	Own sources	6,55,000	6,05,000	9,40,000	11,88,000	52,27,200	1,19,192	4,52,509
2.	Assigned Revenues	2,25,000	2,65,000	3,05,500	6,45,736	3,00,000	5,22,140	4,29,142
3.	Grants	1,16,98,250	1,73,92,330	93,54,750	2,09,21,736	1,00,57,800	96,79,408	1,14,14,152
	Total	**1,25,78,250**	**1,82,62,330**	**1,06,00,250**	**2,27,55,472**	**1,55,85,000**	**1,03,27,740**	**1,22,95,803**

Table – 7.15

Financial Resources of Chennuru Mandal Parishad, Cuddapah District

S.No.	*Item*	*1995-96*	*1996-97*	*1997-98*	*1998-99*	*1999-2000*	*2000-01*	*2001-02*
1.	Own sources	9,603	5,341	8,732	5,412	-	10,786	-
2.	Assigned Revenues	2,04,222	2,44,098	2,64,420	2,76,846	2,72,787	2,79,588	3,03,732
3.	Grants	92,87,101	89,67,670	84,84,821	82,01,168	89,47,925	90,87,815	99,14,777
	Total	**95,00,926**	**92,17,109**	**1,87,57,973**	**84,83,426**	**92,20,712**	**93,78,189**	**1,02,18,509**

Table – 7.16

Financial Resources of Siddhavatam Mandal Parishad, Cuddapah District

S.No.	*Item*	*1995-96*	*1996-97*	*1997-98*	*1998-99*	*1999-2000*	*2000-01*	*2001-02*
1.	Own sources	8,672	14,632	7,540	-	5,872	9,312	-
2.	Assigned Revenues	1,27,087	1,86,161	2,52,619	2,58,242	2,19,043	2,83,333	2,90,168
3.	Grants	87,02,284	89,87,653	90,83,709	92,30,834	88,28,043	79,33,826	87,12,933
	Total	**88,38,043**	**91,88,446**	**93,43,868**	**94,89,076**	**90,52,958**	**82,26,471**	**90,03,101**

Table – 7.17

Financial Resources of Hasanaparthi Mandal Parishad, Warangal District

S.No.	*Item*	*1995-96*	*1996-97*	*1997-98*	*1998-99*	*1999-2000*	*2000-01*	*2001-02*
1.	Own sources	5,872	6,323	6,450	5,004	6,100	9,864	10,126
2.	Assigned Revenues	1,50,430	2,14,893	1,08,494	1,21,190	40,048	2,72,619	2,42,085
3.	Grants	72,87,101	1,69,67,670	1,26,77,828	1,26,02,043	1,65,68,482	2,72,619	20,03,035
	Total	**94,43,403**	**1,71,88,886**	**1,76,98,492**	**1,27,28,237**	**1,66,04,630**	**1,89,71,380**	**2,02,84,146**

Table – 7.18

Financial Resources of Kuravi Mandal Parishad, Warangal District

S.No.	*Item*	*1995-96*	*1996-97*	*1997-98*	*1998-99*	*1999-2000*	*2000-01*	*2001-02*
1.	Own sources	8,718	9,623	10,281	-	9,813	8,763	-
2.	Assigned Revenues	2,06,510	1,94,034	2,65,423	2,78,708	2,92,295	3,03,535	5,22,821
3.	Grants	84,12,062	94,09,912	91,60,950	1,18,67,875	90,84,023	97,46,596	1,19,18,624
	Total	**86,27,290**	**96,13,569**	**94,36,654**	**1,21,46,583**	**93,86,131**	**1,00,58,894**	**1,24,41,445**

Table – 7.19

Sources of Income, Zilla Parishad, Eluru, West Godavari District

Item	*1995-96*	*1996-97*	*1997-98*	*1998-99*	*1999-2000*	*2000-01*	*2001-02*
Own sources	6,88,696	6,06,869	7,08,531	7,41,265	9,40,169	11,00,000	11,00,000
Assigned Revenues	1,94,05,380	2,41,39,251	2,17,74,541	3,12,19,922	3,15,00,429	3,70,95,700	3,78,45,700
Grants	35,92,44,803	39,75,00,659	58,66,09,162	63,35,24,991	36,09,26,719	113,32,77,500	115,71,85,500
Total	**37,93,38,879**	**42,22,46,779**	**60,90,92,234**	**66,54,86,178**	**39,33,67,317**	**117,14,73,200**	**119,61,31,200**

Table – 7.20

Sources of Income, Zilla Parishad, Cuddapah

Item	*1995-96*	*1996-97*	*1997-98*	*1998-99*	*1999-2000*	*2000-01*	*2001-02*
Own sources	59,12,920	80,84,249	80,06,668	83,37,501	23,99,300	39,20,000	46,00,000
Assigned Revenues	1,10,81,248	2,32,64,419	1,79,71,664	3,56,12,198	1,54,96,000	1,30,28,000	1,35,22,000
Grants	44,68,79,204	66,49,00,914	44,77,54,461	69,01,39,840	119,24,90,000	192,52,74,000	128,36,59,000
Total	**46,38,73,372**	**69,62,49,582**	**47,37,32,793**	**73,40,89,539**	**1,21,03,85,300**	**194,22,22,000**	**130,17,81,000**

Table - 7.21

Source of Income Zilla Parishad, Warangal

Item	*1995-96*	*1996-97*	*1997-98*	*1998-99*	*1999-2000*	*2000-01*	*2001-02*
Own sources	1,83,000	2,45,000	3,31,000	3,14,000	1,98,000	6,78,000	3,03,000
Assigned Revenues	70,40,000	73,75,000	86,75,000	1,64,20,000	2,23,50,000	2,30,50,000	5,04,47,680
Grants	87,58,57,000	82,39,25,820	102,98,34,400	115,04,40,000	93,78,67,600	78,94,23,174	112,52,22,657
Total	**88,30,80,000**	**83,15,46,620**	**103,88,40,400**	**116,71,74,000**	**96,04,15,600**	**80,59,42,600**	**117,59,73,337**

References

1. Kautilya, *Arthashastra* translated by Shoma Sastry, Raghuveer Printing Press, Mysore, 1956, p.65.
2. Quoted by M.P. Sharma, *Public Administraiton Theory and Practice*, Kitab Mahal, Allahabad, 1978, p.449.
3. Governemtn of India, *Report of the Taxation Enquiry Committee*, New Delhi, 1953-54.
4. Government of India, *Report of the Study Team on Panchayati Raj Finances*, Ministry of Community Development, 1963.
5. Government of India, *Report of the Committee to Review the Existing Administrative Arrangements for Rural Development and Poverty Allevieation Programmes (CAARD)*, Department of Rural Development, Ministry of Agriculture, New Delhi, 1985.
6. For Instance, the study of finances of four gram Panchayats in West Bengal indicated a steep rise in the income of gram panchayats over a period of 5 years. See A.C. Jena, *Panchayati Raj Finances in West Bengal – A Status Study*, National Institute of Rural Development, Hyderabad, 1999.
7. Ashok Mehta Committee in its sutdy of the financial resources of Panchayati Raj Bodies, found that a substantial proportion of the income of gram panchayats was drawn from taxes and fees. See Government of India, Report of the Committee on *Panchayati Raj Institutions*, *Op.Cit.*, p.103.
8. C.P. Vithal, "Financial Resources of Panchayati Raj Institutions in Andhra Pradesh: A Case for Resource Mobilization and Utilization" in Atmanand (ed.), *Financing of Panchayati Raj*, Excel Books and Co., New Delhi, 1999, p.166.
9. G. Thimmaiah, "Democratic Decentralisation: The Panchayati Raj Experiment in India", in Dr. Atmanand (ed.), *Financing of Panchayati Raj*, Excel Books and Co., New Delhi, 1999, p.19.
10. Constitution (seventy-third) Amendment Act, 1992, Article 243-I.
11. Andhra Pradesh Panchayati Raj Act, 1994 Section 235 (1) and (2).

12. G.O.Ms.No.367, dt. 22-6-1994, Panchayati Raj, Rural Development and Relief (Mandals – III) Department, Government of Andhra Pradesh, Hyderabad.
13. G.O.Ms.No.683, dt. 25-10-1994, Panchayat Raj, Rural Development and Relief (Mandals-III) Department, Government of Andhra Pradesh, Hyderabad.
14. Government of Andhra Pradesh, *Report of the First State Finance Commission,* Commissioner of Printing, Stationery and Stores, Hyderabad, May 1997.
15. See Government of Andhra Pradesh, *Recommendations of the Cabinet Sub-Committee on the Report of the State Finance Commission,* Commissioner of Printing, Stationery and Stores, Hyderabad, November 1997.
16. B.K. Chandrasekhar (ed.), *Panchayat Raj in India: Status Report 1999,* Task Force on Panchayat Raj, Rajiv Gandhi Foundation, New Delhi, March 2000, p.36.
17. G.O.Ms.No.511, dt.8.12.1998, G.O.Ms.No.515, dt. 21.12.1998, and G.O.Ms.No.107, dt. 18.3.1999, Panchayat Raj and Rural Development (Mandals-III) Department, Government of Andhra Pradesh, Hyderabad.
18. Government of Andhra Pradesh, *Report of the Second State Finance Commission,* Commissioner of Printing, Stationery and Stores, Hyderabad, August 2002, pp.244-256.

8

Perceptions on Panchayati Raj Institutions

The Panchayati Raj Institutions are designed to bring about rapid development in the countryside with the participation of officials, elected members and rural population. One of the objectives of the study is to ascertain the perceptions of various groups about the working of Panchayati Raj Institutions in Andhra Pradesh. The opinion of people, people's representatives and officials on Panchayati Raj system in the State was elicited. It was carried out with the help of three separate interview schedules for the people, people's representatives and the officials. Their view points on powers, functions, personnel, financial resources and overall performance are presented in this chapter.

People's Perceptions

It was planned to elicit the opinion of 300 people from each district. Finally we were able to approach 869 people in the three districts. The break-up of people respondents is given below:

West Godavari	281
Cuddapah	334
Warangal	254
Total	**869**

The opinion of the people was elicited on the issue powers of Panchayati Raj Institutions i.e. adequacy of powers devolved upon Panchayati Raj Institutions, the need to give some more powers and the nature of powers to be given. An overwhelming majority of the respondents (94 per cent) expressed the view that the powers given to the Panchayati Raj Institutions were not adequate (Table – 8.1). Most of them (92 per cent) also observed that some more powers should be given to Panchayati Raj Institutions (Table –8.2). The respondents have, however, no idea about the nature of powers devolved upon, and to be transferred to Panchayati Raj Institutions.

The people were asked about the transfer of functions to the Panchayati Raj Institutions. About 96 per cent of the respondents observed that all the functions which are supposed to be entrusted to the Panchayati Raj Institutions were not transferred (Table - 8.3). When they were asked about the functions being performed by the Panchayati Raj Institutions at present, they reported that only few functions like drinking water supply, maintenance of village roads and street lighting are being undertaken by the Panchayati Raj Institutions particularly by Gram Panchayats. They felt that there is a need to transfer some more functions to Panchayati Raj Institutions (Table – 8.4). However, they do not have any idea about the nature of functions to be transferred to Panchayati Raj Institutions.

The opinion of respondents on Panchayati Raj personnel is positive. Ninety per cent of the total respondents reported that there was no shortage of staff (Table - 8.5). About 84 per cent of respondents reported that the Panchayati Raj officials were helpful towards people's problems (Table – 8.6). Some of the respondents observed that the officials of Panchayati Raj Institutions were very helpful.

The opinion that the financial resources available to Panchayati Raj Institutions were not adequate was expressed by about 87 per cent of total respondents (Table – 8.7). This clearly shows that adequate funds were not given to Panchayati Raj Institutions. When the attention of the respondents was drawn about the major source of revenue for Panchayati Raj Institutions, majority of them observed that the government grants would be the major source (Table –8.8). The respondents were asked to give suggestions to strengthen the financial position of Panchayati Raj Institutions. Most of them suggested that the Central and State Government should provide financial resources to meet the needs of Panchayati Raj Institutions and implement various rural development programmes.

Eighty per cent of total respondents were happy with the overall performance of Panchayati Raj Institutions (Table –8.9). Some of them (22 per cent) reported that they were satisfied with the performance of Panchayati Raj Institutions to a greater extent (Table –8.10).

Perception of People's Representatives

The target to elicit the opinion of 300 people's representatives was achieved to a greater extent. We are able to meet 283 Panchayati Raj leaders spreading over three districts. The people's representatives interviewed include ward members of Gram Panchayats, Sarpanches, Mandal Parishad Territorial Constituency (MPTC) members, Mandal Parishad (MP) Presidents and Zilla Parishad Territorial Constituency (ZPTC) members. The number of respondents in each category and district are given in Table - 8.11

For the question whether Panchayati Raj Institutions were given adequate powers, the majority of people's representatives gave negative reply (Table –8.12). Sixty seven per cent from West Godavari district, 66 per cent from Cuddapah district and 86 per cent from Warangal district of Panchayati Raj leaders felt that adequate powers were not devolved upon their institutions. Hence, an overwhelming majority (87 per cent) of them opined that more and more powers should be given to Panchayati Raj Institutions (Table – 8.13). Similarly 64 per cent of the Panchayati Raj leaders wanted all the items mentioned in the Eleventh Schedule of the Constitution transferred to Panchayati Raj Institutions (Table – 8.14). There is, however, variation in the number or percentage of respondents who expressed this view i.e. 51 per cent (45 out of 88) in West Godavari district, 63 per cent (57 out of 91) in Cuddapah district and 76 per cent (79 out of 104) in Warangal district.

Nearly three-fourths of the respondents thought that the present staff pattern of Panchayati Raj Institutions was satisfactory (Table – 8.15). More or less same percentage of the respondents opined that there was adequate staff for Panchayati Raj Institutions (Table –8.16).

Half of the respondent people's representatives thought that the finances at the command of Panchayati Raj Institutions were adequate (Table –8.17). There is, however, variation from district to district in the number or percentage of respondents who gave this opinion. In West Godavari district 66 out of 88 (75 per cent), in Cuddapah district 29 out of 91 (32 per cent) and in Warangal district 49 out of 104 (47 per cent) respondents felt that the financial resources of Panchayati Raj Institutions were adequate. More than three-fourth (78 per cent) of total respondents observed that the Panchayati Raj Institutions were given funds as recommended by the national and state finance commissions (Table - 8.18). The opinion of the respondents on the extent of transfer of funds was also elicited. More than one-third of the respondents felt that the funds were transferred to a greater extent (Table –8.19). Only a negligible number of respondents felt that the funds were not transferred to Panchayati Raj Institutions. More than three fourths of the total respondents (77 per cent) were satisfied with the performance of Panchayati Raj Institutions (Table – 8.20). Some of them were satisfied with the performance of Panchayati Raj Institutions to a great extent (Table – 8.21).

Officials' Perception

A sample of 125 officials of Panchayati Raj Institutions from the three districts were interviewed. In the selection of officials attention was focused on two aspects: decision-making and implementation. The officials whose opinion was elicited are Chief Executive Officer, Deputy Executive Officer, Education Officer, Accounts Officer, Executive Engineer and Office Superintendents of all the three selected Zilla Parishads, Mandal Parishad Development Officers, Rural Development Officers, Education Officers and Engineers at Mandal level and Panchayat Secretaries. The institution or designation wise distribution of Panchayati Raj officials can be seen from the Table -8.22.

The officials were asked whether their institutions were given adequate powers. Only one-third of them replied positively. In other words, majority of the officials (65 per cent) felt that the Panchayati Raj Institutions were not given adequate powers (Table – 8.23). On an average more than 85 per cent of the respondent officials wanted all the 29 items mentioned in the Eleventh Schedule transferred to the Panchayati Raj Institutions (Table – 8.24). About 83 per cent of the officials were happy with the present bureaucratic set-up of the Panchayati Raj Institutions (Table – 8.25). However, about one-fourth of the officials felt that there was shortage of staff (Table – 8.26).

About 60 per cent of official respondents agreed with the view that the biggest drawback of Panchayati Raj system today was the lack of adequate financial resources (Table – 8.27). Majority of the officials (64 per cent) reported that the funds, as recommended by the National Finance Commission and State Finance Commission were given to Panchayati Raj Institutions

(Table – 8.28). More than one-third of them observed that the recommended funds were transferred to a greater extent (Table – 8.29). The official respondents were divided on the issue of main source of revenue of Panchayati Raj Institutions (Table – 8.30). About 53 per cent of them expressed their view that the government grants should be main source of revenue.

On an average seventy nine per cent of officials expressed their satisfaction with the overall performance of Panchayati Raj Institutions (Table – 8.31). Their percentage is highest i.e. 91 per cent in West Godavari district. More than half of them were satisfied to a greater extent with the performance of Panchayati Raj Institutions (Table – 8.32).

The above analysis makes it clear that the powers devolved on, functions transferred to and financial resources made available to Panchayati Raj Institutions are not adequate. The staff position and overall of Panchayati Raj Institutions are, however, satisfactory. There is, of course, variation in the number or percentage of respondents who expressed the opinion on a particular aspect. For instance, 94 per cent of people, 79 per cent of people's representatives and 64 per cent of officials expressed the opinion that the powers devolved upon the Panchayati Raj Institutions were not adequate. Similarly, the inadequacy of financial resources was reported by 87 per cent of people, 50 per cent of people's representatives and 60 per cent of officials. There is also variation in the district-wise opinion in each category of respondents. For instance, the percentages of official respondents who reported that the staff of Panchayati Raj Institutions were adequate are 67.5, 75 and 80 respectively from Cuddapah, Warangal and West Godavari districts. The percentages of respondent people's representatives who were satisfied with the overall performance of Panchayati Raj Institutions are 84, 76 and 72 respectively from West Godavari, Cuddapah and Warangal districts.

Table – 8. 1

Do you think that the powers devolved on PRIs are adequate?

	West Godavari		*Cuddapah*		*Warangal*		*Total*	
	No. of Respondents	*Per cent*	*No. of Respondents*	*Per cent*	*No. of Respondents*	*Per cent*	*No. of Respondents*	*Per cent*
Yes	263	93.55	301	90.1	249	98.03	813	93.55
No	18	6.45	33	9.9	5	1.97	56	6.45
Total	**281**	**100.00**	**334**	**100.00**	**254**	**100.00**	**869**	**100.00**

Table – 8.2

Do you think that some more power shall be given to PRIs?

	West Godavari		*Cuddapah*		*Warangal*		*Total*	
	No. of Respondents	*Per cent*	*No. of Respondents*	*Per cent*	*No. of Respondents*	*Per cent*	*No. of Respondents*	*Per cent*
Yes	261	92.88	298	89.22	238	93.70	797	91.71
No	20	7.12	36	10.78	16	6.30	72	8.29
Total	**281**	**100.00**	**334**	**100.00**	**254**	**100.00**	**869**	**100.00**

Table – 8.3

Do you think that all the intended functions are transferred to PRIs?

	West Godavari		*Cuddapah*		*Warangal*		*Total*	
	No. of Respondents	*Per cent*	*No. of Respondents*	*Per cent*	*No. of Respondents*	*Per cent*	*No. of Respondents*	*Per cent*
Yes	273	97.15	308	92.22	250	98.43	831	95.62
No	8	2.85	26	7.8	4	1.57	38	4.38
Total	**281**	**100.00**	**334**	**100.00**	**254**	**100.00**	**869**	**100.00**

Table – 8.4

Do you think that some more functions shall be transferred to PRIs?

	West Godavari		*Cuddapah*		*Warangal*		*Total*	
	No. of Respondents	*Per cent*	*No. of Respondents*	*Per cent*	*No. of Respondents*	*Per cent*	*No. of Respondents*	*Per cent*
Yes	272	96.79	306	91.81	250	98.43	828	95.29
No	9	3.21	28	8.38	4	1.67	41	4.71
Total	**281**	**100.00**	**334**	**100.00**	**254**	**100.00**	**869**	**100.00**

Table – 8.5

What is your opinion on the staff strength of PRIs?

	West Godavari		*Cuddapah*		*Warangal*		*Total*	
	No. of Respondents	*Per cent*	*No. of Respondents*	*Per cent*	*No. of Respondents*	*Per cent*	*No. of Respondents*	*Per cent*
Adequate staff	249	88.61	310	92.81	223	87.80	782	89.99
Shortage of Staff	32	11.39	24	7.19	31	12.20	87	10.01
Total	**281**	**100.00**	**334**	**100.00**	**254**	**100.00**	**869**	**100.00**

Table – 8.6

What do you think about the attitude of the officials towards people?

	West Godavari		*Cuddapah*		*Warangal*		*Total*	
	No. of Respondents	*Per cent*	*No. of Respondents*	*Per cent*	*No. of Respondents*	*Per cent*	*No. of Respondents*	*Per cent*
Adequate staff	249	88.61	310	92.81	223	87.80	782	89.99
Shortage of Staff	32	11.39	24	7.19	31	12.20	87	10.01
Total	**281**	**100.00**	**334**	**100.00**	**254**	**100.00**	**869**	**100.00**

Table – 8.7

Do you think that the financial resources available to PRIs are adequate?

	West Godavari		*Cuddapah*		*Warangal*		*Total*	
	No. of Respondents	*Per cent*	*No. of Respondents*	*Per cent*	*No. of Respondents*	*Per cent*	*No. of Respondents*	*Per cent*
Yes	46	16.37	22	6.59	40	15.75	108	12.43
No	235	83.63	312	93.41	214	84.75	761	87.57
Total	**281**	**100.00**	**334**	**100.00**	**254**	**100.00**	**869**	**100.00**

Table – 8.8

What would be in your opinion the major sources of revenue for the PRIs?

	West Godavari		*Cuddapah*		*Warangal*		*Total*	
	No. of Respondents	*Per cent*	*No. of Respondents*	*Per cent*	*No. of Respondents*	*Per cent*	*No. of Respondents*	*Per cent*
Govt. grants	173	61.56	219	65.56	169	66.54	561	28.01
Own sources	108	38.44	115	34.44	85	33.46	308	35.44
Total	**281**	**100.00**	**334**	**100.00**	**254**	**100.00**	**869**	**100.00**

Table – 8.9

Are you satisfied with the overall performance of PRIs in your State?

	West Godavari		*Cuddapah*		*Warangal*		*Total*	
	No. of Respondents	*Per cent*	*No. of Respondents*	*Per cent*	*No. of Respondents*	*Per cent*	*No. of Respondents*	*Per cent*
Yes	253	90.03	257	76.95	187	73.62	697	80.20
No	28	9.97	77	23.05	67	26.38	172	19.80
Total	**281**	**100.00**	**334**	**100.00**	**254**	**100.00**	**869**	**100.00**

Table – 8.10

If yes, to what extent you are satisfied?

	West Godavari		*Cuddapah*		*Warangal*		*Total*	
	No. of Respondents	*Per cent*	*No. of Respondents*	*Per cent*	*No. of Respondents*	*Per cent*	*No. of Respondents*	*Per cent*
To a great extent	62	24.51	63	30.00	30	12.85	155	22.24
To some extent	152	60.07	130	61.91	199	85.1	481	69.51
Total	**253**	**100.00**	**210**	**100.00**	**234**	**100.00**	**697**	**100.00**

Table - 8. 11

Respondent People's Representatives

Sl No.	*Position*	*Districts*			
		West Godavari	*Cuddapah*	*Warangal*	*Total*
1.	Ward members	36	39	38	113
2.	Sarpanches	17	18	24	59
3.	MPTC Members	15	14	19	48
4.	MP Presidents	10	10	13	33
5.	ZPTC Members	10	10	10	30
	Total	88	91	104	283

Table – 8.12

We would like to know whether the PRIs were given adequate powers

	West Godavari		*Cuddapah*		*Warangal*		*Total*	
	No. of Respondents	*Per cent*	*No. of Respondents*	*Per cent*	*No. of Respondents*	*Per cent*	*No. of Respondents*	*Per cent*
Yes	29	32.95	31	34.07	18	17.31	78	27.56
No	59	67.0	60	65.93	86	86.69	205	72.4
Total	**88**	**100.00**	**91**	**100.00**	**104**	**100.00**	**283**	**100.00**

Table – 8.13

Do you feel think that more powers are to be given to PRIs?

	West Godavari		*Cuddapah*		*Warangal*		*Total*	
	No. of Respondents	*Per cent*	*No. of Respondents*	*Per cent*	*No. of Respondents*	*Per cent*	*No. of Respondents*	*Per cent*
Yes	79	89.8	78	85.71	84	80.77	246	86.93
No	9	10.2	13	14.29	20	19.23	37	13.07
Total	**88**	**100.00**	**91**	**100.00**	**104**	**100.00**	**283**	**100.00**

Table – 8.14

Do you want all the 29 items mentioned in the Eleventh Schedule be transferred to PRIs?

	West Godavari		*Cuddapah*		*Warangal*		*Total*	
	No. of Respondents	*Per cent*	*No. of Respondents*	*Per cent*	*No. of Respondents*	*Per cent*	*No. of Respondents*	*Per cent*
Yes	45	51.14	57	62.64	79	75.96	181	63.96
No	43	48.86	34	37.36	25	24.04	102	36.04
Total	**88**	**100.00**	**91**	**100.00**	**104**	**100.00**	**283**	**100.00**

Table – 8.15

Do you think the present staff pattern in PRIs is satisfactory?

	[illegible]st Godavari		*Cuddapah*		*Warangal*		*Total*	
	No. of Respondents	*Per cent*	*No. of Respondents*	*Per cent*	*No. of Respondents*	*Per cent*	*No. of Respondents*	*Per cent*
Yes	69	78.40	57	62.64	84	80.77	210	74.20
No	19	21.60	34	37.36	20	19.23	73	25.80
Total	**88**	**100.00**	**91**	**100.00**	**104**	**100.00**	**283**	**100.00**

Table – 8.16

What is your opinion on staff strength of PRIs?

	West Godavari		*Cuddapah*		*Warangal*		*Total*	
	No. of Respondents	*Per cent*	*No. of Respondents*	*Per cent*	*No. of Respondents*	*Per cent*	*No. of Respondents*	*Per cent*
Adequate staff	48	54.55	67	73.63	88	84.62	203	71.73
Shortage of staff	40	45.45	24	26.37	16	15.38	80	28.27
Total	**88**	**100.00**	**91**	**100.00**	**104**	**100.00**	**283**	**100.00**

Table – 8.17

Do you think that the finances at the command of PRIs are adequate?

	West Godavari		*Cuddapah*		*Warangal*		*Total*	
	No. of Respondents	*Per cent*	*No. of Respondents*	*Per cent*	*No. of Respondents*	*Per cent*	*No. of Respondents*	*Per cent*
Yes	66	75.0	29	31.87	49	47.12	144	50.88
No	22	25.0	62	68.13	55	52.88	139	49.12
Total	**88**	**100.00**	**91**	**100.00**	**104**	**100.00**	**283**	**100.00**

Table – 8.18

Do you feel that the funds, as recommended by National Finance Commissions and State Finance Commissions, have been given to PRIs?

	West Godavari		*Cuddapah*		*Warangal*		*Total*	
	No. of Respondents	*Per cent*	*No. of Respondents*	*Per cent*	*No. of Respondents*	*Per cent*	*No. of Respondents*	*Per cent*
Yes	70	79.5	75	82.42	76	73.08	221	78.09
No	18	20.5	16	17.82	28	26.92	62	21.91
Total	**88**	**100.00**	**91**	**100.00**	**104**	**100.00**	**283**	**100.00**

Table – 8.19

If yes, to what extent the funds have been transferred?

	West Godavari		*Cuddapah*		*Warangal*		*Total*	
	No. of Respondents	*Per cent*	*No. of Respondents*	*Per cent*	*No. of Respondents*	*Per cent*	*No. of Respondents*	*Per cent*
To a great extent	32	36.36	37	40.66	35	33.65	104	36.75
To some extent	34	38.64	25	27.47	43	135	102	36.04
To a little extent	14	15.91	21	23.08	26	25.00	61	21.55
Not transferred	8	9.09	8	8.79	-	-	16	5.65
Total	**88**	**100.00**	**91**	**100.00**	**104**	**100.00**	**283**	**100.00**

Table – 8.20

Are you satisfied with the overall performance of PRIs in our State?

	West Godavari		*Cuddapah*		*Warangal*		*Total*	
	No. of Respondents	*Per cent*	*No. of Respondents*	*Per cent*	*No. of Respondents*	*Per cent*	*No. of Respondents*	*Per cent*
Yes	74	84.1	69	75.82	75	72.12	218	77.03
No	14	15.90	22	24.18	29	27.88	65	22.97
Total	**88**	**100.00**	**91**	**100.00**	**104**	**100.00**	**283**	**100.00**

Table – 8.21

If yes, to what extent you are satisfied?

	West Godavari		*Cuddapah*		*Warangal*		*Total*	
	No. of Respondents	*Per cent*	*No. of Respondents*	*Per cent*	*No. of Respondents*	*Per cent*	*No. of Respondents*	*Per cent*
To a great extent	23	31.08	19	27.54	27	36.00	69	31.65
To some extent	24	32.43	22	31.88	28	37.33	74	33.94
To a little extent	27	36.49	28	40.58	20	26.67	75	34.41
Total	**74**	**100.00**	**69**	**100.00**	**75**	**100.00**	**218**	**100.00**

Table – 8.22
Distribution of Officials

Sl No.	*Designation / Institution*	*Districts*			
		West Godavari	*Cuddapah*	*Warangal*	*Total*
1.	Panchayat Secretaries	13	15	15	44
2.	Mandal Parishad Officers	10	8	7	25
3.	Mandal Parishad Development Officers	12	9	8	29
4.	Zilla Parishad Officers	10	8	10	27
	Total	45	40	40	125

Table – 8.23

Do you think that PRIs are given adequate powers?

	West Godavari		*Cuddapah*		*Warangal*		*Total*	
	No. of Respondents	*Per cent*	*No. of Respondents*	*Per cent*	*No. of Respondents*	*Per cent*	*No. of Respondents*	*Per cent*
Yes	18	40.0	14	35.0	12	30.0	44	35.2
No	27	60	26	65.0	28	70.0	81	64.8
Total	**45**	**100.00**	**40**	**100.00**	**40**	**100.00**	**125**	**100.00**

Table – 8.24

Do you want all the 29 items mentioned in the Eleventh Schedule be transferred to PRIs?

	West Godavari		*Cuddapah*		*Warangal*		*Total*	
	No. of Respondents	*Per cent*	*No. of Respondents*	*Per cent*	*No. of Respondents*	*Per cent*	*No. of Respondents*	*Per cent*
Yes	40	88.9	34	85.0	33	82.5	107	85.6
No	5	11.1	6	15.0	7	17.5	55	14.4
Total	**45**	**100.00**	**40**	**100.00**	**40**	**100.00**	**125**	**100.00**

Table – 8.25

Are you satisfied with the present bureaucratic set-u of PRIs?

	West Godavari		*Cuddapah*		*Warangal*		*Total*	
	No. of Respondents	*Per cent*	*No. of Respondents*	*Per cent*	*No. of Respondents*	*Per cent*	*No. of Respondents*	*Per cent*
Yes	39	86.6	32	80.0	33	82.5	104	83.2
No	6	13.4	8	20.0	7	17.5	21	16.8
Total	**45**	**100.00**	**40**	**100.00**	**40**	**100.00**	**125**	**100.00**

Table – 8.26

What is your opinion on staff strength of PRIs?

	West Godavari		*Cuddapah*		*Warangal*		*Total*	
	No. of Respondents	*Per cent*	*No. of Respondents*	*Per cent*	*No. of Respondents*	*Per cent*	*No. of Respondents*	*Per cent*
Adequate staff	36	80.0	27	67.5	30	75.00	93	74.4
Shortage of staff	9	20.0	13	32.50	10	25.00	32	25.6
Total	**45**	**100.00**	**40**	**100.00**	**40**	**100.00**	**125**	**100.00**

Table – 8.27

The biggest drawback in regard to Panchayati Raj system today is the lack of adequate financial resources. Do you agree with this view?

	West Godavari		*Cuddapah*		*Warangal*		*Total*	
	No. of Respondents	*Per cent*	*No. of Respondents*	*Per cent*	*No. of Respondents*	*Per cent*	*No. of Respondents*	*Per cent*
Yes	29	64.44	20	50.0	26	65.0	75	60.00
No	16	35.56	20	50.0	14	35.0	50	40.00
Total	**45**	**100.00**	**40**	**100.00**	**40**	**100.00**	**125**	**100.00**

Table – 8.28

Do you feel that the funds, as recommended by National Finance Commission and State Finance Commissions, have been given to PRIs?

	West Godavari		*Cuddapah*		*Warangal*		*Total*	
	No. of Respondents	*Per cent*	*No. of Respondents*	*Per cent*	*No. of Respondents*	*Per cent*	*No. of Respondents*	*Per cent*
Yes	32	71.11	25	62.5	23	57.5	80	64.0
No	13	28.89	15	37.5	17	42.5	45	36.0
Total	**45**	**100.00**	**40**	**100.00**	**40**	**100.00**	**125**	**100.00**

Table – 8.29

If yes, to what extent the funds have been transferred?

	West Godavari		*Cuddapah*		*Warangal*		*Total*	
	No. of Respondents	*Per cent*	*No. of Respondents*	*Per cent*	*No. of Respondents*	*Per cent*	*No. of Respondents*	*Per cent*
To a great extent	9	28.13	8	32.0	11	40.0	28	35.00
To some extent	21	65.63	12	48.0	10	50.0	43	53.75
To a little extent	2	6.24	5	20.0	2	10.0	9	11.25
Total	**32**	**100.00**	**25**	**100.00**	**23**	**100.00**	**80**	**100.00**

Table – 8.30

What would be the main source of revenue for PRIs?

	West Godavari		*Cuddapah*		*Warangal*		*Total*	
	No. of Respondents	*Per cent*	*No. of Respondents*	*Per cent*	*No. of Respondents*	*Per cent*	*No. of Respondents*	*Per cent*
Govt. grants	22	48.89	21	52.50	23	57.50	66	52.80
Own sources	23	51.11	19	47.50	17	42.50	59	47.20
Total	**45**	**100.00**	**40**	**100.00**	**40**	**100.00**	**125**	**100.00**

Table – 8.31

Are you satisfied with the overall performance of PRIs in our State?

	West Godavari		*Cuddapah*		*Warangal*		*Total*	
	No. of Respondents	*Per cent*	*No. of Respondents*	*Per cent*	*No. of Respondents*	*Per cent*	*No. of Respondents*	*Per cent*
Yes	41	91.1	28	70.0	30	75.0	99	79.20
No	4	8.9	12	30.0	10	25.0	.26	20.80
Total	**45**	**100.00**	**40**	**100.00**	**40**	**100.00**	**125**	**100.00**

Table – 8.32

If yes, to what extent you are satisfied?

	West Godavari		*Cuddapah*		*Warangal*		*Total*	
	No. of Respondents	*Per cent*	*No. of Respondents*	*Per cent*	*No. of Respondents*	*Per cent*	*No. of Respondents*	*Per cent*
To a great extent	28	68.29	18	64.28	17	56.66	63	63.64
To some extent	7	17.07	7	25.00	13	43.34	27	27.27
To a little extent	6	14.64	3	10.72	-	-	9	9.09
Total	**41**	**100.00**	**28**	**100.00**	**30**	**100.00**	**99**	**100.00**

9

Summary and Conclusions

The Seventy-third Constitution Amendment Act conferring constitutional status to PRIs is a land mark in the history of democratic decentralization. Based on the framework provided in the Amendment, the state governments initiated measures and gave shape to the concept of local governance through legislations and rules. The Government of Andhra Pradesh joined the company of other state governments in giving effect to the implementation of the Amendment Act. The system of panchayati raj organized in conformity with the Seventy-third Constitution Amendment Act and Andhra Pradesh Panchayati Raj Act, 1994 comprises gram panchayat at the village level mandal parishad at mandal level and zilla parishad at district level.

Organisation, Powers and Function of PRIs

A gram panchayat consists of members ranging from 5 to 21 depending upon its population. The members of the gram panchayat are elected by the voters of the village from the wards. The chairperson of the gram panchayat is elected by all the registered voters. The Up-sarpanch of a gram panchayat is, however, elected by the ward members. The gram panchayat shall meet once a month. A number of functions relating to development, maintenances, regulating and civic amenities are to be performed by the gram panchayats. Apart from the functions mentioned in the Eleventh Schedule of the Constitution, the State Act listed out a wide array of functions of gram panchayatss. They include 12 obligatory and 27 optional functions.

The number of ward members of the 12 gram panchayats, selected for the study, varies from 8 to 16. The gram panchayats, under study, met more than prescribed number of times in the year 2002. The activities undertaken by the gram panchayats during a period of 7 years from 1995-96 to 2001-02 are more or less similar. The supply of drinking water was received utmost attention by the gram panchayats. Street lighting and cleaning streets were undertaken by all the gram panchayats. Laying and maintenance of roads and culverts in the village is another important function of the gram panchayats.

A mandal parishad is constituted for a revenue mandal in rural areas. The Mandal Parishad consists of MPTC members, MLA and MP having jurisdiction over the mandal and one co-opted member belonging to minorities. The district collector, sarpanchs of GPs and the presidents of agricultural marketing committees in the mandal are the permanent invitees to the mandal parishad meetings.

A mandal parishad is supposed to hold one ordinary meeting every month. It can also convene special meetings. It exercises all the powers conferred on and perform all functions entrusted to it. The mandal parishad may levy a duty in the form of surcharge on any tax levied by the GPs. The mandal parishad performs a number of functions ranging from community development to self-help programmes and management of trusts.

On an average, the MPs convened 12 ordinary and 6 special meetings in the year 2002. Many resolutions were passed by the MPs in these meetings. More than half of the resolutions are on agriculture. All the six MPs reported that they had undertaken many rural development programmes like SGSY, Janmabhoomi, Food for Work, Clean and Green, Neeru – Meeru, Adarana etc.

The ZP is the apex panchayati raj institution. It is constituted for a district. It consists of ZPTC members, MLAs and MPs from the district and two co-opted members. The ZP shall meet at least once in a month. There are 7 standing committees in the ZP. The functions of ZP are mainly coordinating, advisory and supervisory in nature. The ZPs in the state including the ZPs in the districts of West Godavari, Cuddapah and Warangal adhered to the schedule laid down by the statute for holding meetings and held some more ordinary as well as special meetings. The important items on which discussions were held and resolutions passed in the meetings are administration of primary health centers, veterinary hospitals, drinking water supply, expansion of educational facilities, etc. The ZPs are concerned with many issues of people. However, the programmes undertaken by them are very few and very limited activities are being undertaken by them.

Panchayati Raj Personnel

The administrative personnel working in PRIs in various states belongs to broadly two categories. One category is of those deputed bythe state government to occupy posts created for PRIs and also posts transferred by the State Government to the PRIs due to delegation of certain functions to them. The second category of the personnel comprises those occupying posts created for the PRIs and recruited and controlled by PRIs.

Andhra Pradesh has created three cadres for the panchayati raj personnal – State, district and mandal cadres. The state cadre comprises chief executive officer of ZP, mandal parishad development officer and extension officers. The district cadre consists of the clerical staff in the ZP and mandal parishad. The lower level class IV staff have been placed in the mandal cadre.

The Panchayat Secretary is an official functionary of the GP. He provides necessary assistance to the sarpanch in matter of GP administration. In addition to panchayat secretary, there are officials like sanitary inspector, bill collectors and office staff in larger panchayats.

The administrative machinery of mandal parishad is spear-headed by the MPDO. He is supported by Mandal Engineering Officer, Mandal Education Officer and Extension Officer (Panchayati Raj and Rural Development). In addition to these officers, there are office and field personnel under the jurisdiction of MP.

The administrative machinery of ZP is headed by the CEO. The CEO is supported bythe Deputy CEO, Accounts Officer and ZP Education Officer. The subordinate staff at the ZP level include superintendents, senior assistants, junior assistants, typists, record assistants, etc. The officers and employees working in the MPs are under the management of ZP. All the officers of the ZP including the CEO are under the administrative control of the District Collector.

There are some other important officers working in the Panchayati Raj Department. The Commissioner of Panchayati Raj is the head of the Department for the three-tier system of Panchayati Raj and is the Government's agent for implementing the State Act. To assist him as also the District Collectors, there are departmental officers viz., District Panchayat Officer at the district level, and Divisional Panchayat Officer at divisional level.

Financial Resources

In the three-tier system of panchayati raj in Andhra Pradesh, only gram panchayats are empowered to levy taxes. The MPs and ZPs have no taxation powers. The MPs have been permitted to impose surcharge on the taxes levied by the GPs. The sources of income of the PRIs in the state are derived from their own sources, assigned revenues and grants. The main own sources of GPs include income from house tax and kolagaram tax. The assigned revenues such as entertainment tax, profession tax, surcharge on stamp duty and per capita grant are very lucrative sources of revenue for some GPs. The salary grant and JRY grant are some of the grants sanctioned to GPs. The information on income from different sources shows that there are wide variations in the GPs and also in the annual income of the GPs from year to year. The year-wise income of GPs does not reveal any trend – either increase or decrease. It is also found in the study that there is no uniform pattern in the percentage of income under each category of source of income.

The own sources of MPs include the rents on shops, fees, fines and income from auction of fruit bearing trees and fish ponds. Under the assigned revenues, the MPs receive income from land or local cess, surcharge on stamp duty, entertainment tax, seignorage tax, mineral cess and per capita grant. The grants are released to MPs for the purposes of salaries, social welfare, community development, minor irrigation, roads and bridges and rural water supply. The source-wise income of 6 MPs for the years 1995-96 to 2001-02 shows that the MPs are more dependent on government grants than on their own sources and assigned revenues. It is also evident from the data that there are fluctuations from year to year in the income of MPs.

The own sources of ZPs are obtained from rents on buildings, guest houses, quarters, tools and plants, and commercial complexes, fee from markets, ferries and revenue from auctions of fish fonds, fruit bearing trees and land leases. The assigned revenues consist of surcharge on stamp duty, tax on minor minerals, entertainment tax, land cess, seignorage cess, profession tax compensation and per capita grant. Grants are released to ZPs for development works under various programmes such as construction of roads and bridges, social welfare, minor irrigation, rural water supply, rural sanitation, etc. The income of ZPs varies from year to year. The annual income also varies from ZP to ZP. The ZPs are mostly financed by government grants. The government grants constitute, in the years, 2001-02, 95 per cent, 96 per cent and 78 per cent for the ZPs of Warangal, West Godavari and Cuddapah districts respectively.

Perceptions on PRIs

One of the objectives of the study is to ascertain the perceptions of various groups about the working of PRIs in Andhra Pradesh. The opinion of 869 people, 283 peoples representatives and 125 officials. Their view points on powers, functions, personnel, financial resources and overall performance of PRIs in the state were elicited. The majority of respondents expressed the view that the powers devolved on, functions transferred to and the financial resources made available to PRIs are not adequate. They are, however, [1]satisfied with the staff position and overall performance of PRIs. There is, of course, variation in the number or percentage of respondents who expressed opinion on a particular aspect. There is also variation in the district-wise opinion in each category of respondents.

Conclusions

The PRIs were not able to acquire the status and dignity of viable and responsible people's bodies due to a number of reasons including absence of regular elections, prolonged suppressions, insufficient representation of weaker sections like scheduled castes, scheduled tribes and women, inadequate devolution of powers and lack of financial resources. In view of these shortcomings and in order to impart certainty, continuity and strength to PRIs certain basic and essential features were enshrined in the Constitution by the 73rd amendment. The 73rd amendment to the Constitution which confers constitutional status on and protection to the PRIs is undoubtedly a landmark in the process of democratic decentralization in decision-making.[1] It facilitated emergence of vibrant, meaningful and effective units of rural local government. In conformity to this amendment, the States are expected to take necessary measures to empower PRIs.

There are achievements in many aspects of working of PRIs in various states in India including Andhra Pradesh. The grassroots bodies have now acquired a permanent place within the Indian state. Today elections to PRIs for every five years have the become a regular feature. The state governments had tried to postpone them. The civil society organizations took the initiative to fight this by filing public interest litigation. The judiciary at different levels intervened effectively[2]. The constitutional bodies such as the State Finance Commission and State Election Commission are now firmly placed. The SEC had taken up the Panchayati raj elections seriously giving a lot of credibility to the grassroot level democratic process. The SFC had given useful recommendations to strengthen the PRIs financially. There is also steady progress in the representation of women and weaker sections in PRIs. Women have got the maximum mileage. One-third of the seats as well as positions in panchayats at different levels – village, mandal and district levels – have been reserved for women. The scheduled castes, scheduled tribes and backward classes equally secured their due share. Although there were positive notes about some achievements, there is a general feeling today that the 73rd Constitution Amendment Act was not implemented in letter and spirit. The grassroot democratic institutions depend heavily even today on State Government.

The 73rd Constitution Amendment Act makes it clear that 29 types of powers and functions shall be transferred to the PRIs. In addition to these powers and functioned the Andhra Pradesh Panchayati Raj Act listed 12 obligatory and 27 optional functions for gram panchayats. The State Act empowers the Mandal Parishad to exercise powers and perform functions specified in Schedule II. A list of 16 functions of the Zilla Parishad is given in the Section 192 of the State Act. Defying the provisions of constitutional and also the State Act has become routine in most states including Andhra Pradesh. The devolution of powers to PRIs remains in many respects a distant dream. The findings of the study reveal that the PRIs in Andhra Pradesh have been exercising very few powers and perform very few functions. An overwhelming majority of people respondents (94 per cent), 78 per cent of people's representatives and 65 per cent of official respondents opined that the PRIs were not given adequate powers. Similarly 96 per cent of people respondents and 64 per cent of people's representatives observed that the intended functions were not transferred to PRIs. One of the main reasons reported by both official and non-officials was the government's reluctance to devolve powers on and transfer functions to PRIs.

The Government of Andhra Pradesh is not willing to forego the important items like education and public distribution system. The State Government is delaying the devolution of many powers. The PRIs are not happy with the transfer of less important items like libraries and adult education. Though the PRIs were given powers on agriculture and water resources, their powers have been restricted due to the formation of water users associations in every village. The emergence of parallel structures had hampered effective decentralization. The powers of selection of beneficiaries under various schemes were given to panchayats. However, the appointment of nodal officers had reduced the power of sarpanchs. The much-publicized Janmabhoomi programme was entrusted to regular bureaucracy but not the PRIs. The State Government obviously preferred the collector raj to panchayati raj. In the name of giving powers to local bodies powers were snatched from the elected representatives and handed over to the government servants i.e. village secretary, MPDO and CEO of GP, MP and ZP respectively. The cheque power was given to the executive officers of PRIs.

The autonomy of PRIs has been crippled by the enormous overlap between their functions and those of the administrative machinery. The DRDA has been vested with control over developmental activities at the district level. This is in clear violation of the 73rd Constitution Amendment Act, which stipulates the integration of the functions of the DRDA with the Zilla Parishad. The DRDAs are being given distinctive identity from the PRIs in the name of professionalising and strengthening the administration. The funds given by the Centre are being spent through the DRDAs. The District Collectors are the Chairmen to the DRDAs. A DRDA administration above the democratically elected body at the district level would make a mockery of democracy.

Another area of utter neglect is the state finance commission reports for devolution of funds to the PRIs. They are not taken seriously at all by the State Governments. The Government of Andhra Pradesh had not accepted most of the recommendations of the first State Finance Commission[3]. The State Election Commission which is an independent constitutional body is also working under severe limitations. The State Government had tried in 2001 to twist its arms whether it is with regard to delimitation, declaring election results or other related issues.

The Chief Minister, Nara Chandrababu Naidu, and his TDP Government stated many times that the Government was committed to strengthen local bodies by giving them more powers and resources. The Chief Minister promised wide-ranging powers to GPs in future saying the elected bodies should implement whatever was decided by people. Also powers for administrative and technical sanction of works would be given to local bodies. The Government had agreed to initiate steps for giving more administrative and financial powers in tune with the recommendations of the SFC and the TFC.

There were agitations for devolution of powers, functions and funds. The Lok Satta under the banner of Local Bodies Empowerment Forum launched the one crore-signature campaign in August 2003 to press for devolution of powers to local bodies. The Sthanika Prabhutvala Sadhikaraka Samakhya and the Zilla Parishad Chair-persons' Forum had filed writ petitions against the State Government in High Court and Supreme Court, seeking implementation of Constitutional amendment. The Andhra Pradesh Sarpanchs Association also demanded several times for the transfer of powers and funds to the PRIs.

The Centre noticed that many states were found dragging their feet on transferring 29 items to the panchayats to which they were entitled as per the 73rd Constitution Amendment Act. It expressed its anguish many times about slow progress in this aspect. A formal request was made to the states to expedite the issues of sharing powers and resources with local bodies. The Centre also proposed an amendment to the Act making it mandatory for all state governments to transfer powers to PRIs. Inspite of the Governments' promise for more powers and the public demand for the same it seems that the state government is reluctant to transfer powers, thus, defeating the objectives of the 73rd Constitution Amendment Act. Even after 10 years of the package of the constitutional amendment and 7 years from the implementation of State Act, the government had claimed that 17 items were transferred to PRIs. The transfer of other 12 items is under consideration. Most of the Gos transferring 17 items were not yet implemented. The general observation is that the PRIs have become local agencies for implementing central and state government schemes.[4] But in Andhra Pradesh even the implementing role was not assigned to the PRIs.

The permance and reasonable guarantee of continuity of PRIs is an irreversible achievement of the 73rd Constitution Amendment Act. It is the devolution of their sphere of authority that needs priority attention. At present, the statute of the state governing PRIs explicitly provides for specific items of responsibilities and powers of each of the three layers of Panchayati Raj. Mere enumeration of sectors or prescribing a list of functional responsibilities for the PRIs may not facilitate meaningful devolution. The State Governments were fully empowered to adopt legislations in their respective Assemblies to transfer powers to local bodies. It is possible for the Government of Karnataka to transfer all 29 items, Goa and Kerala many items from the list laid down in Article 243(G) of the constitution. A number of offices, institutions and personnel were transferred to the control of the local bodies in Kerala. The President of the local bodies was declared the executive authority with full administrative control, including powers of disciplinary action over staff. But the Government of Andhra Pradesh is reluctant to do so. This is a matter of concern and needs further research.

The PRIs implement schemes with a greater sense of responsibility. Even under the existing severely constrained panchayati raj regime, numerous elected PRIs have shown the willingness and the ability to decide on projects appropriate to local needs, mobilize local resources for such projects and to take the responsibility for implementing government sponsored projects. Works taken up by them have been found to be completed faster, better and cheaper than those of the government agencies. Hence, many works relating to water works, sanitation programme, schools and hospitals could also come under their active supervision and control. The PRIs may also be involved in the effective implementation of the public distribution system, food for work, and other poverty alleviation programmes. This would influence fresh vigour and democratic accountability in the panchayati raj system.

As the PRIs are expected to play a catalyst role in the planning and development of a plethora of rural development programmes and schemes, they should be necessarily be equipped with adequate responsibilities and powers. The popularly elected PRIs need to be given specific functional responsibilities and powers to fulfill these responsibilities. This would have to be done soon as the expectations of the people from the newly created PRIs in the areas of socio-economic development and equity are very high. If this happens, the panchayati raj bodies will be fully empowered to function as local self-governments.

The PRIs would have to be streamlined and strengthened with necessary administrative and technical staff to equip them fully to function as effective instruments of economic development and social justice. This calls for a rational reorganization of the administrative set-up at all levels, viz. ZP, MP and GP levels. During the field visits for the study it was noticed that there were vacancies in many PRIs. Some GPs were put under the in-charge of village secretary of neighboring GPs and MPs under the control of the incharge MPDOs. According to a recent announcement of the State Government, out of 21,943 GPs in the State, the Government had so far filled 13,247 posts of village secretary while 8096 were yet to be filled. There is a dire need to provide proper administrative machinery at the grassroot level. To realize this objective, full-time officers should be appointed for the PRIs. A proper administrative machinery at the grassroot level would ensure proper maintenance of records, full collection of taxes, etc.

Whatever may be the transfer of powers and functions, the PRIs get relief if their financial opportunities are improved. The PRIs have, however, a very weak resource base. The number and nature of the tax sources allocated to them are few and less elastic. The gram panchayats alone are vested with certain powers, while the middle and apex layers of panchayati raj are assigned some non-tax revenues. The revenue which the PRIs mobilize through exercise of their revenue powers is not commensurate their expenditure needs. The quantum of resources actually mobilized by the PRIs constitute an insignificant proportion of their total income. Even in the case of GPs which were empowered to levy and collect taxes, the percentage of income from their own sources is not significant. Out of 12 GPs under study for only one GP namely Gummampadu GP in West Godavari District, the own sources constituted more than half of its total income. There was virtual absence of income from own sources for the PRIs in Cuddapah and Warangal districts.

Even in respect of the few sources allocated to the PRIs, there has been gradual encroachment by the state government. The State Government had diverted in the year 2002 the EFC and SGRY funds of gram panchayats to the construction of individual sanitary latrines and school toilets. Diverting them for other programmes of the State Government amounted to the denial of the rights of local bodies. Octrai duty was one of the major sources of income for panchayats. The Government has exempted the panchayats from collecting this duty from trucks. The Government took the decision bowing to pressure from truckers who went on strike in the year 2003.

As for the existing system of state-aid, it should be admitted that it suffers from certain shortcomings. PRIs are not involved in fixing or alerting the rates of the surcharge or cess that are levied and collected by the state governments for being distributed to the former. The State Government are also reluctant to share a part of the revenue from some of its own productive tax sources. In regard to the grants-in-aid of the PRIs it should be admitted that they are inadequate, uncertain and are not based on any objective criteria. The PRIs particularly the MPs and ZPs depend on State Governments for the finance of the entire gamut of their activities. The position is further aggravated when it is found that even the promised assistance from the government departments is not released in time or in full and the assistance has too many strings attached to it. The people's representatives agitated many a time for the release of funds due to their institutions.

Consistent with their new role as institutions for social and economic development of rural areas, the flow of funds to PRIs would have to be adequate and regular to enable them to play this role affectively. The funds should be commensurate with the functions entrusted to them and their availability should be ensured. Nevertheless, it should be emphasized that there is need for allocating additional tax sources to the PRIs which are productive, simpler to administer, locally feasible and economical to collect at the local level. A large proportion of the state revenue has to be transferred to local bodies to cater to the public expenditure needs at local level. It seems to be reasonable to transfer 40-50 per cent of sales tax revenue and 30-40 per cent of state excise duty to local governments in rural as well as urban areas. Keeping in view the wide magnitude of local functions, the above could help match the financial needs of the local governments.

At the same time, the grants-in-aid have a greater role in strengthening the fiscal position of PRIs. They have largely been depending on grants-in-aid either directly from the centre or from state government. Even in the developed countries like the USA the dependency on federal or state grants has been increasing. More than 50 per cent of local level revenue is mobilized through grants. Majority of the respondents of the study observed that the government grants should be the major source of revenue for PRIs. So the governments - both central and state - maximize their assistance to the PRIs. The PRIs will also have to raise their own resources so as to enjoy some degree of financial autonomy. Hence, one of the emerging tasks of PRIs would be to adopt various measures and to augment their financial resources.

References

1. Jagannath Mishra, "Strengthening Panchayati Raj Institutions" in Atmanand (ed.), *Financing Panchayati Raj*, Excel Books, New Delhi, 1999, p.100.
2. George Mathew, "Ten Years On", *The Hindu*, Visakhapatnam edition, December 27, 2002, p.10.
3. Government of Andhra Pradesh, *Report of the Second State Finance Commission*, Hyderabad, 2002, p.82.
4. Pran Chopra, "Clouds over Panchayati Raj", *The Hindu*, Visakhapatnam edition, September 13, 2003, p.10.

Appendix I

STUDY TEAMS, WORKING GROUPS AND COMMITTEES ON PANCHAYATI RAJ

1. Team for the Study of Community Projects and National Extension Service, 1957.
2. Study Team on Panchayats, 1958.
3. Committee on Rationalisation of Panchayat Statistics, 1960.
4. Working Group on Panchayats and Coopertives, 1961.
5. Study Team on Panchayati Raj Administration, 1961
6. Study Team on Nyaya Panchayats, 1962.
7. Study Team on the Position of Gram Sabha in Panchayati Raj Movement, 1963.
8. Study Group on Budgeting and Accounting Procedure of Panchayati Raj Institutions, 1963.
9. Study Team on Panchayati Raj Finances, 1963.
10. Committee on Panchayati Raj Elections, 1965.
11. Study Team on the Audit and Accounts of Panchayati Raj Bodies, 1965.
12. Evaluation Committee on Panchayati Raj Training Centres, 1966.
13. Study Team on the Role and Functions of Panchayati Raj Institutions in Planning and Development, 1966.
14. Study Team on Involvement of Community Development Agency and Panchayati Raj Institutions in the Implementaiton of Basic Land Reform Measures, 1969.

15. Working Group for Formulation of Fifth Five Year Plan on Community Development and Panchayati Raj, 1972.
16. Committee on Community Development and Panchayati Raj, 1976.
17. Committee on Panchayati Raj Institutions, 1978.
18. Committee to Review the Existing Administrative Arrangements for Rural Development and Poverty Alleviation Programmes, 1985.
19. L.M. Singhvi Committee, 1986.
20. P.K. Thungon Committee, 1988.

Appendix II

THE CONSTITUTION (SEVENTY-THIRD AMENDMENT) ACT, 1992

An Act further to amend the Constitution of India
Be it enacted by Parliament in the Forty-Third Year of the Republic of India as follows –

1. Short title and commencement – (1) This Act may be called the Constitution (Seventy-third Amendment) Act, 1992.
2. It shall come into force on such date as the Central Government may, by notification in the Official Gazette, appoint.
3. **Insertion of new Part IX** – After part VIII of the Constitution, the following Part shall be inserted, namely –

PART IX
THE PANCHAYATS

243. Definitions – In this part unless the context otherwise requires -

(a) "district" means a district in a State;

(b) "Gram Sabha" means a body consisting of persons registered in the electoral rolls relating to a village comprised within the area of Panchayat at the village level;

(c) "intermediate level" means a level between the village and district levels specified by the Governor of a State by public notification to be the intermediate level for the purposes of this Part;

(d) "Panchayat" means an institution (by whatever name called) of self-Government constituted under Article 243-B, for the rural areas;

(e) "Panchayat area" means the territorial area of a Panchayat;

(f) "population" means the population as ascertained at the last preceding census of which the relevant figures have been published;

(g) "village" means a village specified by the Governor by public notification to be a village for the purpose of this part and includes a group of villages so specified.

243-A. Gram Sabha

A Gram Sabha may exercise such Powers and perform such functions at the village level as the legislature of a State may, by law, provide.

234-B. Constitution of Panchayats

1. There shall be constituted in every State Panchayats at the village, intermediate and district levels in accordance with the provisions of this Part.
2. Notwithstanding anything in Clause (1), Panchayats at the intermediate level may not be constituted in a State having a population not exceeding twenty lakhs.

243-C. Composition of Panchayats

1. Subject to the provisions of this Part, the Legislature of a State may, by law, make provisions with respect to the composition of Panchayats provided that the ratio between the population of the territorial area of a Panchayat at any level and the number of seats in such Panchayat to be filled by election shall so far as practicable be the same throughout the State.

2. All the seats in a Panchayat shall be filled by persons chosen by direct election from territorial constituencies in the Panchayat area and for this purpose, each Panchayat area shall be divided into territorial constituencies in such manner that the ratio between the population of each constituency and the number of seats allotted to it shall, so far as practicable, to the same throughout the Panchayat area.

3. The Legislature of a State may, by law, provide for the representation

   (a) of the Chairpersons of the Panchayats at the village level, in the Panchayats at the intermediate level or, in the case of a State not having Panchayats at the intermediate level, in the Panchayats at the district level;

   (b) of the Chairpersons of the Panchayats at the intermediate level, in the Panchayats at the district level;

   (c) of the members of the House of the People and the members of the Legislative Assembly of the State representing constituencies which comprise wholly or partly a Panchayat area at a level other than the village level, in such Panchayat;

   (d) of the members of the Council of States and the members of the Legislative Council of the State where they are registered as electors within

      (i) a Panchayat area at the intermediate level, in Panchayat at the intermediate level;

      (ii) a Panchayat area at the district level, in Panchayat at the district level.

4. The Chairperson of a Panchayat and other members of a Panchayat whether or not chosen by direct election from territorial constituencies in the Panchayat area shall have the right to vote in the meetings of the Panchayats.

5. The Chairperson of –
   (a) a Panchayat at the village level shall be elected in such manner as the Legislature of a State may, by law, provide and
   (b) a Panchayat at the intermediate level or district level shall be elected by and from amongst, the elected members thereof.

243-D. Reservation of seats

1. Seats shall be reserved for –
   (a) the Scheduled Castes; and
   (b) the Scheduled Tribes -

   in every panchayat and the number of seats so reserved shall bear, as nearly as may be, the same proportion to the total number of seats to be filled by direct election in that Panchayat as the population of the Scheduled Castes in that Panchayat area or of the Scheduled Tribes in that Panchayat area bears to the total population of that area and such seats may be allotted by rotation to different constituencies in a Panchayat.
2. Not less than one-third of the total number of sets reserved under Clause (1) shall be reserved for women belonging to the Scheduled Castes, or, as the case may be, the Scheduled Tribes.
3. Not less than one-third (including the number of seats reserved for women belonging to the Scheduled Castes and the Scheduled Tribes) of the total number of seats to be filled by direct election in every Panchayat shall be reserved for women and such seats may be allotted by rotation to different constituencies in a Panchayat.
4. The offices of the Chairpersons in the Panchayats at the village or any other level shall be reserved for the Scheduled Castes, the Scheduled Tribes and women in

such manner as the Legislature of a State may, by law, provide;

Provided that the number of offices of Chairpersons reserved for the Scheduled Castes and the Scheduled Tribes in the Panchayats at each level in any State shall bear, as nearly as may be, the same proportion to the total number of such offices in the Panchayats at each level as the population of the Scheduled Castes in the State or of the Scheduled Tribes in the State bears to the total population of the State;

Provided further that no less than one-third of the total number of offices of Chairpersons in the Panchayats at each level shall be reserved for women;

Provided also that the number of offices reserved under this clause shall be allotted by rotation to different Panchayats at each level.

5. The reservation of seats under clauses (1) and (2) and the reservation of office of Chairperson (other than the reservation for women) under clause (4) shall cease to have effect on the expiration of the period specified in Article 334.
6. Nothing in this part shall prevent the Legislature of a State from making any provision for reservation of seats in any Panchayat or office of Chairpersons in the Panchayats at any level in favour of backward class of citizens.

243-E. Duration of Panchayats, etc.

1. Every Panchayat, unless sooner dissolved under any law for the time being in force, shall continue for five years from the date appointed for its first meeting and no longer.
2. No amendment of any law for the time being in force shall have the effect of causing dissolution of a Panchayat

at any level, which is functioning immediately before such amendment, till the expiration of the duration specified in Clause (1).

3. An election to constitute a Panchayat shall be completed
   (a) before the expiry of its duration specified in Clause (1);
   (b) before the expiration of a period of six months from the date of its dissolution;
   Provided that where the remainder of the period for which the dissolved Panchayat would have continued is less than six months, it shall not be necessary to hold any election under this clause for constituting the Panchayat.

4. A Panchayat constituted upon the dissolution of a Panchayat before the expiration of its duration shall continue only for the remainder of the period for which the dissolved Panchayat would have continued under Clause (1) had it not been so dissolved.

243-F. Disqualifications for membership

Subject to the provisions of the Constitution, the Legislature of a State may, by law, endow the Panchayats with such powers and authority as may be necessary to enable them to function as institutions of self Government and such law may contain provisions for the devolution of powers and responsibilities upon Panchayats at the appropriate level, subject to such conditions as may be specified therein, with respect to –

(a) the preparation of plans for economic development and social justice;

(b) the implementation of schemes for economic development and social justice as may be entrusted to them including those in relation to the matters listed in the Eleventh Schedule.

243-H. Powers to impose taxes by, and Funds of, the Panchayats

The Legislature of a State may, by law –

(a) authorise a Panchayat to levy, collect and appropriate such taxes, duties, tolls and fees in accordance with such procedure and subject to such limits;

(b) assign to a Panchayat such taxes, duties, tolls and fees levied and collect by the State Government for such purposes and subject a such conditions and limits;

(c) provide for making such grants-in-aid to the Panchayats from the Consolidated Fund of the State; and

(d) provide for constitution of such Funds for crediting all moneys received respectively, by or on behalf of the Panchayats and also for the withdrawal of such moneys therefrom.

As may be specified in the law.

243-I. Constitution of Finance Commission to review financial position

1. The Governor of a State shall, as soon as may be within one year from the commencement of the Constitution (Seventy-third Amendment) Act, 1992 and thereafter at the expiration of every fifth year, constitute a Finance Commission to review the financial position of the Panchayats and to make recommendations to the Governor as to –

   (a) the principles which should govern –

      (i) the distribution between the State and the Panchayats of the not proceeds of the taxes, duties, tolls and fees leviable by the State, which may be divided between them under this Part and the allocation between the Panchayat at all levels of their respective shares of such proceeds;

(ii) the determination of the taxes, duties, tolls and fees which may be assigned to, or appropriated by, the Panchayats;

(iii) the grants-in-aid to the Panchayats from the Consolidated Fund of the State.

(b) the measures needed to improve the financial position of the Panchayats;

(c) any other matter referred to the Finance Commission by the Governor in the interests of sound finance of the Panchayats.

2. The Legislature of a State may, by law, provide for the composition of the Commission, the qualifications which shall be requisite for appointment as members thereof and the manner in which they shall be selected.

3. The Commission shall determine their procedure and shall have such powers in the performance of their functions as the Legislature of the State may, by law, confer on them.

4. The Government shall cause every recommendation made by the Commission under this article together with an explanatory memorandum as to the action taken thereon to be laid before the Legislature of the State.

243-J. Audit of Accounts of Panchayats

The Legislature of a State may, by law, make provisions with respect to the maintenance of accounts by the Panchayats and the auditing of such accounts.

243-K. Elections of the Panchayats

1. The superintendence, direction and control of the preparation of electoral rolls for, and the conduct of, all elections to the Panchayats shall be vested in a State Election Commission consisting of a State Election Commissioner to be appointed by the Governor.

2. Subject to the provisions of any law made by the Legislature of a State, the conditions of service and tenure of office of the State Election Commissioner shall be such as the Governor may by rule determine;

   Provided that the State Election Commissioner shall not be removed from his office except in like manner and on the like grounds as a Judge of a High Court and the conditions of service of the State Election Commissioner shall not be varied to his disadvantage after his appointment.

3. The Governor of a State shall, when so requested by the State Election Commission, make available to the State Election Commission such staff as may be necessary for the discharge of the functions conferred on the State Election Commission by Clause (1).

4. Subject to the provisions of this Constitution, the Legislature of a State may, by law, make provision with respect to all matters relating to or in connection with, elections to the Panchayats.

243-L. Application to Union Territories

The provisions of this Part shall apply to the Union territories and shall, in their application to a Union territory, have effect as if the references to the Governor of a State were references to the Administrator of the Union territory appointed under Article 239 and references to the Legislature or the Legislative Assembly of a State were references, in relation to a Union territory having a Legislative Assembly, to that Legislative Assembly:

Provided that the President may, by public notification, direct that the provisions of this Part shall apply to any Union Territory or part thereof subject to such exceptions and modifications as he may specify in the notification.

243-M. Part not to apply to certain areas

1. Nothing in this Part shall apply to the Scheduled Areas referred to in Clause (1) (2), of Article 244.
2. Nothing in this Part shall apply to –
   (a) the States of Nagaland, Meghalaya and Mizoram;
   (b) the Hill Area in the State of Manipur for which District Council exist under any law for the time being in force.
3. Nothing in this Part -
   (a) relating to Panchayats at the district level shall apply to the hill areas of the District of Darjeeling in the State of West Bengal for which Darjeeling Gorkha Hill Council exists under any law for the time being in force;
   (b) shall be construed to affect the functions and powers of the Darjeeling Gorkha Hill Council constituted under such law;
4. Notwithstanding anything in this Constitution –
   (a) the Legislature of a State referred to in sub-clause (a) clause (2) may, by law, extend this Part to that State, except the areas, if any, referred to in clause (1), if the Legislative Assembly of that State passes a resolution to that effect by a majority of not less than two-thirds of the members of that House present and voting;
   (b) Parliament may, by law, extend the provisions of this part to the Scheduled Areas and the tribal areas referred to in clause (1) subject to such exceptions and modifications as may be specified in such law, and no such law shall be deemed to be an amendment of this Constitution for the purposes of Article 368.

243-N. Continuance of existing laws and Panchayats

Notwithstanding anything in this Part, any provision of any law relating to Panchayats in force in a State immediately before the commencement of the Constitution (Seventy-third Amendment) Act, 1992, which is inconsistent with the provisions of this Part, shall continue to be in force until amended or repealed by a competent Legislature or other competent authority or until the expiration of one year from such commencement, whichever is earlier:

Provided that all the Panchayats existing immediately before such commencement shall continue till the expiration of their duration, unless sooner dissolved by a resolution passed to that effect by the Legislative Assembly of that State or, in the case of a State having a Legislative Council, by each House of the Legislature of that State.

243- O. Bar to interference by Courts in electoral matters

Notwithstanding anything in this Constitution –

(a) the validity of any law relating to the delimitation of constituencies or the allotment of seats to such constituencies, made or purporting to be made under Article 243-K, shall not be called in question in any Court;

(b) no election to any Panchayat shall be called in question except by an election petition presented to such authority and in such manner as is provided for by or under any law made by the Legislature of a State.

Amendment of Article 280

In Clause (3) of Article 280 of the Constitution, after sub-clause (b), the following sub-clause shall be inserted, namely – "(bb) the measures needed to augment the Consolidated Fund of a State to supplement the resources of the Panchayats in the State on the basis of the recommendations made by the Finance Commission of the State"

Addition of Eleventh Schedule

After the Tenth Schedule to the Constitution, the following Schedule shall be added, namely –

ELEVENTH SCHEDULE

(Article 243-G)

1. Agriculture, including agricultural extension
2. Land improvement, implementation of land reforms, land consolidation and soil conservation
3. Minor irrigation, water management and watershed development
4. Animal husbandry, dairying and poultry
5. Fisheries
6. Social forestry and farm forestry
7. Minor forest produce
8. Small scale industries, including food processing industries
9. Khadi, village and cottage industries
10. Rural housing
11. Drinking water
12. Fuel and fodder
13. Roads, culverts, bridges, ferries, waterways and other means of communication
14. Rural electrification, including distribution of electricity
15. Non-conventional energy sources
16. Poverty alleviation programme
17. Education, including primary and secondary schools
18. Technical training and vocational education
19. Adult and non-formal education
20. Libraries
21. Cultural activities
22. Markets and fairs
23. Health and sanitation, including hospitals, primary health centers and dispensaries

24. Family welfare
25. Women and child development
26. Social welfare, including welfare of the handicapped and mentally retarded
27. Welfare of the weaker sections, and in particular of the Scheduled Castes and the Scheduled Tribes
28. Public distribution system
29. Maintenance of community assets

Appendix III

IMPORTANT PROVISIONS OF THE ANDHRA PRADESH PANCHAYATI RAJ ACT, 1994

4. Constitution of Gram Panchayats for village and their incorporation

(1) A Gram Panchayat shall be deemed to have been constituted for a village on the date of publication of the notification under Section 3 in respect of that village and the special officer appointed under sub section (1) of Section 143 shall make arrangements for the election of the members and of the Sarpanch of the Gram Panchayat as provided in that Section.

(2) Subject to the provisions of the Act, the administration of the village shall vest in the Gram Panchayat.

(3) Every Gram Panchayat shall be a body corporate by the name of the village specified in the notification issued under Section 3, shall have perpetual succession and a common seal, and subject to any restriction or qualification imposed by or under this Act or any other law.

8. Election of Members: All members of the Gram Panchayat shall be elected by the registered voters in the Ward by the method of secret ballot and in accordance with such rules as may be made in this behalf.

13. Term of office of memebrs. (1) Save as otherwise provied in this Act the term of office of members elected at ordinary elections shall be five years from the date appointed by the Commissioner for the first meeting of the Gram Panchayat after the ordinary elections.

14. Election and term of office of Sarpanch (1) There shall be a Sarpanch for every Gram Panchayat, who shall be elected in the prescribed manner by the persons whose names appear in the electoral roll for the Gram Panchayat, from among themselves. A person shall not be qualified to stand for election as Sarpanch, unless he is not less than twenty-one years of age.

30. Appointment of executive officers for certain Gram Panchayats

(1) A whole time or a part-time executive officer shall be appointed by the Commissioner for any Gram Panchayat or for any group of contiguous Gram Panchayats, which may be notified by him in this behalf.

(2) In the case of every Gram Panchayat not so notified and also in the case of any Gram Panchayat so notified if there is no executive officer incharge, the Sarpanch of the Gram Panchayat shall, subject to such rules as may be prescribed, exercise the powers and perform the functions of the executive officer.

36. Officers and other employees of Gram Panchayat

(1) Subject to such rules as may be made under the proviso to Article 309 of the Constitution, the Government, shall fix and may alter the number, designations and grades of and the salaries, fees and allowances payable to such officers and other employees of a Gram Panchayat as may be prescribed.

45. Duty of Gram Panchayat to provide for certain matters

(1) Subject to the provisions of this Act and the rules made thereunder, it shall be the duty of a Gram Panchyat within the limits of its funds to make reasonable provisions for carrying out the requirements of the village in respect of the following matters, namely –

(i) the construction, repair and maintenance of all buildings vested in the Gram Panchayat and of all public roads in the village (other than the roads vested in the Mandal Parishad and Zilla Parishad and the roads classified by the Government as National and State Highways) and of all bridges, culverts, road, dams and cause ways on such roads;

(ii) the lighting of public roads and public places;

(iii) the construction of drains and their maintenance and the disposal of drainage water and sullage;

(iv) the cleaning of streets, the removal of rubbish heaps, jungle growth and prickly-pear, the filling in of the disused wells, unsanitary ponds, pools, ditches, pits or hollows and other improvements of the sanitary condition of the village;

(v) the provision of public latrines and arrangements to clean latrines whether pubic or private;

(vi) the opening and maintenance of cremation and burial-grounds, and the disposal of unclaimed dead bodies of human beings or of animals;

(vii) preventive and remedial measures connected with any epidemic or with malaria;

(viii) the sinking and repairing of wells, the excavation, repair and maintenance of ponds or tanks and the construction and maintenance of water works, for the supply of water for washing an bating purposes and protected water for drinking purposes;

(ix) the conservation of manurial resources, preparation of compost and sale of manure;

(x) the registration of births and deaths;

(xi) the establishment and maintenance of cattle pounds; and

(xii) all other matters expressly declared obligatory by or under this Act or any other law.

(2) Apart from the matters specified in sub-section (1), the Government may, subject to such rules as may be made in this behalf, entrust the Gram Panchayats with any functions in relations to the subjects specified in Schedule-1.

60. Taxes Leviable by Gram Panchayats

(1) A Gram Panchayat shall levy in the village

(a) a House tax;

(b) kolagaram, or katarusum that is to say, tax on the village produce sold in the village by weight measurement or number subject to such rules as may be prescribed;

(c) such other tax as the Government may, by notification, direct any Gram Panchayat or class of Gram Panchayats to levy subject to such rules as may be prescribed;

2. A duty shall also be levied on transfers of property situated in the area under the jurisdiction of the Gram Panchayat in accordance with the provisions of Section 69.

3. Subject to such rules as may be prescribed the Gram Panchayat may also levy in the village-

(i) a vehicle tax;

(ii) a tax on agricultural land of a specific purpose;

(iii) a land against the rate of two naya paise in the rupee on the annual rental value of all occupied lands, which are not occupied by or adjacent and appurtenant to, buildings;

(iv) fees for use of porambokes or communal lands under the control of the Gram Panchayat;

(v) fees for the occupation of building including chavadies and sarais under the control of the Gram Panchayat.

4. Every Gram Panchayat may also levy a duty in the form of a surcharge on the seigniorage fees collected by the Government on materials other than minerals and minor minerals quarried in the village;

148. Constitution and incorporation of Mandal Parishads

(1) There shall be constituted by the Government by notification from time to time, and with effect on and from such date, as may be specified therein constitute a Mandal Parishad for each Mandal.

149. Composition of Mandal Parishad

(1) Every Mandal Parishad shall consist of the following members, namely –

(i) persons elected under Section 151;

(ii) the Member of the Legislative Assembly of the State representing a constituency which comprises either wholly or partly the Mandal concerned;

(iii) the Member of the House of the People representing a constituency which comprises either wholly or partly the Mandal concerned;

(iv) Any Member of the Council of States who is a registered voter in the Mandal concerned;

(v) One person belonging to minorities to be co-opted in the prescribed manner by the members specified in clause (i) from among persons who are registered voters in the Mandal and who are not les than 21 years of age.

161. Powers and functions of a Mandal Parishad

(1) Subject to the provisions of this Act, the administration of Mandal shall vest in the Mandal Parishad. Every Mandal Parishad shall endeavour to instill among people within its jurisdiction spirit of self help and initiative and harness their enthusiasm for raising the standard of living, it shall exercise all the powers conferred on, and perform all the functions as may be conferred on, and entrusted to it by the Government for carrying out the purposes of this Act, but it shall not exercise the powers or perform the functions expressly assigned by or under this Act, or any other law to its President or to the Mandal Parishad Development Officer or to the Zilla Parishad or any other authority, it shall do extension and review functions at the Mandal level effectively. It may, with the previous approval of the Government and subject to such terms and conditions as may be prescribed borrow moneys for carrying out the purposes of this Act. It shall also exercise and perform such of the powers and functions of the District Board including the powers to levy any tax or fees as may be transferred to it under this Act.

(2) Every Mandal Parishad shall exercise such powers and perform such functions as may be entrusted to it by rules made in this behalf in regard to the subjects enumerated in schedule-I. In particular, the mandal Parishad shall exercise the powers and perform the functions specified in schedule –II.

(3) Notwithstanding anything in this Act, the Mandal Parishad may with the prior approval of the Zilla Parishad levy contributions from the funds of the Gram Panchayats in the Mandal.

(4) Every Mandal Parishad may levy with the prior sanction of the Government a duty in the form of a surcharge on

any tax imposed by a Gram Panchayat or on land cess or local cess levied within its jurisdiction in such manner and subject to such maximum as may be prescribed.

167. Powers and functions of the Mandal Parishad Development Officer

(1) The Mandal Parishad Development Officer shall be the Chief Executive Officer of the Mandal Parishad. He shall be responsible for implementing the resolutions of the Mandal Parishad and shall also exercise such powers and perform such functions as may be entrusted to him by the Government. He shall also exercise such powers of supervision over the Gram Panchayts in the Mandal as may be prescribed.

172. Income and expenses of Mandal Parishad

((1) The sources of income of Mandal Parishad shall consist of;

- (i) funds relating to institutions and schemes transferred by the Government or Heads of Departments of the Government to the Mandal Parishad;
- (ii) funds relating to the community development programmes;
- (iii) Central and State aid and aid received from the all India bodies and institutions for the development of cottage and village industries, khadi, silk, coir, handicrafts and the like;
- (iv) Donations and contributions received by the Mandal Parishad from Gram Panhayats or from the public in any form;
- (v) Such income of the Mandal Parishad as the Government may, by order, allocate to it;
- (vi) Such share of land revenue, state taxes or fees as may be prescribed;

(vii) Proceeds from taxes, surcharge or fee which the Mandal Parishad is empowered to levy under this Act or any other law;

(viii) Such contributions as the Mandal Parishad may levy from Gram Panchayats;

(ix) Any other income from remunerative enterprises and the like.

(2) Government shall also make annual grant at the rate of five rupees per person residing in the Mandal calculated on the basis of the last preceding census of which figures are available.

(3) The expenses of the Mandal Parishad shall include the salaries and allowances of its officers and other employees, the allowances to be paid under Sections 159 and 170 any item of expenditure directed by the Government for carrying out the purposes of this Act and such other expenses as may be necessary for such purposes.

177. Constitution, incorporation and composition of Zilla Parishad

(1) There shall be constituted by the Government by notification a Zilla Parishad for a District with effect from such date as may be specified therein.

(2) Every Zilla Parishad shall, by the name of the District for which it is constituted, be a body corporate having perpetual succession and a common seal with power to acquire, hold and dispose of property and to enter into contracts and may by its corporate name, sue and be sued.

(3) Every Zilla Parishad shall consist of the following members, namely-

(i) Persons elected under Section 179

(ii) The Member of the Legislative Assembly of the state representing the constituency which comprises either wholly or partly the district concerned.

(iii) The Member of the House of People representing the constituency which comprises either wholly or partly the district concerned.

(iv) Two persons belonging to minorities to be co-opted in the prescribed manner by the members specified in clause (i) from among persons who are registered voters in the District and who are not less than 21 years of age.

186. Appointment of Chief Executive Officer and his powers and functions

(1) There shall be Chief Executive Officer for every Zilla Parishad who shall be appointed by the Government.

(2) Every Chief Executive Officer shall be liable to be transferred by the Government.

(3) Save as otherwise expressly provided by or under the Act, the executive power for the purpose of carrying out the provisions of this Act, shall vest in the Chief Executive Officer.

192. Powers and functions of the Zilla Parishad

(1) Every Zilla Parishad shall exercise such powers and perform such functions as may be entrusted to it by rules made in this behalf with regard to the subjects enumerated in the First Schedule. The Zilla Parishad shall also have the power to,

(i) Examine and approve the budgets of Mandal Parishads in the district;

(ii) Distribute the funds allotted to the district by the (iii) Co-ordinate and consolidate the plans prepared in respect of the Mandals in the district and prepare plans in respect of the entire district;

iv) Secure the execution of plans projects, schemes or other works either solely relating to the individual

Mandals or common to two or more Mandals in the district;

(v) Supervise generally the activities of the Mandal Parishads in the district;

(vi) Exercise and perform such of the powers and functions of the District Board including the powers to levy any tax or fees, as may be transferred to it under this Act;

(vii) exercise and perform such other powers and functions in relating to any development programme as the Government may by notification confer on or entrust to it;

(viii) advise Government on all matters relating to development activities and maintenance of services in the district, whether undertaking by local authorities or Government;

(ix) advise Government on the allocation of work among Gram Panchayats and Mandal Parishads and co-ordination of work between the said bodies and among the various Gram Panhayats themselves;

(x) advise government on matters concerning the implementation of any statutory or executive order specially referred by the Government to the Zilla Parishad;

(xi) collect such data as it deems necessary;

(xii) publish statistics or other information relating to the activities of the local authorities;

(xiii) require any local authority to furnish information regarding its activities;

(xiv) accept trusts relating exclusively to the furtherance of any purpose for which its funds may be applied;

(xv) establish, maintain, or expand secondary, vocational and industrial schools;

(xvi) borrow money for carrying out the purposes of the Act with the previous approval of the Government and subject to such terms and conditions as may be prescribed.

((2) The Zilla Parishad may, with the approval of the Government, levy contributions from the funds of the Mandal Parishads in the district.

198. Income and expenses of a Zilla Parishad

(1) The source of income of Zilla Parishad shall consist of –

(i) the Central or State Government funds allotted to the Zilla Parishad;

(ii) grants from All India bodies and Institutions for the development of cottage, village and small scale industries and the likes;

(iii) such share of the land cess or local cess, State taxes or fees as may be prescribed;

(iv) proceeds from taxes or fees which the Zilla Parishad may under any law levy;

(v) income from endowments or trusts administered by the Zilla Parishad;

(vi) Such income of the District Board as the Government may by order, allocate to it;

(vii) Donations and contributions from the Mandal Parishads or from the public in any form;

(viii) Such contributions as the Zilla Parishad may levy from the Mandal Parishad with the previous approval of the Government;

(2) The Government shall also make an annual grant at the rate of two rupees per person residing in the District calculated on the basis of the last preceding census of which figures are available.

(3) The expenses of the Zilla Parishad shall include the salaries and allowances of the officers and other employees, the allowances to be paid under Section 189 and Section 196, any item of expenditure directed by the Government

for carrying out the purposes of this Act and such other expenses as may be necessary for such purposes.

201. Powers and functions of the State Election Commissioner

(1) All elections to the Panchayat Raj Institutions shall be held under the supervision and control of the State Election Commission and for this purpose it shall have power to give such directions as it may deem necessary to the Commissioner, District Collector or any officer or servant of the Government and the Panchayati Raj Institutions, so as to ensure efficient conduct of the elections under this Act.

(2) The preparation of electoral rolls for the conduct of all elections under the Act shall be done under the supervision and control of the State Elections Commission.

(3) For the purpose of this section the Government shall provide the State Election Commission with such staff as may be necessary.

(4) On the request of the State Election Commission, the State Government shall place at the disposal of the Commission such staff of the State Government, Gram Panchayats, Mandal Parishads and Zilla Parishads for the purpose of conduct of elections under this Act.

(5) The State Election Commissioner may, subject to control and revision, delegate his powers to such officers as he may deem necessary.

235. Constitution of Finance Commission

(1) The Governor shall on the recommendation of the State Government constitute a Finance Commission as soon as may be within one year from the date of commencement of the Constitution (Seventy-third) Amendment Act, 1992 and thereafter on the expiration of every fifth year.

(2) The Finance Commission shall consist of a Chairman and four other members of whom one shall be the Member Secretary. The Governor shall by order appoint on the recommendation of the Government the Chairman and other members of the Commission.

(3) The Government shall make available to the Finance Commission such staff as may be necessary for the discharge of the functions conferred on the Finance Commission.

Appendix - IV

ELECTED MEMBERS OF ZILLA PARISHADS

ZPTC Members, Zilla Parishad, West Godavari, Eluru

S.No.	*Name*	*Mandal*
1.	Sri D. Mangi Setty	Achanta
2.	Smt. Tota Annapurna	Bulusumudi
3.	Smt. B. Bullemma	Attili
4.	Smt. G. Sesharatnam	Bhimadolu
5.	Smt. B. Bharata Lakshmi	Bhimavaram
6.	Sri D. Sunkurudu	Buttayagudem
7.	Sri K. Babu Rao	Chagallu
8.	Smt. T. Devamani	Chintalapudi
9.	Sri G. Someswara Rao	Denduluru
10.	Sri Ch Subba Rao	Devarapalli
11.	Sri D. Pera Swamy Chowdary	Dwaraka Tirumala
12.	Sri G. Jayaraju	Yelamanchili
13.	Sri G. Kasi Viswanadha Rao	Eluru
14.	Sri S. Govinda Rao	Ganapavaram
15.	Sri U. Subhas Chandra Bose	Gopalapuram

(Contd.)

(Contd. Table)

S.No.	Name	Mandal
16.	Sri Y. Satyanarayana	Iragavaram
17.	Sri M. Srinivasa Rao	Jangared dygudem
18.	Sri G. Ravi Kumar	Jeelugumilli
19.	Smt. A. Padmavathi	Kalla
20.	Sri G. Murali Ramakrishna	Kamavarapukota
21.	Sri Y. Ranga Rao	Kovvuru
22.	Smt. R. Padmavathi Subhadra Devi	Koyyalagudem
23.	Sri N. Nageswara Rao	Lingapalem
24	Smt. N. Lakshmi Devi	Mogalturu
25.	Sri B. Appa Rao	Nallagerla
26.	Sri K. Surayya	Narasapuram
27.	Smt. P. Srilatha	Nidadavolu
28.	Smt. I. Kanakadurga Mani	Nidamarru
29.	Sri K. Kasiviswanadham	Palakoderu
30	Smt. S. Ratnasuseela Devi	Palakollu
31.	Sri K. Lakshminarayana Chowdary	Nayudugudem
32.	Smt. T. Sridevi	Cheravegi
33.	Smt. D. Krishnaveni	Pentapadu
34.	Sri P. Trimurthulu	Penugonda
35.	Sri Ch. Tataji	Penumantra
36.	Sri K. Venkata Satyanarayana	Peravalli
37.	Sri B. Saradhi	Polamuru
38.	Smt K. Venkateswari	Polavaram
39.	Smt. D. Jayalakshmi	Unguturu
40.	Smt. V. Vijayalakshmi	Veeravasaram

(Contd.)

(Contd. Table)

S.No.	*Name*	*Mandal*
41.	Sri M. Sampath Kumar	Tadepalligudem
42.	Sri N. Sreeramulu	Tallapudi
43.	Sri K. Surya Rao	Tanuku
44.	Sri A. Lakshmaiah	D. Narsapuram
45.	Sri K. Mahankali	Undi
46.	Sri N. Venkateswara Rao	Undrajavaram

ZPTC Members Zilla Parishad, Cuddapah

S.No.	*Name*	*Mandal*
1	K. Suresh Babu	Cuddapah
2	I Govinda Reddy	Khajipet
3	M Varalakshmi	Pendlimarri
4	P. Ravindranath Reddy	C.K. Dinne
5	P. Madhuri	Yerraguntla
6	T. Annaiah	Veeraballi
7	P. Nagi Reddy	Chinnamandem
8.	K. Surendra	Sambepalli
9.	B. Sarojamma	Penagalur
10.	K. Ayyavaramma	Pullampet
11.	P. Sreenivasulu	Kodur
12.	P. Ramakrishna Reddy	Atloor
13.	C.C. Padmanabhaiah	Jammalamadugu
14.	S. Ramadevi	Muddanuru
15.	A. Krishnaiah	Mylavaram
16.	C.M. Ramachandra Reddy	Kondapuram
17.	S. Sadasiva Reddy	Proddatur
18.	R. Bhaskar	Rajupalem
19.	I. Veeramma	Duvvur
20	D. Jyothi	Pulivendla
21.	G. Sambasiva Reddy	Simhadripuram

(Contd.)

(Contd.Table)

S.No.	Name	Mandal
22.	S.F. Basha	Vaimpalli
23.	M. Raja Reddy	Vemula
24.	N. Chandrasekhar Reddy	Lingala
25.	V. Sivamohan Reddy	Thondur
26.	B. Anantharamaiah	Vontimitta
27.	K. Sarveswar Reddy	Chennur
28.	G. Rajeswaramma	V.N. Palli
29.	Y. Reddaiah	L.R. Palli
30.	V. Siddaiah	Ramapuram
31.	T. Radhakrishnaiah	Charayapet
32.	K. Ameena	Galiveedu
33.	S. Subramanyam	Rayachoty
34.	M. Bhudevi	Tsundupalli
35.	C. Saraswathamma	Rajampet
36.	E. Venkateswarlu	Nandalur
37.	K. Balaji	Chitvel
38.	K. Nageswara Rao	O.V. Palli
39.	Y. Prasad	Badvel
40.	B. Rama Subba Reddy	B. Mattam
41.	Y. Kumari	B. Kodur
42.	B. Sunanda	Porumamilla
43.	N. Venkata Subba Reddy	Kalasapadu
44.	K. Nagalakshumma	S.A. Kasinayana
45.	V. Subbamma	Gopavaram
46.	C. Chalamaiah Yadav	Siddhavatam
47	R. Narasimhudu	Peddamudium
48.	L. Gangulaiah	Chapadu
49.	B. Peddireddy	Mydukur
50.	K. Suseelamma	Valluru
51.	V. Pitchi Reddy	Kamalapuram

(Contd.)

ZPTC Members, Zilla Parishad,Warangal

S.No.	*Name*	*Mandal*
1.	K. Sambaiah	Hanamkonda
2.	V. Venkateswarlu	Hasanparthi
3.	K. Bhagyalakshmi	Athmakur
4.	V. Kavitha	Geesugonda
5.	E. Baswa Reddy	Sangem
6.	G. Yadaiah (Yadagiri)	Ghanapur (ST)
7.	K. Sambalaxmi	Dharmasagar
8.	K. Dargaiah	Zafeergadh
9.	K. Prabhakar	Wardhannapet
10.	N. Naresh Reddy	Raiparthy
11.	U. Panthulu	Parvathagiri
12.	A. Rama	Duggondi
13.	B. Prabhakar	Janagaon
14.	M. Rambabu	Raghunathpally
15.	G. Kistaiah	Lingal Ghanpur
16.	K. Narsinga Rao	Cherial
17.	J. Siddaiah	Maddur
18.	M. Bhumaiah	Bachannapet
19.	K. Prathap Reddy	Narmetta
20.	N. Praveen Kumar	Kodakandla
21.	L. Shirisha	Devaruppula
22.	G. Parvathi	Palakurthi
23.	J. Venkateswarlu	Mahabubabad
24.	K. Surender	Kesamudram
25.	J. Srinu	Dornakal
26.	A. Veerabadram	Korivi
27.	B. Srinivas	Maripeda

(Contd.)

(Contd.Table)

S.No.	*Name*	*Mandal*
28.	G. Kamsala	Nellikudur
29.	B. Nalini Devi	Narsimhulapet
30.	J. Venkatesh	Thorpur
31.	N. Dharma Reddy	Gudur
32.	K. Madhusudhan Reddy	Kothaguda
33.	G. Balu	Khanapur
34.	P. Sudershan Reddy	Nallabelli
35.	B. Agaiah	Narsampet
36.	V. Tejavath	Nekkonda
37.	B. Vijaya	Chennaraopet
38.	B. Gopal Reddy	Mulug
39.	A. Veeralaxmi	Ghanapur (Mulug)
40.	A. Sarojana	Govindaraopet
41.	M. Amaravathi	Venkatapur
42.	G. Somaiah	Mangapet
43.	B. Narsimulu	Eturunagaram
44.	R. Srinivas Reddy	Tadvai
45.	L. Laxmibai	Parkal
46.	B. Kanaka Laxmi	Shayampet
47.	S. Samma Rao	Regonda
48.	A. Rajyalaxmi	Chityal
49.	K. Lachamma	Mogullapally
50.	J. Sarojana	Bhupalpally

Appendix - V

INTERVIEW SCHEDULES

INTERVIEW SCHEUDLE: I - PEOPLE

Background

1. Name
2. Age
3. Sex
4. Education
5. Main Occupation
6. Land holding
7. Income
8. Religion Hindu/Muslim/Christian/ Any other (specify)
9. Caste/Social Status SC/ ST/ BC/ OC
10. Association with Social/Cultural/Voluntary/Political Organisations.

Structure

1. Do you notice any changes in the Panchayati Raj system in Andhra Pradesh after 73rd Constitution Amendment Act? Yes/No/DK

   If yes, give the changes noticed by you.

   1..

   2.

   3.

2. Do you think that present three-tier system of Panchayati Raj is effective? Yes/No/NR

   If no, give reasons

   1.

   2.

3. Do you want the present system be continued?

   Yes/No/NR

   If no, suggest the changes to be made in the system.

Powers:

1. What would you say are the most important powers given to Panchayati Raj Institutions?
2. What are the powers normally exercised by Panchayati Raj Institutions?
3. Do you think that some more powers shall be given to Panchayati Raj Institutions? Yes/No/NR
4. Please give the nature of powers yet to be given to Panchayati Raj Institutions.

   1.

   2.

Functions

1. What would say are the most important functions transferred to Panchayati Raj Institutions?
2. What are the functions normally performed by the Panchayati Raj Institutions?
3. Do you think that some more functions shall be transferred to Panchayati Raj Institutions?

   Yes/No/NR

4. Please give the nature of functions yet to be transferred to the Panchayati Raj Institutions.

   1.

   2.

Personnel

1. What is your opinion on the present staff pattern of Panchayati Raj system in the State?

   Very effective   Effective

   Not Effective   No idea

2. What is your opinion on the staff strength?

   Surplus staff   Adequate Staff

   Shortage of Staff   No Staff

3. What impressions do you have on the efficiency of the staff?

   Very good   Good   Fair

   Bad   Very bad

4. What do you think about the attitude of the officials towards people?

   Very Helpful   Somewhat Helpful

   Unhelpful   Indifferent

Finance

1. What according to you, are the major sources of income for Panchayati Raj Institutions?

2. Do you think that the financial resources available to Panchayati Raj Institutions are adequate?

   Yes/No/DK

3. What are the additional sources to be transferred to the Panchayati Raj Institutions?

   1.

   2.

   3.

4. Give suggestions to strengthen the financial position of Panchayati Raj Institutions.

   1.

   2.

Performance

1. How much attention do you think that panchayati Raj Institutions pay towards problems?
   Good deal Some what
   Not much No attention
2. Do you agree that the new Panchayati Raj system in general provided opportunities to the people in managing their own affairs? Agree/Disagree/DK
3. Are you satisfied with the overall performance of Panchayati Raj Institutions in our State? Yes/No/DK
   If yes, to what extent you are satisfied?
   Very satisfied/Some what Satisfied/Dissatisfied.

INTERVIEW SCHEUDLE: II - PEOPLE'S REPRESENTATIVES

Background

1. Name
2. Designation/Position
3. Age
4. Sex : Male / Female
5. Education
6. Land holding
7. Main Occupation
8. Monthly/Annual Income :
9. Religion : Hindu/Muslim/Christian/ others (specify)
10. Caste/Social Status : SC/ ST/ BC/ OC
11. Association with Social/Cultural/Voluntary Organisations.
12. Political Experience

Structure

1. Do you think that the 73rd Constitution Amendment Act was implemented in Andhra Pradesh in letter and spirit? Yes/No/DK

2. Do you notice any significant changes in the Panchayati Raj System of Andhra Pradesh after the enactment of 73rd Constitution Amendment Act, 1992?

Yes/No/DK

3. Do you think that the present structure of Panchayati Raj system is effective?

Yes/No/DK

4. Do you suggest any change in the composition of Panchayati Raj Institutions?

Yes/No/NR

5. Do you agree that the infrastructural facilities in the offices of Panchayati Raj Institutions are adequate?

Agree/Disagree/NR

Powers

1. What would you say are the most important powers given to Panchayati Raj Institutions?
2. What are the powers normally exercised by Panchayati Raj Institutions?
3. Do you think that some more powers shall be given to Panchayati Raj Institutions?

Yes/No

4. Do you feel that loans and subsidies in regard to different schemes be kept at the disposal of Panchayati Raj Institutions?

Yes/No/NR

Functions

1. We would like to know what are the most important functions transferred to Panchayati Raj Institutions?
2. What are the functions normally performed by the Panchayati Raj Institutions?
3. Do you want all the 29 items mentioned in Eleventh Schedule be transferred to Panchayati Raj Institutions?

Yes/No/NR

4. Do you want all the Rural Development Programmes be transferred to Panchayati Raj Institutions?

Yes/No/NR

Personnel

1. Do you think the present staff pattern in Panchayati Raj Institutions is satisfactory?

Yes/No/NR

If not, give your suggestion for a particular pattern.

2. What is your opinion on staff strength?

Surplus staff   Adequate Staff
Shortage of staff   No staff

3. What impressions do you have on the efficiency of the Panchayati Raj Personnel?

Very good   Good   Fair
Bad   Very Bad

4. What is, in your opinion, the attitude of officials towards the problems of the people?

Very helpful   Helpful
Unhelpful   Indifferent

Finance

1. Do you think that the finances at the command of Panchayati Raj Institutions are adequate?

Yes/No/DK

2. What are your suggestions to improve their financial position?

3. Do you feel that the funds, as recommended by National Finance Commission and State Finance Commissions, have been given to Panchayati Raj Institutions?

Yes/No/DK

If yes, to what extent the funds have been transferred?

To a greater extent   To some extent
To a little extent   Not transferred

Performance

1. How much attention do you think that Panchayati Raj Institutions pay towards problems?

   Good deal Some what

   Not much No attention

2. Do you agree that the new Panchayati Raj system in general provided opportunities to the people in managing their own affairs?

   Agree/Disagree/DK

3. Do you think that the Panchayati Raj has been able to achieve its goals?

   Yes/No/DK

   If yes, how far it has been able to active its goals?

   Fully Partially Not at all

   If not, give reasons.

   1.

   2.

4. Are you satisfied with the overall performance of Panchayati Raj Institutions in our State?

   Yes/No/NR

   If yes, to what extent you are satisfied?

   Very satisfied/Some what Satisfied/Dissatisfied.

INTERVIEW SCHEDULE: III - OFFICIALS

Background

1. Name
2. Designation
3. Age
4. Sex
5. Education
6. Rural/Urban Background
7. Occupation of father/parents/family

8. Land Holding
9. Monthly salary
10. Other Income
11. Religion
12. Caste
13. Association with social/cultural/voluntary/political organizations
14. Service Experience
15. Have you attended any training programme after you were posted in Panchayati Raj Institutions?

Yes/No

If yes, give the nature of training and period of training.

Structure:

1. Do you think that the 73rd Constitution Amendment Act was implemented in Andhra Pradesh in letter and spirit?

Yes/No/DK

2. Do you notice any significant changes in the Panchayati Raj System of Andhra Pradesh after the enactment of 73rd Constitution Amendment Act, 1992?

Yes/No/DK

If yes, what are the changes noticed by you?

1.

2.

3. Do you think that the present structure of Panchayati Raj system is effective?

Yes/No/DK

If not, suggest alternative structural arrangement

1.

2.

4. Do you suggest any change in the composition of Panchayati Raj Institutions?

Yes/No/DK

If yes, what are your suggestions?

1.

2.

5. Do you agree that the infrastructural facilities in the offices of Panchayati Raj Institutions are adequate?

Agree/Disagree/DK

6. There is general apprehension that there won't be proper co-ordination among the three-tiers of Panchayati Raj System. Do you agree with this statement?

Strongly Agree | Agree
Disagree | Strongly disagree

7. Do you like the Panchayati Raj representatives involve actively in decision-making and policy implementation?

Yes/No

If no, why

1.

2.

8. Do you feel the Panchayati Raj representatives co-operate with officials?

Yes/No/DK

Powers:

1. Do you think that the 73rd Constitution Amendment Act and the State Act have given adequate powers to Panchayati Raj Institutions?

Yes/No/DK

2. What are the Powers given to Panchayati Raj Institutions in the State?

3. Please mention the powers to be given yet to Panchayati Raj Institutions?

4. Do you feel that loans and subsidiaries in regard to different rural development programmes should be kept at the disposal of Panchayati Raj Institutions?

Yes/No

Functions:

1. We would like to know what are the most important functions transferred to Panchayati Raj Institutions?
2. What are the functions normally performed by the Panchayati Raj Institutions?
3. Do you like to transfer all 29 items mentioned in Eleventh Schedule to Panchayati Raj Institutions?

   Yes/No
4. Do you want all the Rural Development Programmes be transferred to Panchayati Raj Institutions?

   Yes/No/NR

Personnel

1. Are you satisfied with the present bureaucratic set-up of Panchayati Raj Institutions?

   Yes/No

   If not, please give suggestions for a change in the present bureaucratic set up.

   1.

   2.
2. What is your opinion on staff strength?

   Surplus staff — Adequate staff

   Shortage of staff — No staff

Finance

1. The biggest drawback in regard to Panchayati Raj system today is the lack of adequate financial resources. Do you agree with this view?

   Yes/No

   If yes, please tell us, on the basis of your experience, the methods to solve the financial problems of Panchayati Raj Institutions.
2. Tax collection, imposition and collection are very poor in Panchayati Raj Institutions. Do you agree with this view?

   Yes/No

3. Do you feel that the funds, as recommended by National Finance Commissions and State Finance Commissions, have been given to Panchayati Raj Institutions?

Yes/No/DK

If yes, to what extent the funds have been transferred?

To a greater extent   To some extent
To a little extent   Not transferred

Performance

1. How much attention do you think that Panchayati Raj Institutions pay towards problems?

Good deal   Some what
Not much   No attention

2. Do you agree that the new Panchayati Raj system in general provided opportunities to the people in managing their own affairs?

Agree/Disagree/DK

3. Do you think that the Panchayati Raj has been able to achieve its goals?

Yes/No/NR

If yes, how far it has been able to achieve its goals?

Fully   Partially   Not at all

If not, give reasons.

1.
2.

4. Are you satisfied with the overall performance of Panchayati Raj Institutions in our State?

Yes/No/DK

If yes, to what extent you are satisfied?

Very satisfied/Some what Satisfied/Dissatisfied.

Bibliography

Abhijit Datta, "Constitutional Status of Local Government of India", *The Indian Journal of Public Administration*, Vol.XXXIII, No.2, April-June, 1987.

Abida Samiuddin, *A Critique of Panchayati Raj with special reference to Uttar Pradesh*, Sahitya Bhawan, Agra, 1976.

Anil, K. Singh, *State Panchayati Acts*: *A Critical Review*, Voluntary Action Network India, New Delhi, 1995.

Aurcliano Fernandes, "Changing Role of Panchayats in the New Millennium", *Kurukshetra*, November 2001.

Arjun Y. Darshankar, *Leadership in Panchayati Raj: A Study of Beed District of Maharastra*, Panchsheel Prakashan, Jaipur, 1979.

Atmanand (Ed.), *Financing of Panchayati Raj*, Excell Printers, New Delhi, 1999.

Bhargava, B.S., *Politico-Administrative Dynamics in Panchayati Raj System*, Ashish Publishing House, New Delhi, 1978.

Biju, M.R., "Decentralised Planning Process in Kerala: A Unique Experiment of Participaiton Democracy" in M.R. Biju (ed.), *Decemntralisaiton: An Indian Experience*, New Delhi, National Publishing House, 2007.

Chokshi, H.P., *A Study of Mobilisation of Resources for Village Panchayats in Baroda District*, Planning Commission, New Delhi, 1971.

Chandrasekhar, B.K., (ed.), *Panchayat Raj in India: Status Report 1999*, Task Force on Panchayat Raj, Rajiv Gandhi Foundation, New Delhi, March 2000.

Chopra, Pran., "Clouds over Panchayati Raj", *The Hindu*, Visakhapatnam edition, September 13, 2003.

Desai, Vasant, *Panchayati Raj: Power to the People,* Bombay, Himalaya, 1990.

District Collector, *The Hand Book of Statistics* – Cuddapah, 1996-97.

District Industries Centre, *Progress Report on Industries*, Cuddapah, 1998.

Dubey S.N., and Ratna Murdia, *Structure and Process of Decision Making in Panchayati Raj Institutions*, Somiya Publications, Bombay, 1976.

George Mathew, "Ten Years On", *The Hindu*, Visakhapatnam edition, December 27, 2002.

Government of Andhra Pradesh, *Economic Survey 2003-2004*, A.P. Secretariat, Planning Department, Hyderabad, 2004.

Government of Andhra Pradesh, *High Power Committee on Panchayati Raj*, Panchayati Raj Department, Hyderabad, 1981.

Government of Andhra Pradesh, *Recommendations of the Cabinet Sub-Committee on the Report of the State Finance Commission,* Commissioner of Printing, Stationery and Stores, Hyderabad, November 1997.

Government of Andhra Pradesh, *Report of the First State Finance Commission,* Commissioner of Printing, Stationery and Stores, Hyderabad, May 1997.

Government of Andhra Pradesh, *Report of the Second State Finance Commission,* Commissioner of Printing, Stationery and Stores, Hyderabad, August 2002.

Government of Andhra Pradesh, *Statistical Abstracts of Andhra Pradesh 2003,* Directorate of Economics and Statistics, Hyderabad, 2003.

Government of India, *Census of India 2001,* series-29, Andhra Pradesh, Provisional Population Totals, Director of Census Operations, New Delhi.

Governemtn of India, *Report of the Taxation Enquiry Committee*, New Delhi, 1953-54.

Government of India, *Report of the Committee on Administrative Arrangements for Rural Development and Poverty Alleviation Programmes* (Chairman: G.V.K. Rao), Ministry of Agriculture, Department of Rural Development, New Delhi, 1985.

Government of India, *Report of the Committee on Panchayati Raj* (Chairman: L.M. Sighvi), Ministry of Agriculture, Department of Rural Development, New Delhi, 1986.

Government of India, *Report of the Committee on Panchayati Raj Institutions*, Department of Rural Development, Ministry of Agriculture, New Delhi, August, 1978.

Government of India, *Report of the Study Team on Panchayati Raj Finances*, Ministry of Community Development, New Delhi, 1963.

Government of India, *Report of the Team for the Study of Community Projects and National Extension Service,* Vol.I, New Delhi, Committee on Plan Projects, 1957.

Government of Rjasthan, *Report of the Administrtive Reforms Commission*, Jaipur, 2001.

Grover, V.P., et al., *Panchayati Raj Administration in Rajasthan*, Lakshmi Narayan Aggarwal, Delhi,1972.

Hanson, A.H., and Janet Douglas, *India's Democracy,* Vikas, Delhi, 1972.

Harichandran, C., *Panchayati Raj and Rural Development: A Study of Tamil Nadu*, Concept Publishing Co., New Delhi, 1986.

Henry Maddick, *Panchayati Raj: A Study of Rural Local Government in India*, Longman, London, 1970.

Inamdar, N.R., *Functioning of Village Panchayats*, Popular Prakashan, New Delhi, 1970.

Iqbal Narain, "A Perspective on Research in Panchayati Raj" in S.L. Verma (ed.), *Panchayati Raj, Gram Swaraj and Federal Polity,* Rawat, Jaipur, 1990.

Iqbal Narian, Susil Kumar and M.V. Mathur, *Panchayati Raj Administration*, Indian Institute of Public Administraiton, New Delhi, 1970.

Jain, S.P. and Thomas W. Hochgesang (Ed.), *Emerging Trends in Panchayati Raj in India,* National Institute of Rural Development, Hyderabad, 1995.

James Manor, "Democratic Decentralisation in Two Indian States: Past and Present", *The Indian Journal of Political Science*, Vol.63, No.1, March 2002.

Jathar, R.V., *Evolution of Panchayati Raj in India*, J.S.S. Institute of Economic Research, Dharwar, 1964.

Jena, A.C., *Panchati Raj Finances in West Bengal – A Status Study*, National Institute of Rural Development, Hyderabad, 1999.

Joshi, R.P., (ed.), *Constitutionalization of Panchayati Raj : A Reassessment*, Rawat Publicaitons, New Delhi, 1998.

Kailash C. Sharma, *Leadership in Panchayati Raj: A Study of Chitturgarh District*, Printwell, Jaipur, 1996.

Kautilya, *Arthashastra* translated by Shoma Sastry, Raghuveer Printing Press, Mysore, 1956.

Khanna, B.S., *Rural Local Government in India and South Asia,* Deep & Deep Publications, New Delhi, 1999.

Khanna, R.L., *Panchayati Raj in Punjab and Harayana,* Mohindra Capital Publishers, Chandigarh, 1966.

Kumar, Sushil and K. Venkataraman, *State-Panchayati Raj Relations: A Study of Supervision and Control in Tamil Nadu*, Asia Publshing House, Bombay, 1974.

Mahajan, V.S. (Ed.), *Agriculture, Rural Development and Panchayati Raj – Regional Level Strategies and Policies*, Vols I and II, Deep & Deep Publications, New Delhi, 1996.

Maheswari, B., *Studies in Panchayati Raj*, Metropolitan, Delhi, 1963.

Maheswari, Sriram, *Local Government in India*, Lakshmi Narain Agarwal, Agra, 2005.

Mahipal, *Gap Between Needs and Resources of Panchayats in India*, Mittal Publications, New Delhi, 2003.

Mahipal, "From Raj Governance to Swaraj Governnce", *Kurukshetra,* August 2004.

Mishra, Jagannath, "Strengthening Panchayati Raj Institutions" in Atmanand (ed.), *Financing Panchayati Raj*, Excel Books, New Delhi, 1999.

Misra, S.N., and S.S. Singh, *Roads to Model Panchayati Raj*, Mittal Publications, New Delhi, 1993.

Muthaya, B.C., *Panchayat Taxes Factors Influencing their Mobilisation: A Study in three Panchayats in East Godavari Andhra Pradesh*, National Institute of Community Department, Hyderabad, 1972.

Naganathan, M and Jothi Sivagnanam, K, "Decentralised Governance: Tamil Nadu Experience", in M.R. Biju (ed.), *Decentralisation: An Indian Experience*, New Delhi, Ntional Publishing House, 2007.

Nandekar, V.G., *Local Government: Its Role in Development Administration*, Concept Publishing Co., Delhi, 1979.

Narayana, E.A., "The Role of Zilla Praja Parishad in Rural Development" in G. Vidyasagar et al. (eds.), *Rural Development and Local Participation*, Anmol Publications, New Delhi, 1992.

Narayana, E.A., "Panchayati Raj Institutions in Andhra Pradesh: An Analysis of their Powers, Functions and Finance" in M.R. Biju (ed.), *Decentralisaiton: An Indian Experience*, National Publishing House, New Delhi, 2007.

National Institute of Rural Development, *Panchayati Raj Institutions in Select States: An Analytical Study*, Hyderabad, 1995.

Norman D. Palmer, *The Indian Political System*, Boston, Houghton, Miffin.

Palanithurai, G., Dwaraki, B.R., and Narayanaswamy, S. (eds.), *Major Issues in New Panchayati Raj System*, Kanishka Publishers, Delhi, 1997.

Palanithurai, G., *Empowering People for Prosperity: A Study in New Panchayati Raj System,* Kanishka Publisher, Delhi, 1994.

Prasad, V.S., *Panchayats and Development*, Light & Life Publishers, New Delhi, 1981.

Raghavulu C.V., and Narayana, E.A., "Reforms in Panchayati Raj: A Comparative Analysis of Andhra Pradesh, Karnataka and West Bengal", *The Indian Journal of Public Administration*, Vol.XXXVII, No.1, January-March, 1991.

Raghavulu, C.V. and Narayana, E.A., "Mandal System in Andhra Pradesh: An Appraisal", *ISDA* Journal, Vol. 2, No. 2, April-June 1992.

Raj Singh (Ed.), *New Panchayati Raj : A Functional Analysis*, Anmol Publications Pvt. Ltd., New Delhi, 2000.

Rajeswar Dayal, *Panchayati Raj in India*, Metroplitan, Delhi, 1970.

Ram Reddy G. and Seshadri, K., *The Voter and Panchayati Raj,* National Institute of Community Development, Hyderabad, 1972.

Ram Reddy, G., (ed.), *Patterns of Panchayati Raj*, Macmillan, Delhi,1977.

Sandeep Joshi, *Panchayati Raj Institutions and Poverty Alleviation*, Rawat Publications, New Delhi, 2000.

Sharma, Shakuntala, *Grassroot Politics and Panchayati Raj*, Deep and Deep Publications, New Delhi, 1997.

Sharma, Sudesh Kumar, *Panchayati Raj in India,* Trimurti Publications, New Delhi, 1976.

Singh, S.S., and Suresh Misra, *Legislative Framework of Panchayati Raj in India*, Intellectual Publishing House, New Delhi, 1993.

Singh, Surat, "Functioning of Panchayati Raj Institutions in Himachal Pradesh", *Kurukshetra,* Vol.XXXVI, No.3, December 1987.

Srinivas Reddy, G., "Panchayati Raj Reforms in Andhra Pradesh: A Critique" in M. Kistaiah (ed.), *Administrative Reforms in a Developing Society*, Sterling, New Delhi, 1990.

Thimmaiah, G., "Democratic Decentralisation: The Panchayati Raj Experiment in India", in Dr. Atmanand (ed.), *Financing of Panchayati Raj*, Excel Books and Co., New Delhi, 1999.

Thomas, E.M. "Decentralised Planning nd Transfer of Development Functions: A Case Study of Four Village Panchayats in Kerala", *Administrtive Change,* Vol.XXXI, No.2 and Vol.XXXII, No.1, January-December 2004.

Venkatarangaiah, M., and Ram Reddy, G., *Panchayati Raj in Andhra Pradesh,* Andhra Pradesh Chamber of Panchayati Raj, Hyderabad, 1967.

Venkatarangaiya, M., and Pattabhiram, M., (eds.), Local Government in India, Select Readings, Applied Publishers, Calcutta, 1969.

Venkatesan, V., *Institutionalizing Panchayati Raj in India,* Concept, New Delhi, 2002.

Vijay Kumar, A., and Sudhakar, E., "Role of Panchayat Secretary in Andhra Pradesh: A Study", *The Indian Journal of Public Administration*, Vol.XLIX, No.2, April-June, 2002.

Vithal, C.P., "Financial Resources of Panchayati Raj Institutions in Andhra Pradesh: A Case for Resource Mobilization and Utilization" in Atmanand (ed.), *Financing of Panchayati Raj*, Excel Books and Co., New Delhi, 1999.

Acts:

Andhra Pradesh Panchayat Samithis and Zilla Parishads Act, 1959.

Andhra Pradesh Gram Panchayats Act, 1964.

Andhra Pradesh Mandal Praja Parishads, Zilla Parishads and Zilla Pranalika Abhivrudhi Mandals Act, 1986.

Andhra Pradesh Local Bodies Electoral Reforms Act, 1989.

Andhra Pradesh Panchayati Raj Act, 1994.

Seventy-third (Constitution Amendment) Act, 1992.

Government Orders:

G.O.Ms.No.367, dt. 22-6-1994, Panchayati Raj, Rural Development and Relief (Mandals – III) Department, Government of Andhra Pradesh, Hyderabad.

G.O.Ms.No.683, Panchayat Raj, Rural Development and Relief (Mandals-III) Department, Government of Andhra Pradesh, Hyderabad, dt. 25-10-1994.

G.O.Ms.No.511, dt.8.12.1998, Panchayat Raj and Rural Development (Mandals-III) Department, Government of Andhra Pradesh, Hyderabad.

G.O.Ms.No.515, dt. 21.12.1998, Panchayat Raj and Rural Development (Mandals-III) Department, Government of Andhra Pradesh, Hyderabad.

G.O.Ms.No.107, dt. 18.3.1999, Panchayat Raj and Rural Development (Mandals-III) Department, Government of Andhra Pradesh, Hyderabad.

G.O. M.S. No.369, dt. 12-12-01, Panchayati Raj and Rural Development (Mdl-II) Department, Government of Andhra Pradesh, Hyderabad.

G.O. Ms.No.384, dt. 22-12-01, Panchayati Raj and Rural Development (Estt. – IX) Department, Government of Andhra Pradesh, Hyderabad.

Index

J

K

L

M